What others are saying about

"Smashing the Wall of Fear"
by Sean Hockensmith

"*Smashing the Wall of Fear* is a brilliant guide to self-empowerment. This excellent book is chock-full of inspiring stories and practical tips. I strongly recommend this book for anyone seeking to grow beyond their limits and step into their magnificence."

Alan Cohen
Author of *The Dragon Doesn't Live Here Anymore*

"A wonderful book filled with helpful, practical spiritual nuggets."

Gerald G. Jampolsky, M.D.
Author of the international bestseller *Love is Letting Go of Fear*

"Practical, positive, and provoca....... ..... *The Wall Of Fear* will guide you through issu..... your life."

Eric Allenba......
Author of *Wa......*

"In *Smashing the Wall of Fear*, Sean Hockensmith explores many of the obstacles that hold people back, and in convincing fashion offers antidotes."

Jeff Davidson MBA, CMC
Author of 24 books including *Breathing Space*

"*Smashing the Wall of Fear* contains a lot of wisdom. Let us hope the needy read it and apply it to their lives."

Bernie Siegel, M.D.
Bestselling Author of *Love, Medicine, and Miracles*

Smashing the Wall of Fear
Dynamic Strategies to Overcome the Obstacles in Your Life

by
Sean Hockensmith

Published by: **Dynamic Life Publishing, 429 Clearwater St., Johnstown, PA 15904.**

Library of Congress Catalog Card Number: 96-86670

Publisher's Cataloging in Publication
(Prepared by Quality Books Inc.)

Hockensmith, Sean
    Smashing the wall of fear : dynamic strategies to overcome the obstacles in your life / Sean Hockensmith. -- 1st ed.
    p.cm.
    Includes bibliographical references and index.
    ISBN 0-9651246-5-7 (hardcover)
    ISBN 0-9651246-8-1 (softcover)

    1. Fear. 2. Success.   I. Title.
BF575.F2H63 1997   152'.46
                                   QBI96-40370

ATTENTION CORPORATIONS, ASSOCIATIONS, AND OTHER ORGANIZATIONS: Quantity discounts are available on bulk purchases of this book for educational purposes, fund raising, or gift giving. For information call **1-888-925-5762** or contact: Dynamic Life Publishing, 429 Clearwater St., Johnstown, PA 15904-1340.

ACKNOWLEDGMENTS

To put it simply, this book could not have been completed without the help of many different people. Unfortunately, it is impossible to acknowledge everyone who has been influential in this project. Nonetheless, it is necessary to mention a few.

To Gina Leis, you have done more than just brilliantly edit this book. You have been a dynamic role model for me to follow. Words cannot express the impact you have had on my life. Thank you for your unconditional love. You are a giant in my life!

To Eric Bowser, your wisdom shines forth from every page of this book. Your assistance in this project has been nothing less than paramount. Thank you for *living* what you believe instead of merely *saying* what you believe. Most of all, thank you for teaching me about the power of a dream. You are a diamond in the rough!

To Diana Barth who did a fine job copyediting this book. Thank you for your attention to the details.

To Phil Langerholc and Nathan Smith, my computer consultants and friends who spent many hours counseling me. Thank you for sharing your wisdom with me and guiding me in the right direction.

To Thomas and Mary Jo Hockensmith, my parents and my friends. Thanks for reading an early draft of this book and giving me some suggestions. Thanks, Mom, for believing in me and supporting me even when you didn't understand how I could possibly achieve my dreams. You taught me about the power of faith. Thanks, Dad, for having the courage to tell me what you really thought. It would have been easy for you to hide behind a wall. Instead, you taught me that if I am going to succeed, I had to be extremely courageous.

To Mark Cable, thank you for giving me my first personal development book, *The Game of Life and How to Play It* by Florence Scovel Shinn. In a way, you helped launch my career.

To all those people who read bits and pieces of early drafts. Thank you Mike Sekela, Trudy Dilling, and Bill Harris.

To Kevin Gabrovsek, thank you for having the audacity to challenge many of my strategies and ideas. You have helped me to refine them and make them more effective.

To Jim Bowser who taught me the difference between a habit and a ritual. Thanks for your advice.

To my many teachers and mentors along my journey through life. Although I may or may not know you, I thank you nonetheless. Without you, *Smashing the Wall of Fear* could not exist.

To Tony Robbins, thank you for coaching me to access more of my personal power.

To Les Brown, thank you for providing me with additional motivation to live my dreams.

To Marianne Williamson, thank you for educating me about the relationship between love and fear.

To Charles Givens, thank you for teaching me about business success and the importance of taking total responsibility for my life.

To Bernie Siegel, thank you for inspiring me to be my own unique person despite pressure from my peers.

To Susan Jeffers, thank you for showing me that fear is usually an educational problem, not a psychological problem, and that I must "feel the fear and do it anyway."

To Wayne Dyer, thank you for uncovering the unlimited power of a thought. I challenge you to a game of tennis.

To Mark Victor Hansen and Jack Canfield, thank you for giving me real life references of people who have overcome major obstacles on the way to achieving their dreams. Your books and tapes are a source of motivation for me whenever I encounter a wall.

To Napoleon Hill, Maxwell Maltz, and Norman Vincent Peale, thank you for the outstanding foundation you laid in the area of personal development.

To Zig Ziglar, thank you for making the distinction between positive thinking and positive believing.

To Denis Waitley, thank you for demonstrating the importance of meticulous research.

To Morris Goodman, thank you for revealing the power of the human spirit and the resiliency of the human body.

To Rich Ruffalo, thank you for showing me that vision is more important than eyesight.

To Stephen Covey, thank you for instructing me that my character is much more important than my personality.

To Robert Schuller, thank you for teaching me to see the possibilities in my life.

To Norman Cousins, thank you for harnessing the power of laughter.

To Shakti Gawain, thank you for your example of dynamic living.

To great teachers like Joan Borysenko, Louise Hay, and Deepak Chopra, thank you for teaching me how to channel the power of my mind and spirit.

To Jim Rohn and Shad Helmstetter, thank you for demonstrating the power of spoken words.

ACKNOWLEDGMENTS

To Robert Fulghum, thank you for reminding me that I can live dynamically by excelling in the simple fundamentals of life.

To the rural country roads of Pennsylvania where I rode thousands of miles on my bicycle. Thank you for being a part of my rejuvenation and inspiration. You refreshed my mind and body, which allowed me to write closer to my potential.

To all those people in the comfort zone who consciously or unconsciously did their best to pull me down to a life of mediocrity. Thank you for supplying me with extra motivation to achieve my dreams.

Most of all, to my Creator who inspired me and guided me to write this book. You made me realize how precious the gift of desire really is. Thank you for choosing me as the one to bring this book into existence. What an honor it is to serve you!

*Dedicated to the unlimited wall smashing ability
that exists within you.
Let it rest no more!*

TABLE OF CONTENTS

PREFACE

This book simply HAD to be written. The vast majority of our society does not understand the real purpose and intent of fear in their life. As a result, fear has devastated the lives of millions of people and it has undoubtedly had some negative effect upon your life as well. Fear might be causing you to settle for a lackluster, complacent existence when you could be enjoying a dynamic, fulfilling life.

The good news is that it is possible for you to learn how to handle your fears. It does not matter how badly fear has hurt you in your past. You can still learn how to overcome the obstacles in your life (smash your walls of fear) and live your dreams. No longer do you have to settle for a life of mediocrity. There is still time for you to change your life regardless of your current age, knowledge, or experience. *Smashing the Wall of Fear* contains the specific strategies and ideas that you need to move beyond your current fears, whatever they may be.

My motivation to write this book stemmed from the toll that fear has taken upon my own life. Fear has caused me so much emotional, mental, and physical pain that I became passionate about discovering a way to avoid feeling fear in my life. I assumed that by eliminating fear from my life, I could avoid a significant amount of pain and discomfort as well.

After a long period of research combined with many personal experiences, I found that my assumption was wrong! There is no permanent way to avoid feeling fear. Fear is a part of life that will never go away.

Although I never found a way to rid my life of fear, I did make an amazing discovery in the process. I discovered that fear was not the enemy I had originally believed it to be. Instead, it was my friend, a friend who could literally transform the quality of my life.

At first, the thought of accepting fear as a friend seemed unheard of, until I began to experiment with the idea. The results were nothing less than amazing. I began to see my life with a whole new perception. Suddenly, I found myself enjoying certain fearful situations that once had been unpleasant and painful for me. Although I still felt fear in many different situations, I learned to handle it and even thrive upon it at certain times. Eventually, I began to link excitement to fear rather than the agony and misery I had once associated with fear.

Smashing the Wall of Fear contains those same cutting edge strategies that I adhere to every day of my life. It is my honor to make these strategies available to you. I know you can benefit from this book as much as I have. It only takes a small investment of your time to reap enormous benefits.

In this day and age of information overload, few of us can keep up to date in even one field. Thus, you need simple practical strategies that you can easily apply in your life without taking away from your already limited amount of time. *Smashing the Wall of Fear* was written in everyday common language so that you can easily understand and more importantly, apply the strategies to your own life to make changes today. By applying the strategies contained within these pages, the benefits that you receive will begin to spill over into every area of your life.

Every fiber of my being went into this book project so that you can benefit from this information as much as I have. During my writing process, I focused on one primary question, "Will this be useful to YOU?" From there, I eliminated everything that did not pass the test. As a result, you now have the key information that, when applied, can make your life more exciting, creative, adventurous, and dynamic.

INTRODUCTION

Welcome to the world of wall smashing! You are about to depart on a thrilling journey through your dynamic zone, the place where you overcome those fearful obstacles in your life that are blocking you from the attainment of your dreams. As you prepare for your adventure, keep in mind that it is you alone who will determine to what heights you will soar. This book can only supply you with the specific ideas and strategies that it takes to succeed; the rest is up to you. You alone must be the one who smashes the walls in your life.

Walls are simply the obstacles you have in your life. Your walls could be a lack of money, a lack of experience, a challenging relationship, a disability, health problems, discouragement from a loved one, a "dead end" job, or anything else that blocks you from achieving your dreams. To achieve your dreams, your only choice is to smash through those walls that are in your way. This is done by listening to the expert guidance of your special friend who will accompany you throughout your journey. This friend is none other than fear itself. Yes, your fear will direct you to the right walls at the right time so that you can consistently move closer to the attainment of your dreams.

Chances are, you are probably saying, "Fear is anything but a friend in my life!" Well, I agree. Fear is indeed wreaking havoc upon the lives of millions of people and it has undoubtedly left its marks upon your life as well. But this does not have to be the case! Most of your pain associated with fear likely stems from your misunderstanding of the real purpose of fear. Instead of perceiving fear as a friend that you listen to and learn from, you probably perceive fear as an enemy that you should avoid. To correct this situation, you must gain the proper knowledge about fear so that you can rid your life of this "enemy" and transform it back into the friend it was originally meant to be.

Smashing the Wall of Fear teaches you how to understand the emotion of fear so that you can begin to use it as a friend in your daily life. Using fear as a friend will transform the quality of your life, forever. It will also pay you dividends of joy for the rest of your life. You will be free to live the kind of dynamic life that you may have given up on long ago.

Although these strategies are written specifically for you, they also can benefit any relationship, family, business, organization, community, or country. These principles are universal in their application and, therefore, any group of people would stand to benefit from their applications. Nonetheless, you must realize that before change can occur on a large scale, you must first ignite your own changes at the personal level. Only by taking control of your own life and learning how to smash your own walls of fear can you ever influence other people to smash their walls. Do your part for the good of the world by reading and, more importantly, applying the strategies tucked away within the pages of this book.

> *"I never teach my pupils; I only attempt to provide the conditions in which they can learn."*
> Albert Einstein

Too many people are being controlled by their fears instead of learning to control them. Rather than facing their fears, many people are resorting to things like legal and/or illegal drugs as a means to avoid their fears. Every day millions of people flock to doctors, pharmacies, liquor stores, and bars across the nation to buy mind-altering substances to relieve them from their fears. Psychiatrists are writing prescriptions for antidepressant drugs like Prozac, Anafranil, Zoloft, Luvox, and Paxil as if they are some type of candy. Dr. Wayne Dyer, author of *Pulling Your Own Strings*, reported, "More than 100 million prescriptions a year are given out for antidepressant and tranquilizing drugs" in the United States alone. In addition, he cites that America is also the home of over 12 million alcoholics. The massive use of prescription drugs and alcohol has grown to deadly proportions. Worse yet is the increasingly widespread use of illegal drugs. It is plain to see that we are facing an epidemic. And a large part of this epidemic is traceable back to our misunderstanding and avoidance of the emotion of FEAR.

It is true that the short-term result of legal drug use is sometimes effective, but the medium and long term results are often extremely ineffective, not to mention dangerous. I'm here to tell you that drugs will never rid you of your fears! The power to overcome your fears can only be found within yourself. You already possess it. Yet, you must exhibit the necessary courage to access this special power.

During these turbulent times, when you feel as if you are barely hanging on, you need something to cling to, some simple reference that teaches you how to thrive on fear instead of "freezing." In short, you need something that will pull you through the hard times. Thus, the creation of *Smashing the Wall of Fear*.

11

A FEW TIPS TO GET THE MOST OUT OF YOUR READING

The following suggestions will help to ensure that you get the most out of this book. These tips will also allow you to make the best use of your time in the process.

The first tip is to make sure that you understand every word that you read. Even though this book is written in non-technical common language, it is possible to misinterpret the meaning of a section if you do not understand the definition of a particular word. To avoid this problem, it would be wise for you to open this book to the glossary and become familiar with the definitions of the key words. If you come to a word in the text not listed in the glossary, by all means, refer to your dictionary. Make sure you understand all of the words so that you can gain a full understanding of the content of this book.

The second tip is to read this book as if it was the first personal development book you ever read. Your enthusiasm, excitement, and energy will cause you to retain more of the information.

The third tip is to read this book in chronological order since each chapter builds on the foundation laid in the previous chapter.

The fourth tip is to have a pen or highlighter nearby so that you can truly "own" this book by marking all the key ideas, strategies, and quotations that specifically speak to you. Also, write notes in the margins as you feel inspired to do so. This book will provoke many creative ideas in your mind. Don't let your inspirations slip away; they may never come back!

The fifth tip is to question everything that you read. That's right! Don't believe a word you read unless it agrees with your own common sense. Keep in mind that there is no such thing as an expert in anything! It does not matter who the author is; you alone are the expert in your own life. Since you are the expert in your life, it is important to realize that different ideas and strategies will "speak" to you at different times along your life's journey. The strategy that is best for you at this particular moment will not necessarily be the best strategy for you after several years of growing, changing, and improving. It all depends upon your current level of mental, emotional, social, and spiritual growth.

"Does this strategy work in my own life?"
The ultimate test

The sixth tip is to read *Smashing the Wall of Fear* as though it cost you $10,000.00. Act as though you had to work for months in order to afford this book. Treat it the same way you would treat your finest antique. This attitude will create a sense of passion that will motivate you to actually use these strategies in your own life. This approach is not unrealistic because any one of these strategies could justifiably warrant the investment of a large amount of money on your part. It just so happened that you got a tremendous bargain and didn't have to pay $10,000.00.

The seventh tip is to read the entire book. Although you made a wise choice in purchasing this book, it was only the first step. The critical question is, "Do you have the discipline and courage to read the entire book?" Research has shown that less than 10% of the people who buy nonfiction books ever read past chapter one. I dare you to become part of the elite 10%. By doing so, you will reap the rewards for a long time to come.

> *"You will never 'find' time for anything. If you want time you must make it."*
> Charles Buxton

This book is not another one of the thousands of books that tell you all about achieving your dreams while forgetting to mention the trials and tribulations that you will encounter along your journey. *Smashing the Wall of Fear* is a book about the truth. At times, you may cringe at the honesty presented in this book, but nothing will be held back. You deserve to know the complete truth about fear and what it takes to move beyond your walls. Those of you who are strong enough to handle the truth will benefit greatly. The process will not be easy, but I guarantee it will be worth it!

The eighth tip is to read another book by a different author while you are reading this book. When you finish each section or chapter of this book, read a section or a chapter of a different book. The contrast will keep your mind alert and you will remember more of the information that you read. In addition, you will also have a more dynamic experience as a result.

The ninth and final tip is simply to enjoy yourself as you read. Life is short. It is absurd not to enjoy everything that you do.

It is now time for you to embark on an exhilarating adventure into your dynamic zone. Join me as you discover how to smash your walls of fear once and for all. Remember, you deserve to achieve your dreams! I now present to you...*Smashing the Wall of Fear*.

"Come to the edge. No, we will fall.
Come to the edge. No, we will fall.
They came to the edge.
He pushed them and they flew."
Guillaume Apollinaire

CHAPTER 1

THE PURPOSE OF FEAR

"Do the thing you fear
and the death of fear is certain."
Ralph Waldo Emerson

There is an outbreak in our society and YOU have been infected! This disease is capable of destroying your life. No, it's not cancer or heart disease. It's something worse! This disease has ruined more lives than any other malady ever known to humankind. There has never been anything like it in the history of the world! In order to save yourself from disaster, you must acquire the vaccine to diminish the effects of this dreadful disease.

Every day, more and more people are giving up on their dreams and settling for a life of mediocrity as a result of this appalling disease. People are living quiet lives of desperation, merely grasping for survival, never aspiring to any kind of greatness. The National Institute of Mental Health estimates that this devastating disease costs our economy about 46 billion dollars a year in lost productivity and medical treatment. This disease is at the heart of all the anxiety disorders including panic disorder, phobias, obsessive-compulsive disorder, post-traumatic stress disorder, and generalized anxiety disorder. It is even largely at fault for the roughly 15 million people in the United States classified as clinically depressed. What is this horrid disease? And more importantly, how can we control it?

Well, the name of this horrid disease is FEAR! You may choose to call it anything from timidity, worry, nervousness, alarm, or distress to terror, panic, horror, or anguish. Some of its basic characteristics include excessive sweating, increased heartbeat, cold hands or feet, uneasy mind, nauseous feelings in the stomach, and tightness in your chest, back, or neck. Although these basic characteristics are uncomfortable in and of themselves, the real tragedy occurs when you hide from your fears instead of facing them.

The moment you allow your fears to cause you to quit pursuing the dreams of your heart, you will begin to feel empty. Eventually, your emptiness will escalate into feelings of worthlessness and uselessness that will cause you to experience the greatest pain of all, the pain of a broken spirit. This pain is much worse than any physical pain you have ever felt; it is a pain that does not go away by itself.

> *Who lived longer, the person who faced her fears and died courageously at 40 or the person who avoided her fears and died a coward at 80?*

Now that you understand a bit about the deadly powers of fear, you deserve to know that there does exist a cure to reverse the horrifying effects of this disease. The cure was discovered many years ago by a fellow named Ralph Waldo Emerson. After many years of research, Emerson came to the conclusion that the only way to cure this wretched disease is to "do the thing we fear!" In recent years psychologist Dr. Susan Jeffers reinforced Emerson's conclusion by coining the phrase "feel the fear and do it anyway."

Every form of effective modern day treatments and therapies for fear stem from this strategy. The most recent breakthroughs in treating fears involve using "virtual reality" computer programs as a form of exposure therapy. This form of treatment allows the patients to gradually face their fears until they eventually become comfortable with them after several sessions of treatment.

Regardless of the many different forms of therapies and treatments for fear, my goal is to supply you with the knowledge you need to treat yourself. This book is not a technical psychology book that makes you aware of all the current psychological services available to you. After all, many of you are already aware of them. Rather, this is a book that you can apply to yourself without having to run to a therapist every time you feel fearful

Now, to address the obvious question, "If we know we can control our fears by 'doing the things we fear,' then why isn't everybody doing it?" Well, it is practically impossible to motivate ourselves to do something that we perceive to be so painful. Many people wrongly believe that it is easier for them to suffer from this dreaded disease than it is to break free from its deadly clutches. Consequently, most people have decided that they would rather give up on their dreams than be courageous enough to face their fears.

It has become all too common for people to avoid doing the things they love, out of fear. People refuse offers for fantastic jobs, decline invitations to parties, and reject opportunities to become involved with certain organizations due to their fear of public speaking, social interactions, confrontations, or anything else for that matter. Other people are so afraid of snakes or bugs that they never allow themselves to experience the joys of hiking, camping, fishing, boating, or hunting. Still others are afraid to ask someone out on a date, drive over a bridge, tell a joke, initiate an intimate discussion, go swimming, take a test, fly in an airplane, ask a particular question, trust a family member, go to the doctor, attend a party, ride in an elevator, achieve a certain level of success, encounter failure, or tell someone "I love you." Many people are even afraid of the actual feeling of fear, as you will discover in a later chapter. There are literally thousands of different things that people fear, any of which are capable of stopping you from doing something that is very important to you.

"Somewhere along the path of growing up and older, we came to believe that fear was an acceptable excuse for inaction and avoidance. It is not."
Charles Givens

The good news is that there is still hope for you. You can learn how to motivate yourself to "do the thing you fear." You simply need to understand that the real purpose of fear in your life is to help you to grow into a more complete person. This will allow you to realize that facing your fears can be a very pleasurable and fulfilling process. Then, you need to apply your new understanding about fear to the obstacles that are preventing you from achieving your dreams. This process is known as "smashing your walls of fear."

As you begin your wall smashing journey, you need to understand that....

FEAR IS YOUR FRIEND

The only reason that fear is the worst disease on the planet is because most people misunderstand its message and consequently take the wrong type of actions. In truth, fear is really one of the best friends you could ever have. You can think of fear the same way you would think of any one of your human friends. Treat it as your own personal companion who is constantly by your side. The only difference between fear and a good human friend is that fear communicates through sensations and feelings instead of words, tonality, and body language. Nevertheless, fear truly wants you to succeed in life every bit as much as your best human friends do.

It is only natural for you to be startled by the preceding paragraph. After all, you have probably spent your entire life perceiving fear as your enemy and the objects of your fear as things that you should avoid. Nonetheless, you will soon realize that the basic nature of fear is to be your friend. Regardless of how bad your current relationship may be with fear, you can still learn how to harness its power.

> *"Before we can make friends with fear, it may be necessary to learn that fear is not the enemy."*
> Peter McWilliams and John-Roger

Fear exists in your life as a means of protection and guidance. It protects you from danger and guides you to the obstacles or "walls" that you need to encounter in your life in order to make you into a more complete person. When you choose not to follow its initial guidance, you force your fear to intensify each subsequent time. It does this as a means to motivate you to "do the thing you fear." However, the longer you wait to obey this guidance, the more it will appear that fear is your enemy.

Your relationship with fear is really no different from the kind of relationship that you have with someone that you love very deeply. Let's suppose that this person is your father. Imagine that your father politely asks you to wash the dishes after supper. You respond by telling him that you will wash them as soon as you make a "quick" phone call.

About a half hour later, there is a knock on your door. In a slightly more intense tonality, your father repeats his original request. Once again, you assure him that you will be there in a few seconds to do the dishes. Meanwhile, you get a few more phone calls and you forget about the dishes once more. This time, you become startled when you hear your father pounding on your door as if he was using a sledgehammer. Upon answering the door, you discover that his face is bright red and he has smoke coming out of his ears. At this point, you can easily interpret the change in the intensity of your father's current emotions. All of a sudden, it seems as though your father, your friend who dearly loves you, has now become your worst enemy. The truth is that he still loves you, but he is extremely angry at you for ignoring his request.

This example illustrates how angry a friend, even your own father, gets when you do not listen to his requests. Fear acts the same way when you continue to ignore its guidance. Every time you ignore the guidance of your fear, it continues to intensify until you finally "do the thing you fear."

It is likely that you are not accustomed to having such a loyal friend, a friend who will not permit you to take the easy way out. Chances are, your human friends do not hold you to such high standards. They probably tell you what you *want* to hear instead of what you *need* to hear. Often, they advise you of the *easiest* rather than the *best* way to do something.

Let's say that your dream is to be an actor. Suppose there is an audition next week. Hundreds of people will be auditioning for one part. Realistically, you have a very slim chance of getting the part since this is your first audition. As you contemplate whether or not you will attend, you feel some fear. In this case, your feelings of fear are guiding you to "do the thing you fear" by attending the audition.

When you mention the challenges involved with the audition to your human friends, most of them politely advise you to skip it. This is not a malicious act on their part. In their minds, they think they are doing you a favor by encouraging you to skip the audition. After all, they want you to avoid the pain of rejection.

Fear, on the other hand, will always encourage you to venture forth into a special place called your "dynamic zone." Your dynamic zone is the place where you take action to smash your walls of fear that are blocking the attainment of your dreams. By guiding you into your dynamic zone, fear is making you aware of what you need to do to improve the quality of your life. How else would you realize what you need to improve upon? If you felt comfortable about every aspect of your life, you would not have any motivation to make the necessary improvements to take your life to the next level.

"Fears that are faced, even if the act is difficult, lead to transformation of attitudes, leaving you with an increased sense of self-worth, control, and inner strength."
Dr. Joan Borysenko

Unfortunately, most of your human friends will encourage you to cling to your "comfort zone" instead of your dynamic zone. Your comfort zone is the place where everything is easy and comfortable, a place where you do not have any walls. It is a place where you do not have to think very much, a place where you can avoid most of your fears. Although your comfort zone is a much needed place for rest, it can also become extremely dangerous when you use it as a place to retreat from the pursuit of your dreams. When you choose not to pursue your dreams, your life begins to lose its meaning and you feel empty inside. Therefore, it is very unwise to listen to the advice of anyone who encourages you to use your comfort zone for that purpose.

Only the best of friends will consistently encourage you to venture forth into your dynamic zone and smash your walls of fear. Even though you will encounter a lot of discomfort and adversity along your journey, it is still the only way to achieve your dreams. As a human being, it is absolutely necessary to your health and happiness to pursue your dreams.

YOU MUST PURSUE YOUR DREAMS IN ORDER TO MOVE BEYOND YOUR CURRENT FEARS

Dreams are what life is all about. The dreams that you possess within your heart are gifts. They are uniquely yours and you owe it to yourself and to the people of this planet to pursue the attainment of these dreams. Without these dreams of yours, it would be impossible for you to motivate yourself to take action and move beyond your current fears.

"Don't let your fears stand in the way of your dreams."
The back of a T-shirt

Maybe your current dream is to develop an intimate relationship with your son, produce a movie, own your own profitable business, write a book, contribute some of your time to a community project, get elected to public office, remodel your bathroom, create an organization to help children who have suffered from child abuse, become financially independent, or to be a part of a dynamic family consisting of a spouse and five children. Maybe you want to achieve all of these dreams and more. Regardless of what your dreams might be, you alone must recognize them and courageously pursue their attainment in order to move beyond your current fears!

The dreams you have while you're awake are more powerful than the dreams you have while you're asleep.

If you choose to dodge your fears and quit pursuing the dreams of your heart, then you create a void in your life. Consequently, something will fill this void. After all, science has proven that a vacuum cannot exist for an extended amount of time. Unfortunately, most people choose to fill this void with false forms of fulfillment like drugs, alcohol, cigarettes, food, crime, gossip, gambling, pornography, or violence.

> *The poorest of them all is the one who is not actively pursuing her dream.*

Fortunately, you can choose to fill this void with joy by facing your fears and actively pursuing your most precious dreams. It doesn't even matter whether your actions are successful or unsuccessful. The fact that you give one hundred percent of your effort to achieve your dreams is enough to fill the void in your life with a "high" greater than any addictive substance, negative behavior, or ineffective habit could ever give you. In fact, pursuing your dreams will allow you to access the "ultimate high" that occurs when you know deep in your heart that you are living your life dynamically.

FEAR GUIDES YOU AND PROTECTS YOU THROUGH FEELINGS

Fear communicates with you through feelings. This can be a sinking feeling in your stomach, a knot in your neck, a lump in your throat, an ache in your back or virtually any kind of unpleasant sensation in your body. These feelings basically exist as a means to provide you with two invaluable services. They both **guide** you as to what you need to do next and **protect** you by warning you of danger. Either way, these feelings prepare you to encounter obstacles in your life.

The only way to distinguish whether your fear is guiding you or protecting you is by asking yourself one important question, "Will I harm myself or anyone else by facing my fear?" If you answer "No" to this question, then your feelings of fear are ones of guidance and you should indulge in the activity. But, if you answer "Yes," then your feelings of fear are ones of protection and you should avoid the activity. Realistically, had it not been for your fears, you would not have lived past your childhood. Surely, you would have died doing something totally illogical like diving into deep water without knowing how to swim, jumping off the roof of a tall building, approaching a dangerous animal, or running out into the middle of a busy intersection. In truth, the protection you receive from your fear is as essential to your well-being as is oxygen.

Imagine for a moment that a runaway car is speeding directly at you. In this case, the runaway car immediately awakens a fear response in your body. This natural response instantly pumps adrenaline throughout your entire body as a desperate means to supply you with enough energy to get out of the way.

Fear is a fight or flight response that urges you to do whatever it takes to save your life. It does so by giving you sensations and feelings that prompt you either to run away and escape the current danger or to stop and put up a fight. In the case of a speeding car, it would obviously be the best choice to run away from the danger.

On the other hand, there will be times when your life will not be in danger, times when the fear that you feel will be guiding you to do something. Let's look at a common fear of public speaking as an example of this guidance.

Suppose you have no experience speaking in public. Then, one day, someone unexpectedly invites you to make a special public presentation. Although you are shocked by the invitation, you nonetheless accept it. Since the event is scheduled almost two months in the future, you feel very little initial fear. All you feel is a slight gnawing in your stomach. Unbeknownst to you, this little gnawing sensation is really a friendly prompting from your fear to get you to prepare for your upcoming speech. Unfortunately, you never understood the real message of fear. As a result, you choose to disregard this subtle feeling of guidance. Instead, you decide to procrastinate.

As you continue to procrastinate, you force your fear to intensify progressively. Within a short period of time, that once slight gnawing sensation in your stomach transforms itself into a very irritating, almost nauseous feeling in your stomach. Furthermore, your chest and neck begin to feel tight. Suddenly, it is much more challenging for you to ignore the guidance of your fear since it feels so uncomfortable. At this point, you will either begin to prepare for your presentation or you will cancel your presentation altogether.

Looking back on this situation, you could have avoided much of your tension simply by following the initial guidance of your fear. All you had to do was to prepare for the presentation for a short period of time each day. By doing so, you could have saved yourself from having to experience such a large amount of fear several weeks later. The following list includes samples of daily actions that you could have taken to get yourself properly prepared for your presentation:

■ Gather information about the audience you will be addressing.
■ Make an outline of the topics you want to cover in your presentation.
■ Listen to several different audiocassette programs on effective public speaking, read books about public speaking, or join Toastmasters or some other local speaking club.
■ Watch video tapes and model techniques from great speakers like Martin Luther King, Marva Collins, Zig Ziglar, Denis Waitley, Bernie Siegel, John F. Kennedy, Lonise Bias, Les Brown, Tony Robbins, Winston Churchill, Wayne Dyer, Marianne Williamson, etc.
■ Spend ten minutes a day rehearsing specific parts of your presentation.

Taking actions like these could have easily saved you from feeling so paralyzed by your fear. In fact, every aspect of your life should follow the creed of "doing the thing you fear." Following this advice will keep your fear under much greater control and it will not seem like such an enemy.

Another example of fear guiding you to take action is when you get a subtle feeling of discomfort in early January about doing your taxes that are due April 15th. Since this feeling is very subtle at first, it is very easy to ignore. However, as time draws closer to the April 15th deadline, your feelings of fear will intensify progressively until they reach a level of pain that finally prompts you to take the necessary action.

To avoid much of this pain, you could obey the initial guidance of your fear and complete your taxes well before the deadline. All it takes is the proper understanding and a little bit of discipline to rid yourself of a significant amount of fear.

Develop an attitude of trust and appreciation for your friend. Realize that your fear will guide you to the most dynamic, fulfilling life you could ever imagine if you only follow its lead. Maybe it is telling you to confront someone about a certain issue. Or, maybe your fear is telling you to accept a new job that requires you to move out of town. Whatever the message, you need to take action upon this guidance.

| *Whatever you fear, is what you need to do next.* |

Avoiding a fearful experience will only stunt your emotional growth and cause you to miss out on a potentially joyful experience. Think about your own life. Don't you always feel better after you do something that you were afraid to do? Remember a time when you did something simple, yet courageous, like "breaking the ice" with a person you could have easily avoided. Even if the exchange was a bit awkward, you probably felt a deep sense of joy and relief afterward. It is only natural to feel good after you do something courageous. In addition to feeling good, you also increase your odds of acting upon an even bigger wall in your future and consequently experiencing even more joy.

Remember, fear is your friend and it would rather communicate with you in a subtle, loving way than a ruthless, demanding way. It wants you to smash your walls of fear and feel the joy of progress as you move closer to the attainment of your dreams. But, when you ignore the message of your fear, you force it to intensify progressively until you finally decide to comply with it.

> *The law of nature is growth and fear enforces this law!*

EVERYONE FEARS UNFAMILIAR SITUATIONS

Regardless of who you are, you will feel fear whenever you face a totally unfamiliar situation. These feelings are absolutely natural and therefore, you should not deny them. However, with the proper preparation, you can significantly lessen the amount of fear that you have to feel.

Take, for example, a woman who has never gone through the experience of childbirth. Undoubtedly, she will feel some degree of fear over such an unfamiliar situation. The only question is, "How much fear will she have to feel?" The answer will be primarily determined by the amount and quality of her preparation. If she visits a well qualified doctor, attends classes, reads books, visualizes everything working out perfectly, and gets advice from the right people, she will likely feel a much lower level of anxiety as she progresses through the various stages of pregnancy. On the other hand, if she asks the "wrong" people for advice, skips her doctor appointments, and imagines the worst possible outcome, then she will likely experience a much higher level of anxiety.

Similarly, if you never spent a significant amount of time away from your family and you suddenly needed to spend a week by yourself in a distant city, then you would also feel some degree of fear. In this case, your fear would be preparing you for the challenges involved in experiencing a different type of lifestyle away from your family. It is only natural for brand new situations to contain the element of fear. Otherwise, you would not have any motivation to properly prepare for the event.

Fearing something unfamiliar does not necessarily mean that it terrifies you. It doesn't even mean that you are displaying any obvious physiological or behavioral signs of fear. It only means that you have some degree of uneasiness about the unfamiliar situation. Remember, the primary goal of this book is not to teach you how to rid yourself of fear, but rather to teach you how to control and handle your fears so that you do not feel overwhelmed by them.

As for now, it is important to realize that everyone fears the unknown and unfamiliar. It is totally natural for you to fear a new experience such as performing in front of an audience, calling a business prospect, discussing important family issues, buying a new home, changing jobs, or opening a business. Even your greatest role models basically have the same fears as you do. The only difference between them and you is that they have acted in the face of fear more often than you have. They are really no different from you. At best, they only have more experience in certain key areas.

The great therapist Carl Rogers once said, "Whatever is most personal is most general." Rogers was referring to the fact that deep down in the most private chambers of our minds, everyone fears the same things. The only difference is that some people have worked through their fears while others have not. The following list includes some of the most common fears initially shared by everyone regardless of their income, social status, religious affiliation, marital status, or career.

- Public speaking
- Failure
- Rejection
- Poor health
- Financial loss
- Death

Since everyone essentially fears the same things, you might as well learn how to thrive upon your fears instead of being paralyzed or frozen by them.

Take public speaking for example. The fear of public speaking is common for all types of people regardless of their income, nationality, sex, or age. It does not matter who you are or what you do, you will feel some degree of fear whenever you speak in public. Statistically, the fear of public speaking continually ranks as the greatest fear in the world. It is more widely feared than death itself! And people will continue to possess this fear and any other fear until they finally access the courage to "do the thing they fear," as Emerson would say.

Even by doing the thing you are afraid to do, it is rare to entirely wipe out your fear of it after only one experience. Usually, a dynamic activity such as public speaking will take numerous efforts before you actually feel some degree of comfort while doing it. In truth, it is actually best to have a small degree of fear before you take part in a dynamic activity. Research has shown that well-managed feelings of fear tend to give you an extra boost of energy that helps you to perform closer to your potential. Many actors, speakers, and entertainers have learned to thrive on this sense of fear that they feel before their performance. The key is to face your fear often enough until you have nothing left, except for a reasonable amount of anxiety that will only help you to do your best.

> *"I decided the best way to get over my fears was to face each one head-on, until the experience or even the anticipation of the experience no longer slowed me down."*
> Charles Givens

The things you fear are indeed the things you need to do. Listen to your fear, take action upon its guidance, and remember that everyone's journey through life is different. You will not necessarily face the same fears at the same time as someone else. Everyone is on her own unique journey; making progress at different speeds, taking different routes, and even using different strategies. Although we all fear the same things, each person will learn to handle certain fears at different points in her life.

A businessman who has never spent time in the woods as a child will certainly experience fear when his family asks him to take them on a camping trip. Since camping is unfamiliar to him, it will trigger feelings of fear as a means to help him to prepare for this new experience. The same would not be true for a man who spent a considerable amount of time camping and experiencing the outdoors as a child. This man would experience little or no fear about taking his family on a camping trip, because camping is a familiar experience for him.

The same holds true for a housewife who has never traveled outside her home state. She will undoubtedly experience some degree of fear the first time she accompanies her husband on a business trip to another country. Since extensive traveling is unfamiliar to this woman, it is natural for her to feel anxious in this situation. Her fear is getting her prepared for the new experience. Everyone fears the unknown. It's human nature.

Even the governor of your state who has acted fearlessly in many different political situations would feel fear if she was asked to sing the national anthem before a crowd of 50 people at a junior high school basketball game. Of course, this is assuming that she has no previous experience singing in public. On the other hand, if the governor's husband, an experienced soloist, was asked to sing at the game, he would experience very little fear over this situation. The reason is simple. Her husband has had plenty of experience singing in front of other people. He has already worked through this particular fear whereas she has not.

The good news is that once you successfully do something, even one time, your fear will lessen the next time you do it. By successfully doing something, your fear no longer has any reason to continue to manifest at such a high intensity. After all, you have already proven that you can handle the situation. You no longer need as much guidance or preparation in the future.

THERE WILL ALWAYS BE FEAR IN YOUR LIFE

Doing the thing you fear is obviously a very uncomfortable process. It is understandable why you may want to hide in your comfort zone to avoid these feelings of discomfort. The flaw with this philosophy is that you cannot escape fear. Even if you hide in your comfort zone, fear will still be present in your life. It doesn't matter what you choose to do, there will always be fear in your life.

Yes, in the short-term, it is possible not to feel fearful by simply avoiding situations that trigger fear, but in the long-term, you will begin to develop a much worse fear. You will fear that you wasted your life away. Suddenly, you will realize that you were alive and breathing for all these years, yet you never took the time to face your fears and pursue your dreams. This pain will hurt at least as much as all the short-term pain you would have felt if you had courageously faced your fears. Often, you can even experience much less pain over the long-term by courageously facing your fears as you encounter them. Knowing this, doesn't it only seem logical to pursue your dreams instead of hiding in your comfort zone?

Honor your dreams more than your comfort zone.

Surely you can remember a friend from your childhood who always talked about pursuing some special dream of hers. It doesn't matter if her dream was to become a famous actor, a world-class chef, or a best-selling author. All that matters is that this person had a dream with a special meaning to her, a dream charged with passion. Then, years later you met up with this person only to find that she had given up her dream and decided to go to college to take up a field that was more acceptable to her family.

This is a prime example of someone who chose the comfortable, rather than the dynamic route, a person who conformed her life to other people's expectations instead of pursuing her own unique dreams. In addition to the fact that she will lack any real fulfillment in her career, she will also experience the same amount of fear as she would have faced if she had followed her dreams. She will only experience her fear over things that are not really that important to her. Worse yet is the wrenching pain she will feel when she realizes that she wasted a portion of her life pursuing something she really did not want.

There is no sense in pursuing something out of a desire to avoid your fears. In reality, it does not matter what you choose to do, fear will still be present in your life, fear will eventually find you. You will always fear something. Remember, fear is an integral part of life. You never conquer it, you only learn to handle it. There is not enough time allotted to you in this short lifetime in order to experience and master every aspect of life, which would be the only way for you to conquer fear. The best you can do is to consistently expand your comfort zone every day of your life.

With this in mind, you might as well do something that will bring you joy instead of something that will bring you pain and boredom. Always move in the direction of your dreams. Since you will feel fear regardless of where you go and what you do, you might as well encounter fear as you are pursuing whatever is most important to you.

INTERPRET FEAR AS EXCITEMENT

Even though fear is an integral part of your life, it is still very possible to experience it in a more bearable way. This is done by changing the labels you attach to fearful situations and experiences. I am suggesting that you learn to associate excitement, adventure, and passion with the uncomfortable situations that you currently associate with fear, dread, and worry.

Begin by realizing that the same sensations that you currently link to fear are not much different from those you associate with excitement. Each of the two emotions involves similar characteristics such as an increased heartbeat, a heightened state of awareness, sweating, shallow breathing, and sudden bursts of energy. The only thing that separates the two emotions from each other is the way you interpret them. When you interpret certain sensations to be fearful, you create tension in your body which produces fear. On the other hand, when you interpret these same sensations as excitement, you create acceptance in your body which allows you to feel excited.

Notice that the sensations do not change. Your heart still beats fast, your awareness is still heightened, your breath is still shallow, you still sweat, and you still get a rush of energy. Everything is the same except for the interpretation or meaning you attach to these sensations. If you interpret the sensations to be fearful, then you feel tension and stress. If you interpret the sensations to be exciting, then you experience acceptance and fun. The reason for this phenomenon is that your mind has been conditioned over the years to accept the emotion of excitement as something pleasurable and to reject the emotion of fear as something painful. Beyond that, excitement and fear are the same emotion.

Consider the high school boy who picks up the telephone to call a girl for his first date. He will undoubtedly feel some strong sensations in his body as he performs this unfamiliar action. He may begin to sweat, get "butterflies" in his stomach, or even feel lightheaded. If he interprets these sensations as being fearful, then he will subsequently tense his body and imagine the worst outcome in his mind, which will cause him to feel fearful. On the other hand, if the boy interprets these sensations as being exciting, his body will remain loose and his mind will visualize a wonderful outcome. Consequently, the boy will actually feel excited, which will increase his odds of getting the date.

Deepak Chopra, author of *Ageless Body, Timeless Mind* and *Unconditional Life,* uses a roller coaster example to illustrate the subtle difference between excitement and fear. Two people are riding a roller coaster. The first person interprets the experience as being fearful. As a result, she tenses her body and generates a flood of stress hormones. This results in feelings of terror. The second person interprets the experience with a sense of excitement. She lets herself go and accepts the sensations produced by the roller coaster ride. This causes her body to produce a flood of positive joyful chemicals like interleukin and interferon that strengthen her immune system and simultaneously cause her to feel excited. Both people feel the same sensations, yet each one interprets them differently, which results in two different experiences. The first person hated the ride while the second person loved it.

Placing the proper labels upon your experiences is absolutely vital to creating a dynamic life for yourself. Quite often, you can feel excited simply by referring to something as being exciting. Since you are the one who operates your mind, you have the right to decide what you will label your feelings, sensations, experiences, and situations. With excitement and fear being the same emotion, you would be a fool to choose to label any sensation or situation as being fearful. Given the choice, your mind will always choose to do something exciting before it chooses to do something fearful.

Did you know that the exact same nerve endings in your body are capable of producing two totally different emotional responses? That's right, both fear and excitement are produced by the same nerve endings. The only difference that determines which emotion you will feel is how your mind interprets the sensation.

> *"The ability to feel is indivisible... The same nerve endings are required for weeping and dancing, fear and ecstasy."*
> Sam Keen

Keep this strategy in mind as you read this book. Remember that any time fear is mentioned, you can easily choose to interpret it as excitement without forfeiting any of its protection or guidance. Doing so will only cause your mind to perceive this guidance as much more pleasurable. Thus, you will feel more inclined to take action and obey its message. Indeed, this strategy will prove invaluable to you in your wall smashing endeavors!

THE TRUTH WILL SET YOU FREE

Suppose you do make the mistake of labeling a certain experience as being fearful instead of exciting. Fortunately, the truth still remains that fear is nothing more than an emotion. It does not have the power to hurt you. This realization is what can free you to act upon any given situation regardless of how fearful you may feel.

Dr. Susan Jeffers, author of the wonderful book, *Feel the Fear and Do It Anyway*, discovered that handling fear is more of an educational than a psychological problem. She explains that there is nothing wrong with fear itself. In fact, it serves many useful purposes. The problem occurs when you misunderstand the real purpose of fear. Instead of feeling the fear and taking action, many people wrongly perceive fear as something that paralyzes them from taking action. The truth is that an emotion is not capable of stopping you from taking action. You always retain the right to act in spite of any fear that you may be feeling. You simply need to educate yourself about this truth.

Maybe one of your fears is approaching a prominent business person to ask her to buy a certain product from you. In this case, you can free yourself to ask this person for an order by understanding that fear is merely an emotion and emotions cannot stop you from taking action. By consistently reminding yourself about this truth, you will come to realize that regardless of someone's status or position, she is only a human being, no different from any other human being, certainly no better than you.

"Ye shall know the truth and the truth shall set you free."
Jesus Christ

It is always wise to look at a situation with an objective viewpoint. Many times the simple realization that fear is only an emotion or that this person is no different from you is enough to get you to take action. The truth has a way of motivating you to take action. Instead of mesmerizing yourself in fear, learn to recognize the truth of any given situation.

Let's suppose you belong to your church choir. You have sung in the choir for seven years and have thoroughly enjoyed it. It is very comfortable for you to sing in front of the members of your church as long as you are alongside the other choir members.

Then, while you are at Tuesday night practice, your pastor approaches you and asks if you would sing solo at a special ceremony being held next Monday. Since you highly respect your pastor, you agree to his request even though you are trembling with fear. As the pastor walks away, immediately you break into a cold sweat, your heart begins to pound, your breathing becomes shallow, and your whole body becomes tense. Fear instantly fills your entire being. Exposing yourself in front of the entire congregation is one of your greatest fears. Nonetheless, you decide to face your fear.

Since you are already familiar with the format of the ceremony and you know all the songs you will be singing, there is very little else you can do to prepare yourself. In this case, you could better cope with your fear by making a list of all the truths about this particular situation. Your list might include the following truths:

- Fear is only an emotion and emotions cannot stop me from taking action.
- I know the format of the ceremony and I know all of the songs that I will be singing. I am totally prepared.

- My pastor must really respect me since he asked me to sing solo at such an important ceremony.
- I am a gifted singer with many years of experience. Hundreds of people have sincerely complimented me on my talents and skills.
- My pastor and many members of the church support me and want me to succeed.
- The members of the church in the audience are no different from me. No one is any better than anyone else.
- I have a wonderful opportunity to give of myself to my church, to my pastor, to the congregation, and to God by singing at this ceremony.
- I really do love to sing.
- As a child, I used to dream of singing solo in front of a large group of people.
- My pastor, the members of my church, my family, and most importantly, myself, will be proud of me.
- I can teach my children to face their walls of fear by using my courage to face my own.
- I will experience so much joy once I get past my initial feelings of anxiety.
- I will feel closer to my creator as a result of this experience.
- I am free to label this situation as being exciting instead of fearful.
- I have agreed to sing, so I might as well not drown myself in fear. After all, I am going to sing no matter how much I focus on my fear.

Once you understand the truth of this particular situation, you set yourself free to feel much less fear for the week preceding your performance. To expand on this strategy, you could carry this list of truths in your purse or wallet for the entire week preceding the ceremony. This way you can refer to these truths at any time throughout the week when you begin to feel a bit fearful. Doing this will remind you about the truth of the situation and will likely put your mind at ease.

It is so easy to imagine ridiculous scenarios and to saturate yourself in fear if you do not take the time to discover the truth. Filling yourself with fear will only make it harder for you to perform at your best. Remember the age-old truth, "Whatever you choose to focus on, you will get more of." With this in mind, learn to focus on the truth of any fearful situation instead of the fear.

THE PURPOSE OF FEAR

THERE ARE THINGS YOU SHOULD FEAR AND THINGS YOU SHOULD NOT FEAR

On the surface, it seems as though everyone should be pursuing their dreams. Although this statement is true, many people do not pursue their dreams because they have learned to fear the very things that they need to do in order to achieve their dreams. The following list includes some of these activities and experiences that should NOT be feared.

- ☑ Public speaking
- ☑ Initiating business ventures
- ☑ Learning new things
- ☑ Expressing your ideas
- ☑ Meeting unfamiliar people
- ☑ Organizing functions
- ☑ Speaking up for yourself
- ☑ Confronting certain people
- ☑ Visiting new places
- ☑ Doing things a different way

Unfortunately, you have made it difficult for yourself to achieve your dreams by adopting many of these "learned fears." After all, it is necessary to take many of these actions in order to smash through the walls in your life.

Although society has either consciously or unconsciously taught you to avoid and fear many vital dynamic activities, you must take it upon yourself to reprogram your own mind to associate pleasure and excitement with these experiences. Blaming society will not change your situation. Even though 99% of your fears are "learned fears," it's still up to you to make the decision as to what you will continue to fear and what you will no longer fear. Fortunately, the simple fact that you are reading this book proves that you are the type of person who is capable of reprogramming your mind.

The things you should continue to fear simply include anything that would harm you or anyone else. Somebody once said, "It is better to be a coward for a moment than to be dead for the rest of your life." This person obviously knew what she was saying. It is certainly much wiser to avoid dangerous situations than it is for you to take unnecessary risks that put your life at stake.

Although it is easy to see why you should avoid situations that put your life in danger, you must also learn to avoid situations that harm your life or the lives of others in less obvious ways. The following list will give you an idea about what kind of additional experiences and situations that you *should* learn to fear:

◊   Creating a miserable atmosphere for your spouse because of something that happened to you at work.

◊   Ignoring your brother because of a small misunderstanding in your past.

◊   Designing a plan to avoid certain responsibilities of your job.

◊   Being a poor role model for your children to follow.

◊   All types of crime and wrongdoing.

The preceding list includes examples of some of the things that you should learn to fear. This is not to imply that it is necessary to develop an uncontrollable phobia about them. It is only to say that it is healthy to fear them to the point where you will avoid them.

In addition to the preceding list of "things you should fear," there does exist one abstract fear that was intentionally omitted. This fear is one of the most important and most beneficial fears you could ever create for yourself. Developing this fear will pay you big dividends in the long run. It is the **FEAR OF DYING BEFORE YOU EVER REALLY LIVED**.

The fear of dying before you ever really lived helps to make sure that you pursue the dreams of your heart on a daily basis. It reminds you that your time on Earth may expire at any moment. This particular fear motivates you to live today as if it was your last day. After all, one of these "today's" will be your last day.

> *There is no greater sin than to be granted the gift of life, only to return it unused.*

Wasting your precious time on this planet really should instill fear in your heart. It should also embarrass you to be given so many talents, only to let them go to waste. Most of us have so much talent that we could virtually do anything we desire. All we have to do is to be willing to feel a little bit of discomfort along our journey. Don't be another person who settles for mere survival rather than a dynamic life. Develop the fear of dying before you ever really lived and use it as motivation to smash through your....WALLS.

CHAPTER 2

WALLS: THE OBSTACLES BLOCKING YOU FROM ACHIEVING YOUR DREAMS

"People come to many walls in their life. Some go around them and some go over them. But I have always chosen to go through them!"
Eric J. Bowser

You are a miracle! The chances of you getting to this point in time where you are right now are literally beyond human comprehension. The hardest part is over. The very fact that you are alive is stunning compared to the overwhelming odds against that happening. Only one out of two hundred million sperm survived long enough to successfully unite with the one fertile egg that eventually made YOU. Therefore, you are a biological rarity!

Even more amazing is the fact that only one out of several million life forms on this planet are actually human beings. This means that you have already won the greatest lottery in existence. The statistical probability of you being where you are is next to nothing, but you have already defied the odds. Furthermore, research has shown that the odds of another person existing with the exact same abilities and talents as you are a staggering 50 billion to one. The mere fact that you exist signifies your authority to break free from the clutches of your fears and achieve your dreams. You need no other reason to achieve every one of your greatest desires. You are meant to be where you are and you are meant to be anywhere you think you can go.

Now that the hard part is over, you simply need to do the easy part, which is smashing your walls of fear. You are already 99.999% of the way to achieving your dreams. You are so close that mere words cannot accurately justify your current level of achievement. Even if you are currently living in absolute poverty, you are still nothing less than 99.998% of the way to achieving your dreams.

Even though you are only a few steps away from achieving your dreams, you still need to follow the primary strategy of this book which is: "Whatever you fear is what you need to do next." If you are afraid of something, then you need to do it! This message will continue to be drilled into your mind until this book runs out of pages.

Take a moment and think about how painful it would be to die and to realize that you were 99.999% of the way to living a dynamic life. Imagine what it would be like to quit your journey before you took the last few steps. Feel the frustration, anguish, and outrage that you would experience. Associate yourself with this mental picture and really feel the pain. Then, use the pain as motivation to take the last few steps along your journey.

Before you begin to overcome these final obstacles in your life, there is one essential point that must be made absolutely clear before you start. No matter what your dreams are, you have the power and potential to achieve them. You do not get inspirations without the corresponding ability to make them come true. Whatever you can dream, you can also achieve. Your creator would not instill a dream within you if you did not possess the ability to make it come true. Thus, you should never cling to feelings of unworthiness. You are better than any wall you will ever face.

Use your mind and detect any feelings of unworthiness that you may experience along the way. Realize that when you decide not to act upon your dream of applying for a prestigious job, you really consider yourself unworthy of the job. The same is true when you do not pursue your other dreams, like asking someone special out on a date, earning a spot on the debate team, or running for the presidency of the local PTA. All of these scenarios reveal your feelings of unworthiness.

Keep in mind that no matter how bad you feel at any one moment or how hard any single obstacle may be to overcome, your life as a whole is much more valuable than any of your experiences. You are indeed worthy of smashing your walls and achieving your dreams!

THE RELATIONSHIP BETWEEN YOUR WALLS AND YOUR DREAMS

Along your journey through life, there can be any number of walls that are blocking you from the attainment of a particular dream. Consider the following examples to help you to better understand the relationship between your walls and your dreams.

DREAM:

You want to weigh 160 pounds and feel great in the process.

WALLS:

→ You have unhealthy eating habits.
→ You rarely exercise.
→ You lack a good role model.

DREAM:

You want to have a monogamous, loving, sexual relationship.

WALLS:

⌘ You have trouble meeting potential partners.
⌘ You have low self-esteem.
⌘ You are extremely afraid of being rejected.
⌘ You have poor communication skills.
⌘ You have very little experience in dating.

DREAM:

You want to make the honor roll at school.

WALLS:

➢ You have poor time management skills.
➢ You have poor study habits.
➢ You miss too many classes.
➢ You have poor reading skills.

DREAM:

You want to live a life free of drugs and alcohol.

WALLS:

* You hang around the wrong type of friends.
* You have poor role models at home.
* You have low self-esteem.

DREAM:

You want to learn how to file your own taxes.

WALLS:

- You do not have enough time to learn.
- You believe that you are not smart enough.
- You do not know of anyone who would teach you.

As you can see by these examples, walls are the obstacles that prevent you from achieving your dreams and your dreams are what you get when you successfully smash your walls. Walls are absolutely necessary to your life. Without walls, you would already possess all of your dreams and there would be no reason for you to live. Walls are what make life so interesting and mysterious. Life would be boring without the existence of walls.

The greatest wall you will ever face is quite simply YOURSELF. If you do not take full responsibility for your own life, then you will never become a true wall smasher. You alone are the only one who can smash your walls of fear. No one else could ever do it for you, nor would it benefit you if someone did. As Dr. Barbara DeAngelis would say, "You must be your own hero."

"The hardest victory is victory over self."
Aristotle

WALLS FORCE YOU TO DELAY GRATIFICATION

Wall smashing is not a means to instant gratification. It is a way of life, a way of pursuing the things that mean the most to you. Wall smashing is a never-ending journey where you access greater depths of joy as you make additional progress. It is a lifelong process much like that of changing your eating patterns. Wall smashing is not like some kind of eccentric diet where you adhere to some radical plan for a few weeks and then resort back to your original ineffective eating habits. It is a daily habit where you face the obstacles in your life and consequently feel an ever greater level of joy.

Real joy could never be experienced if all of your dreams were instantly handed to you. Think about your own life. Did you have to save your money and buy your own car when you turned sixteen or did your parents buy you the car of your choice? If your parents bought you a car, then you would probably admit that you did not feel the same joy of ownership as you did when you actually purchased your own car. Only by actually paying the price do you ever truly learn to appreciate something. Instant gratification is never enough. No matter how much you get, you will never feel truly fulfilled.

Walls are a form of delayed gratification that slow life down so that everything does not happen at once. This way, you get time to enjoy and appreciate each of your triumphs, instead of being overwhelmed with more good than you can absorb. Walls also help you to develop personal qualities like mental toughness, discipline, determination, focus, resiliency, and most of all, character.

> *Walls are those physical and psychological barriers that separate the average from the dynamic!*

Walls make it possible for you to experience joy. Joy is the feeling you get when you finally receive the prestigious promotion that you deserve even though your peers said that you were too young. Joy is the experience of holding your own infant baby in your arms even though you had to endure a long hard pregnancy. Joy is the feeling you get when you attend your son's graduation ceremony even though you originally had doubts about having enough money to finance his education. All of these joyous experiences and the many others like them are made possible by the walls that exist in your life. Nonetheless, you still must be the one to smash them. Walls alone can do nothing for you unless *you* take action on them. They merely present you with an opportunity to take your life to a higher level.

"Judge a man not by what he has but what he had to overcome to make his accomplishment."
George Washington Carver

Quite often, you will find that your most formidable walls are also the same ones that produce the greatest amount of joy in your life. Look back upon your own life and consider which experiences gave you the most joy. It is likely you will discover that your most challenging experiences were also your most fulfilling experiences. Think about how challenging it was for you to get through graduate school. Even though it was difficult, didn't your joy at graduation equal or exceed the price you had to pay? Think about how challenging it was to support your family through some of those "hard years." Wouldn't you do it all over again if you had the chance? Think about the other moments in your life when you felt intense feelings of joy. Weren't they also the result of smashing some very difficult walls?

> *Walls are like uncharted waters*
> *and fear is like the navigator*
> *who acts as your guide.*

Fortunately, everyone has walls in their life. The couple in an unhappy marriage is up against many different walls. The family moving to a new city is facing a wide variety of walls. Even the collegiate golf team that wants to win a national championship has an assortment of walls in front of them. Walls are all around us. There is an endless number of walls in our society and each one of us is progressing through these walls at our own pace, experiencing different walls at different times. The only thing for sure is that if you are alive, then you have more walls to smash.

> *"If you are going to die, you might as well live a life*
> *worth dying for!"*
> David Viscott

YOUR WALLS ARE LOCATED ONE STEP OUT-SIDE YOUR COMFORT ZONE

One step outside your comfort zone on the very edge of your dynamic zone is the place where your initial walls are located. As you know, these walls serve as obstacles that block you from achieving your dreams. Off in the distance of your dynamic zone, you will notice your dreams. You can see them, but you cannot get to them. The only way to get to them is by smashing the walls in front of you. The challenging part is that you cannot go around these walls. You cannot go under these walls. You cannot even climb over these walls. The only way to get by them is to smash through them. Only then will you be permitted to unite with your dreams. The following diagram gives you a visual image of the relationship between your comfort zone, your dynamic zone, your walls, and your dreams.

DYNAMIC ZONE
(THE PLACE WHERE YOU LIVE YOUR DREAMS)

DREAM   *DREAM*   *DREAM*

WALL

WALL   WALL

WALL   WALL   WALL

WALL   WALL   WALL

WALL   WALL   WALL

COMFORT ZONE
(THE PLACE WHERE THINGS ARE EASY AND FAMILIAR, A PLACE OF REST)

Notice in the diagram that there are different numbers of walls that lead to each of your dreams. Depending on the size of your dream, there can be virtually any number and any size of walls that you may encounter along your journey. Usually, the bigger your dream, the more walls you will encounter.

It is also important to realize the need to replenish your strength by spending an ample amount of time in your comfort zone resting. Make sure you get enough rest, but do not spend too much time in your comfort zone or you run the risk of becoming complacent.

As you begin to smash walls, your comfort zone will grow larger and begin to engulf part of your dynamic zone. When this happens, you will find that the activities that you once feared have now become routine.

WALLS PRESENT YOU WITH OPPORTUNITIES TO IMPROVE THE QUALITY OF YOUR LIFE

As a dynamic human being, you were born with a distinct need to express the wonderful talents, abilities, and desires that you were given. In short, you have an inborn need to consistently improve the quality of your life, to tap into more of your potential. When you act upon this inborn urge to tap into your unlimited potential, you tend to feel happy, alive, important, passionate, and overall joyously fulfilled. Rollo May, author of the outstanding book, *Man's Search for Himself*, reports how people become ill to the extent that they do not "fulfill their potentialities." He is quoted as saying, "If any organism fails to fulfill its potentialities, it becomes sick, just as your leg would wither if you never walked."

Norman Vincent Peale, author of *The Power of Positive Thinking*, taught these same fundamentals. He consistently encouraged his students to visit a cemetery to get the feel of what it would be like to have no problems (walls) in their life. Peale was even known to get down on his knees and pray to God for more walls to exist in his life. He believed that God only gave walls to the most qualified people, people strong enough to deal with them. Peale knew that walls were merely opportunities to take his life to the next level.

"Challenge is an invitation to be great."
Alan Cohen

We would surely drift into a "coma of complacency" as dynamic speaker and entrepreneur Bob Harrison would say, if it were not for some type of conflict or obstacle pressing us to express more of our potential. You could never know just how strong you are without the help of walls. Without walls, life would be easy and you would become unmotivated and weak.

"That which does not kill me, makes me stronger."
Nietzsche

Can you recall even one great biblical character who did not encounter and overcome tremendous walls? Is it not true that every notable biblical character gained her or his particular strength by enduring tremendous trials and tribulations? The following examples will prove how their walls made them into the great people that we now consider them to have been.

- ➲ Moses feared public speaking and leadership as much as anyone ever has. Nonetheless, he faced his fear and led his people from Egyptian bondage through the desert to "the promised land." Since this feat took roughly forty years, it obviously required quite a bit of public speaking and leadership skills on his part. Do you think Moses encountered any other adversities along the way? What would you do if you were in charge of a large mass of angry people who were lost in a desert for forty years? Imagine the walls that Moses had to smash on any single day throughout the forty-year journey. He had to deal with issues like revolt, starvation, violence, sickness, disbelief, and death. But without these walls, Moses could have never become the great person that he eventually became.

➲ Mary was an unmarried, shy teenager who became pregnant with Jesus Christ while she was still a virgin. Keep in mind that this happened during a time when the community considered unwed pregnant women to be filth. How many people do you think believed her story about an immaculate conception? How many walls do you think she had to overcome?

➲ The disciples were every bit as afraid of other people's opinions as you and I, but they had faith that they could overcome their walls and achieve their dream of spreading the teachings of Christ. They chose to accept rejection and even persecution from society rather than to relinquish their beliefs. Keep in mind that this occurred during a time when their leader was beaten, nailed to a wooden cross, and left to die. Wouldn't it have been much easier for the disciples to do their worshipping behind closed doors?

➲ Jesus Christ was born in a manger. Imagine being born in a cold barn next to cows and donkeys. From the moment he was born, certain people wanted to kill him. During his life, he encountered many walls including verbal abuse, rejection, humiliation, injustice, and even murder. Jesus was spared no pain. Even his death involved being stripped of his clothes, beaten, and nailed to a wooden cross to die in front of the whole community. Could a person encounter any greater obstacles? Jesus Christ not only faced every type of obstacle, but also conquered them all. There was no obstacle that could prevent him from achieving his purpose on Earth. As a result, Jesus brought the world a set of teachings which have endured and thrived even as I write this paragraph. His walls were the size of mountains, yet he never once uttered a word of complaint! Surely, Jesus could have chosen to take the easy way out.

> *Greatness is merely a fantasy without the presence of adversity.*

These biblical examples, like all dynamic people, rose to the occasion and used their walls as a vehicle to improve the quality of their lives. They gained strength through the adversity that they faced. Consider some of the walls these people smashed: fear of public speaking, lack of leadership skills, unexpected pregnancy, persecution, harassment, discouragement, rejection, injustice, physical abuse, and even murder. Aren't these the same walls that are facing you and me in this day and age? Isn't it true that even though thousands of years have passed, we are still facing the same walls? Therefore, let's begin to learn from the examples of our predecessors and use our walls as a means to improve the quality of our lives.

> *"We only think when we are confronted with a problem."*
> John Dewey

Do something great with your time on this planet! Every wall you have in your life is your personal invitation to be great. Keep in mind that being "great" can mean virtually anything. Reflect upon some of the following examples of greatness:

- Raising a great family
- Donating a small amount of time each week to visit with and assist a handicapped friend
- Taking your disabled grandmother to the grocery store and helping her with her shopping
- Spending two hours on a Saturday morning picking up garbage alongside a highway in your community
- Obtaining a position on your local school board as a means to help create classes that teach goal setting, relationship skills, and strategies to achieve financial independence

Only you know what greatness means to you. No one could ever tell you how to be great. You alone must answer that question. Take a step toward your own unique aspiration of greatness by perceiving your walls as opportunities to improve the quality of your life. Look deep within yourself and begin to express some of that greatness that lies untapped within you.

WALLS UNCOVER THE PURPOSE OF YOUR LIFE

As you pursue the greatness that lies untapped inside of you, you will begin to see yourself more clearly. With each wall that you act upon, you will feel a particular purpose evolving in your life. It will feel as though you are becoming closer and closer to the special person you are meant to be.

"Adversity is the mother of invention."
Denis Waitley

My own unique personal experiences serve as one example of this principle. As a young child, I had a dream of playing professional baseball. One of my goals along the way was to play collegiate baseball for the Miami Hurricanes. Every single day, I would take some kind of worthwhile action toward the attainment of my baseball dream. It didn't matter what the weather was like, how I felt, or who would practice with me. Over the course of a few years, I fielded millions of ground balls and swung my bat a countless number of times apart from any type of formal team practice. For years, I practiced relentlessly, always giving 100%. I did everything in my power to make my dream come true. Unfortunately, it turned out that I did not have enough baseball talent to play at Miami, but I did earn a partial scholarship to a good division II college in Florida.

As the day approached for me to leave for college, I began to feel a great deal of fear. I knew that I was going to encounter many scary walls along my journey. To this day, I can still remember the overwhelming sensation of fear that encompassed my entire body and mind as my parents dropped me off at college. Tears rolled down my face and my heart sank into my stomach as my parents pulled out of the dormitory parking lot. There I stood, an 18-year-old boy 1100 miles from home, feeling overwhelmed with fear. I didn't even know one person on the whole campus. Nonetheless, I chose to face the walls that were blocking the attainment of my baseball dreams.

Unfortunately, my baseball career ended soon thereafter. I was heartbroken! But to my utter amazement, I did not feel as though my journey was a waste of time. In fact, I experienced feelings of genuine joy for having the courage to pursue my dream even though it never materialized.

In a short period of time, I was inspired with a new dream. It happened when I accepted a job at the state fair. There, I met a man who traveled to fairs and festivals across the country setting up food stands. He and his family had developed a very successful business. Immediately, I felt a burning desire to open a similar type of business. With this objective in mind, I proceeded to ask him dozens of questions about his business. As it turned out, he was kind enough to answer my questions and to help me to start my own business.

Although I was only an 18-year-old boy with nothing more than a dream, I decided to take a bold leap into my dynamic zone and open my own business. So, without any business experience and with practically no money, I spent the following summer pursuing my new dream. By now, I was sure that professional baseball was not my true calling in life. After all, I had given baseball every ounce of effort and ability that I possessed and I still came up short. After a year of working my business, I came to the point where I had to decide between building my business or going back to college. Although my family and friends encouraged me to choose school, I listened to my heart and chose my business even though I was afraid of the changes it would involve.

> *"What you are afraid to do is a clear indicator of the next thing you need to do."*
> Dr. Robert Anthony

One year later, I found myself once again in Florida, but this time as a fearful 19-year-old college dropout. I spent the winter traveling from fair to fair operating my concession business. I gave my business all the effort I had, the same way I once did in baseball. As a way to save money to expand my business, I decided to sleep in the back of my cargo van instead of paying for a hotel room or purchasing a camper. Even now, I can recall working 16 hours a day only to return to my cargo van to sleep in a space barely as wide as my shoulders and not even as long as the length of my body. There were nights that were so cold that I wore long underwear, jeans, sweatshirts, a winter coat, hats, and gloves to bed. I would cover myself with a sleeping bag or two and lie awake watching my breath as it encountered the frigid air.

Despite my many hardships, I still focused on my dream of becoming a successful businessperson. I was willing to smash however many walls it took to make my dream come true. Little by little, my purpose in life was unfolding.

Within a couple of years, I succeeded in creating a business that continues to thrive today. In the process, I began to see myself more clearly with each wall that I smashed. Even when I failed to smash a particular wall, I gained valuable inspiration as to what I should do next. I began to realize that I was the kind of person who thrived upon adventure, providing service to others, traveling, and working for myself. I was beginning to see my genuine self more clearly. The real Sean Hockensmith was emerging.

"Every obstacle introduces a person to himself."
John Mason

Once I felt comfortable with my new business success, I realized that I had overcome some very challenging walls up to that point in my life. I was proud of the wisdom I had accumulated and I decided that I wanted to share that wisdom with other people. A new dream was arising inside me. I wanted to share my strategies and wisdom with other people. So, here I am writing *Smashing the Wall of Fear*.

With every wall that I smashed in pursuit of my dreams, I could feel my purpose evolving. Every action I took left me with another clue to my unique calling in life. Only by passionately pursuing my dreams am I now capable of sharing this information with you.

Although my story is hardly amazing by any stretch of the imagination, it is one simple story that can serve as a reminder to consistently pursue your dreams regardless of how "crazy" they may seem. This is the only way you will ever realize your real purpose in life. Keep acting upon the most important wall in your life and you will always be heading in the right direction. With each step that you take, you will become that much closer to seeing the real, dynamic YOU!

WALLS CAN JOLT YOU INTO A NEW REALITY

As you progress along your journey, smashing one wall after another, you will suddenly run into a wall that you did not see, a wall that seemingly came out of nowhere. This unexpected wall will jolt you into a brand new reality by surprising you with something that may seem terrible at first. There will be nothing that you can do about it. Nor will there be anywhere you can hide. You will be forced to deal with this particular wall. The following list includes a few examples of these types of unexpected walls.

∇   Being diagnosed with a serious illness or disease
∇   Getting fired or laid off from your job
∇   One of your parents unexpectedly leaving you
∇   The death of a loved one
∇   An unexpected lawsuit
∇   Discovering your child is taking drugs
∇   An unplanned pregnancy
∇   Being robbed, raped, assaulted or abused in some way

Unexpected walls like these have the power to change your perception of reality in a moment. That is exactly what happened for the families of the 2,400 naval personnel who died when the Japanese unexpectedly bombed Pearl Harbor on the morning of December 7, 1941. A similar type of jolt occurred for most of the world on the day that John F. Kennedy was assassinated. These walls instantly changed the reality of everyone involved. Unexpected walls automatically catapult people out of their comfort zone into their dynamic zone.

It would be cruel for you to tell someone who has run into an unexpected wall to look at the bright side. The best thing you could do is simply to be there for them while they mourn. It is necessary to let the person get over her initial shock of the traumatic experience before you give her any kind of advice. Then, once she makes it through the initial shock, you can begin to help her to create a new, powerful perception of reality. No matter how challenging or terrible a wall may seem, human beings still retain the distinct ability to choose what the experience will mean to them and what they will do about it. Sometimes unexpected walls can even be blessings in disguise, depending on how they are interpreted.

> *"Success is not measured by the heights one attains, but by the obstacles one overcomes in their attainment."*
> Booker T. Washington

For instance, the bombing of Pearl Harbor could be interpreted as an opportunity for America to create improved relations with all the countries of the world. Maybe it could be a call to appreciate life and to stop taking our freedom for granted. Who knows? It could mean something totally different for each person affected by it. For one person, it could be a sign to show love and appreciation to the surviving members of her family. For another, it could be a sign to make amends with someone in their past. The death of Kennedy could have been perceived as a chance for the American people to show the true strength of their country. It also could have been interpreted as a call for unity and resiliency among the American people.

There could literally be millions of different interpretations of any single event. The only thing for sure is that your current perception will be jolted as you feel the initial shock of any unexpected wall. It will force you to see a portion of your life in a way you never experienced.

WALL PREVENTION

Fortunately, it is not always necessary for you to wait for an unexpected wall to knock you down before you can learn your lesson and shift your perception. It is possible to learn a lesson from a wall before you encounter it. However, this requires you to sit down and contemplate your current lifestyle. Look, listen, and feel for any clues that could warn you that a potential wall is close at hand.

"In our pain-avoiding culture, most people think that the mentally healthy life is one characterized by an absence of crises. Nothing could be further from the truth. What characterizes mental health is how early we meet our crises."
M. Scott Peck

For instance, the weird noise under the hood of your car may be telling you to have your engine tuned up. By addressing this issue, you might save yourself from breaking down on a lonely deserted road in the middle of the night. Another example is to take more seriously your boss's remarks about always being five minutes late for work. If you don't, you might find yourself in the unemployment line. Or maybe you should listen a little more closely the next time your spouse tells you that you are not home enough. Maybe you will come home one day to find that your spouse has left you.

This kind of prevention all comes back to the strategy of listening to the soft guidance of your fear. If you feel fear, evaluate your situation and quickly determine whether your fear is guiding you or protecting you. Then, take the appropriate actions. By doing so, you will prevent your walls from growing stronger and your fears from growing more intense. Prevention is always the best medicine.

YOU MUST ADMIT YOU ARE FACING A WALL BEFORE YOU CAN BEGIN TO SMASH IT

When a wall appears in your life, you gain nothing by denying its existence. The only thing denial does is to cause your fear to grow in intensity and your wall to grow in strength. You can only begin to smash a wall once you admit that you are indeed facing a wall. It is a well-known fact that an alcoholic cannot begin to heal until she admits that she has a drinking problem. In a similar way, you must first acknowledge the walls that exist in your life. Walls do not go away by them-

49

selves. The whole process of wall smashing begins with your willingness to admit, "Yes, I am facing a wall." This may seem quite obvious, but there are plenty of examples every day of people who do not understand this truth.

How many married people do you know who consciously avoid confronting their spouse about certain issues? Quite a few, I'm sure. Most of these people are hoping that their differences will disappear magically without any effort on their part. They would rather deny the existence of their walls than go through the pain of facing certain issues. This is one of the major reasons why fifty percent of marriages in the United States end in divorce. Worse yet, of the fifty percent of the couples that stay married, nearly half of them are unhappy and want to get divorced, but for one reason or another they remain married.

The marriage problems of today do not stem from the choice of marriage partners. Rather, this national epidemic is caused by the millions of husbands and wives who refuse to face the walls that jeopardize their relationship. Instead of facing the walls they encounter in their marriage, they choose to avoid them. Then, somewhere down the road, all the avoided walls add up and leave a terribly negative effect on the relationship. At this point, the couple has two realistic choices, either get a divorce or live out an unhappy marriage.

Conversely, the 25% of marriages in America that are happy result from the courage of each partner to face every wall that they encounter in their relationship. Instead of denying the existence of a wall in their life, they openly admit its presence and take action to smash it. If one partner takes offense to a comment made by the other partner, then a discussion that leads to a resolution immediately follows. The same is true if one partner acts in an unacceptable way. Action would be immediately taken by the other partner to correct the situation and to see that it does not happen again. Whatever the case, both partners admit to the presence of a wall and they take action to smash it.

Take a moment and imagine that a bright purple donkey is roaming around your family room. Suppose it is knocking over your lamps, crafts, pictures and end tables. Picture the donkey leaving periodic deposits on your carpet. If this were the case, wouldn't you openly admit that you have a problem? Wouldn't you immediately address the issue by taking action to remove the donkey from your house? Then, why don't you also admit the other obvious walls that are present in your life? How long will you continue to deny that you have a purple donkey in your family room? The only thing ridiculous about this example is the fact that you have been ignoring issues every bit as obvious as that of the purple donkey scenario.

If you are not willing to look at yourself and admit that you have certain walls in your life, then you might as well use the rest of this book as toilet paper. Without this initial confession on your part, this book can do nothing for you. Let your fear point you to the wall you need to smash and when you get there, admit that you have some work to do. You lose your power the moment you deny the presence of a wall in your life.

DON'T PLACE TOO MUCH IMPORTANCE ON SMASHING ANY ONE WALL

Although it is a bad idea to deny the presence of walls in your life, it is just as bad to place too much importance on any one wall. There are about six billion people who inhabit this planet. What makes you think that any one bankruptcy, divorce, or rejection is even slightly important to the overall scheme of life? Your greatest personal walls are practically insignificant when compared to the much larger societal walls like plant and animal extinction, destruction of rain forests, starvation, terrorism, pollution, and even war. In the face of these much more important societal walls, your personal walls pale in comparison. Think about it. No one living on this planet two hundred years from now will even care about your individual problems.

Developing this attitude will help you to view your life with a healthier perspective. It will keep you from thinking that you are the only one with any problems. This is not to say that your walls are not important; of course they are. They simply are not as important as you think. Your life as a whole is much more important than any amount of walls you may encounter.

Realizing this truth will also keep you from getting caught up solely in the smashing of one particular wall. Instead, you will learn to act upon a wide variety of walls. You will begin to smash walls in all the different departments of your life. Life is too beautiful to focus all of your emotional, mental, spiritual, and physical energy on smashing any one wall while you disregard the other walls in your life. Do not become "hung up" on one wall for too long. Determination is great, but while you are being determined, be sure to realize that life is multidimensional. There is more to life than any single challenge facing you. Keep the idea of balance foremost in your mind.

Life is not a race to see who achieves the most honors, gains the most fame, attains the most goals, earns the most money, receives the highest promotions, or finishes the most projects. Instead, life is about having lots of loving fun. There does not exist even one shred of evidence to prove that life is a serious event. You might very well be getting all stressed out about the walls in your life for nothing. Maybe you should be having fun while you tackle your greatest challenges.

Make a decision today to have fun regardless of what challenges you encounter. Along the way, remember to balance your life by spending the appropriate amount of time in your....COMFORT ZONE.

CHAPTER 3

COMFORT ZONE: YOUR PLACE OF REST, RELAXA- TION, AND RECUPERATION

"The pace of modern life must be reduced if we are not to suffer profoundly from its debilitating over-stimulation and super-excitement."
Norman Vincent Peale

The walls in your life can undoubtedly cause you to experience a frenzy of intense fearful emotions. Periodically, you need a place where you can escape from all of this emotional intensity. You need a place to rest, relax, and recuperate—a place of safety, security, and comfort—a place away from the action. This place of rest is your comfort zone. Your comfort zone is a place where you take part in relaxing activities. It might include activities like playing a friendly game of tennis, taking a leisurely walk through the woods, reading a book, watching television, or traveling to the river for a relaxing day of fishing. Everybody has their own unique activities that bring them comfort.

Picture your comfort zone as your own personal island resort where everything is easy, familiar, and comfortable. It is a place where you can easily handle everything that you encounter, a place where you rarely feel any fear. When you are in your comfort zone, there are no demands placed upon you. It is a place where you feel totally in control of your life.

Quite often, nature can be such a place. Many people have discovered the outdoors to be a very effective environment to regain balance and sanity in their life. A day of fishing on the lake can work miracles for the burnt-out salesperson who has been working twelve-hour days for the past week. Hunting, hiking, biking, horseback riding, and white water rafting are a few of the other outdoor activities that produce similar relaxing effects for worn-out executives and frustrated housekeepers alike.

Research has shown that "the outdoors" often produces calming benefits very similar to those of the most advanced forms of meditation. Nature has a way of clearing our vision so that we can easily recognize what is most important to us. It helps us to feel the difference between the dense inner city fog and the refreshing light country air. Spending time in nature allows us to evaluate our own individual life with a clear mind. In essence, it refreshes our body and mind by giving us a place to escape from our daily challenges.

Escapism is a much needed aspect of life. You might even escape more often than you realize. When you buy a house to live in, you are escaping from the weather. When you play music, you are escaping into your imagination. Driving your car is even a form of escapism so you do not have to walk long distances. Escapism is simply a way to rest from any tiring activity.

It is perfectly OK to escape at certain times throughout your day. As a human being, you periodically need to escape from excessive stimulation. The human body can cope with only so much emotional intensity at a time. This is apparent with front-line soldiers during a war. Armies limit the time any single soldier is on the front-line because the intensity of emotion can easily become overwhelming and result in "shell shock." The excessive amounts of fear generated in these types of situations are just too much for the human body to handle for extended periods of time. Emotional and physical illnesses tend to manifest as a result. In order to be healthy, you must balance your life with the right amount of both rest and action.

When you begin to feel fatigued, you need to take part in some relaxing activity. Avoiding proper rest and relaxation only causes your wall smashing skills to become increasingly more ineffective. Human beings do not function properly when they are consistently run ragged. You need to rest when your body sends you signals of fatigue.

Life itself is a never-ending cycle. The sun rises and the sun sets. We breathe in and we breathe out. Winter comes and winter goes. People are born and people die. You must honor the same cyclic process when you deal with fear. You cannot spend too much time face to face with your fears. By the same token, you cannot spend too much time resting or hiding from your fears either. The only answer is to balance your life by spending the right amount of time in both your dynamic zone and your comfort zone.

View your life as a seven day cycle where you need to rest at least one complete day or two half days during the cycle in order to gain a strong sense of balance. Resting for this one day out of the week will give you a much better chance to get the most out of the remaining six days. What would happen to the world champion boxer if he got up the very next morning after a grueling 15 round fight and participated in another championship boxing match? Wouldn't he be much less effective than he was the preceding night? Similarly, how can you expect to perform at your best if you are not getting enough rest? You cannot! Getting the proper amount of rest is the only way of renewing your energy.

Listen to your body and mind; they will tell you when you need to take a break. This break might even be something as simple as a nap. Thomas Edison was famous for taking a nap in the middle of the day so that he might awaken with a fresh mind. Another famous "napper" was Winston Churchill. Over time, his naps became quite legendary.

At other times, you might need to take a vacation. Many of the world leaders take periodical vacations as a means of regrouping and energizing their bodies and minds. For instance, it is very common for the president of the United States to go on a weekend vacation to a place like Camp David in order to get some much needed rest and relaxation. It is really in the best interest of all of America. A president needs balance because she is responsible for the safety and welfare of a nation. No one is capable of performing at optimal levels without getting the proper amount of rest.

Exercise is another great way to break up a long day and to refresh your body and mind. Exercise has been proven to foster advanced levels of emotional stability. This, of course, will permit you to spend a greater amount of quality time in your dynamic zone without feeling overwhelmed by all of the emotion. Motivational expert Zig Ziglar has testified that a short walk around the block is one of the best ways for him to replenish his creative juices when he is writing a book. I have also personally found exercise to be a great way to break up long periods of writing. It gives me a refreshed perspective when I return to my writing. After all, exercise produces a healthier mind and body which means more productivity as well as more fun.

Remove yourself from challenging situations for a short period of time. Allow your body and mind to rest and rejuvenate itself. Doing so will clear your mind and allow yourself to take much wiser, more productive action when you return. Resting and refreshing your body and mind in your comfort zone will pay big dividends in the long run by making your wall smashing time much more productive as well as much more enjoyable.

YOU WERE TAUGHT TO SPEND TOO MUCH TIME IN YOUR COMFORT ZONE

As you know, it is absolutely necessary for you to rest for the right amount of time in your comfort zone. But it is very easy to abuse your comfort zone if you are not careful. Since your comfort zone is so comfortable, it is very tempting to overindulge in it. Slowly but surely, you can become complacent and unmotivated by spending too much time in your comfort zone.

In truth, you have probably already been sucked much too deep into your comfort zone. Instead of using your comfort zone as a temporary place of *rest*, you probably learned to use it as a permanent place of *inhabitancy*. Either consciously or unconsciously society taught you as a child that it is best to give up on your dreams and settle for a mediocre life. Statements like the following likely programmed your mind:

⇒ Don't explore new opportunities. There will be some kind of "catch" and you will end up getting hurt.
⇒ Don't talk to strangers. People cannot be trusted.
⇒ Children are to be seen, not heard. Your ideas are meaningless anyway.
⇒ Don't take chances. If you do, you will lose everything you have.
⇒ Dreams only come true in fairy tales. Dreamers are not realistic.
⇒ Do whatever they tell you to do. Don't question adults. Don't change traditions. Don't challenge experts.
⇒ Don't rock the boat. Be satisfied with the way things are.

Sooner or later, you probably began to accept these types of statements as your beliefs. This explains why you may spend excessive amounts of time in your comfort zone. Each additional belief made it that much more challenging for you to break free from the gravitational pull of your comfort zone.

This process that society used to program your mind is known as *conditioning*. Conditioning causes you to feel specific emotions when you encounter specific stimuli in your environment. Stimuli can be anything in your environment including certain people, sounds, smells, situations, or experiences. Unfortunately, you were conditioned to link fearful emotions to many of the same activities that you need to perform in order to achieve your dreams. Although this societal conditioning was not the result of malicious intent, it is a major reason why most people spend too much time in their comfort zone.

All of this conditioning started many generations ago. Each new generation simply learned what the preceding generation taught them. Unfortunately, the lesson was to avoid anything dynamic and to cling to a life of comfort. In short, you learned to aspire merely to mediocrity. Now, you may be at a place in your life where you want to break free from the clutch of your comfort zone and achieve some worthwhile goals. The major problem is that you are finding it very difficult to take action when you have been conditioned toward comfort all of your life. Cheri Huber, author of *The Fear Book*, accurately summed up this tragedy:

> Children are naturally fearless; they are open to the world and to exploring and learning from it. But when they are repeatedly told that something they have done is stupid and foolish, they are humiliated, so that eventually they no longer find new situations interesting. They stop being excited about exploring the unknown, because the unknown has become another opportunity to be wrong.

As a child, you learned to associate avoidance to many activities in your life that you really should be embracing. This avoidance is what keeps you trapped in your comfort zone. Some of these conditioned activities include: public speaking, opening a business, discussing intimate topics, setting high goals, meeting new people, sharing ideas with people, asking key questions, and negotiating for the things you want. The truth is that many of these types of activities are exactly what you need to do in order to get your life back into balance and to begin living dynamically.

"Man was born to win, but conditioned to lose."
Zig Ziglar

Avoiding dynamic activities is probably the reason why 95% of our population have never risen above middle class. In order to obtain financial independence, it is necessary for you to take some dynamic actions. This is NOT to say that wealth alone is an accurate indicator of a dynamic life. It merely indicates that most people were never taught how to become financially independent. As a result, most people are not financially secure. The same is true with the comfort zone. Most people never learned how to properly use their comfort zone. Consequently, these people are paying the price by living a life that is lacking the kind of fulfillment they deserve.

The good news is that no matter what you were taught, you now possess the information to gain the proper understanding about your comfort zone. No longer do you have any excuse for experiencing a quality of life that is less than you deserve. You have the information you need to take your life to whatever level you desire. All that's left is its application.

THE COMFORT ZONE LOOKS LIKE A GREAT PLACE TO SPEND YOUR LIFE, BUT IT IS DEADLY

Even if you have been conditioned to cling to your comfort zone, that does not mean you lost your dreams. Regardless of how much you have abused your comfort zone in the past, there is still the spark of a dream alive within you. You have probably already sensed this dream. You might have even pursued it briefly until you encountered a wall and decided to retreat into your comfort zone. After several similar experiences, you probably became very disappointed and decided that you were not meant to achieve your dreams anyway. After all, you "tried" to live your dreams, but it was too tough.

As a result, you probably made a decision to stay put in your comfort zone to avoid any more pain. At first, your decision to choose the path of least resistance may have seemed valid. You probably found that nothing was really expected of you and no one bothered you. The only problem is that the comfort zone does not promote physical, emotional, mental, social, or spiritual growth. The comfort zone is static. It is like being stuck in a rut. It violates the law of growth. When you stop growing, you turn into a societal parasite who only takes from the world. Soon you will experience deep feelings of boredom and a lack of fulfillment as a result. These pains will end up hurting much more than would any amount of growing pains.

"A RUT-RUT HERE, A RUT-RUT THERE, HERE A RUT, THERE A RUT, EVERYWHERE A RUT-RUT"
The comfort zone version of "Old MacDonald"

Joy cannot be found in a lopsided life that consists of only comfort. Joy can only be accessed when you give of yourself to make the world a better place. This means that you must get out of your habit of complacency and make yourself into a better person so that you have something to give to this world. If you waste your life away in comfort, then you will ensure one thing, that you will miss out on a substantial amount of joy.

You have a distinct obligation to make your own unique contribution to the world in which you live. Withholding your special talents and abilities out of fear will only disrupt the balance of nature and force you to pay a great price. Eventually, the price will be felt as a feeling of uselessness, hopelessness, despair, and depression that will penetrate your entire being. At this point, you will realize how dangerous it is to inhabit your comfort zone.

Jim McAnarney, a "diamond" in the Amway Corporation, recently passed along a beautiful poem that accurately sums up the comfort zone.

I used to have a comfort zone where I knew I couldn't fail.
The same four walls and busy work were really more like jail.
I longed so much to do the things I've never done before
But I stayed inside my comfort zone and paced the same old floor.
I said it didn't matter that I wasn't doing much.
I said I didn't care for things like goals, and dreams, and such.
I claimed to be so busy with the things inside the zone.
But deep inside I longed for something special of my own.
I couldn't let my life go by just watching others win.
So I held my breath and stepped outside to let the change begin.
I took a step and with new strength I'd never felt before
I kissed my comfort zone goodbye and closed and locked the door.

NEVER RETIRE FROM LIFE

Maybe you are one of the few people who actually defied the odds by stepping outside your comfort zone into the vast wilderness of your dynamic zone. Who knows, maybe you even became financially independent in the process and decided to retire from your particular job, career, business, or occupation. If this is the case, then I congratulate you, but more importantly, I wish to warn you about the pitfalls. Yes, money is fantastic and I hope you "retire" a multimillionaire. But treat your money as an opportunity to purchase more experiences that will cause you to grow. This way, you will be free to pursue many of the wonderful opportunities, expeditions, and learning experiences that life has to offer.

The greatest mistake you could possibly make after acquiring a large amount of money is to retire from life. Retiring from life means that you stop growing, you stop changing, and you stop improving. No longer do you continue to explore your dynamic zone. When you retire from life, you are retiring from the pursuit of new dreams. You are choosing to kill your spirit.

Too many people wrongly believe that at some point in their life they earn the privilege of doing nothing. They think they have added enough value to society. They feel as though they have paid their dues and therefore earned the reward of an "easy life" of instant pleasure.

"Retire from a job, but never retire from life."
Maxwell Maltz

When people quit striving to achieve new dreams, they find themselves lacking the joy of a purposeful journey. Instead of joy, these people feel bored, restless, and even depressed. They soon realize what was meant by the person who said, "The *journey* is more fulfilling than the *destination.*"

Fortunately, some of the people who fall into this trap learn their lessons and quickly reenter their dynamic zones to continue to stretch their abilities. Consequently, they regain their passion and zest for life. As for those who continue to live static lives, they usually end up dying within a short number of years. Although their autopsy may claim that they died from cancer, heart disease, etc., could it be possible that they really died from boredom and a lack of real fulfillment?

The human mind and body need stimulation on a daily basis in order to continue to function properly. The best strategy is to keep doing the things that bring you the most joy. If you work at a job, business, or career that you love, then work there until the day you die. Whatever brings you joy is what you should be doing. Make it a point to continue to add value to society in every way that you can. This decision could save your life.

As long as you are alive, you have more walls to smash. Use all of your successes as opportunities to grow and expand into a more complete person. Invite challenge into your life. Begin today to develop the habit of consistently stretching yourself into your....DYNAMIC ZONE.

CHAPTER 4

DYNAMIC ZONE: EXPLORING THE UNKNOWN

"...growth comes from saying yes to the unknown."
Gloria Steinem

"Dynamic" can be defined as anything that is growing, changing, and improving. In order for you to become dynamic, you must be consistently growing, changing, and improving. To do so, you must first venture forth into an unknown place, your dynamic zone.

The dynamic zone can only be experienced by someone who is courageous, someone who is willing to be the first person on the dance floor. While the other people at the dance are paralyzed by their fear of expressing themselves in front of others, one brave soul acts in the face of her fear and begins to dance. By doing so, she "smashes the wall of fear" in the room and makes it OK for the rest of the people to begin dancing as well.

The dynamic zone is a very emotional place. It is the place to go when you really want to feel alive. After all, life is made real by your emotions. The desire to obtain pleasure and avoid pain is what drives all human behavior. If you could not feel any emotions, whether pleasurable or painful, then you would not be motivated to do anything at all. You would not want to play with your children, exercise, get married, make new friends, read a book, or even eat. Life would indeed become meaningless. Therefore, feeling a wide variety of different emotions on a regular basis is the only way you can possibly live dynamically. Otherwise, you would not be living at all, you would merely be surviving, choosing to avoid the essence of life.

> *"There is no security in this life.*
> *There is only opportunity."*
> Douglas MacArthur

To avoid this tragedy, you must be brave enough to step into your dynamic zone and risk letting both yourself and other people know who you are, what you stand for, and where you are going. In the party of life, you can either be the person who stands in the corner hoping not to be seen or you can be the person who risks expressing your genuine self to everyone you meet. Of course, displaying your genuine self involves feeling some emotional pain at times, but it is well worth it. There is no greater privilege than the freedom of being you. Life is too short to hide your genuine self behind some false image you are portraying.

Become dynamic enough to express your genuine self to everyone you meet. This is the only way you will ever discover who your real friends are. By letting down your guard and being yourself, you free other people to determine whether they like or dislike the real you. Yes, it will be painful, but no longer will you have to put on an act for anybody. Consequently, you will free yourself to live your own unique dynamic life.

DEVELOP MANY DIFFERENT PERSONALITY TRAITS

Developing many different personality traits is a great way to guard yourself against feeling overwhelmed by emotion when you venture into your dynamic zone. Your personality is the way you act. The more personality traits you have to draw from, the better armed you will be to face each new situation that you encounter. Anything can and will happen in your dynamic zone. You need to be as prepared as possible.

It has become all too common for people to mistake their "personality type" as something that is etched in stone. There are many different personality qualities that you can experience and each one allows you to feel a different flavor of emotion. You need to be both cautious and risky, reserved and outgoing, steady and changing, excited and calm, and tough and intimate. Robert Rohm, author of *Positive Personality Profiles*, agrees that it is best to incorporate a wide variety of personality traits into your one dominant personality type.

Let's look at one possible consequence of adopting a single personality label. Shelly is a 14-year-old girl who has consistently been labeled as a very shy personality type ever since she was eight years old. In her mind, she believes that she is shy. As a result, she feels powerless every time she encounters a wall that calls for an outgoing action on her part. After all, a shy person is not capable of taking a bold action.

Once again, the problem of developing too narrow of a personality lies in part with your parents, teachers, coaches, and friends. They were the ones who disabled you as a child through the use of negative labels. They told you that you were shy, unintelligent, overactive, and learning disabled among other negative labels. As a result, you lived up to their expectations of you. This is a terrible disservice to any child's growth and development. Children tend to believe exactly what others tell them. If you choose to give your children labels, give them positive labels like:

☺ You are so honest.
☺ You are such a beautiful person.
☺ You are extremely talented.
☺ You are smart.
☺ You are so creative.
☺ You are a very loving person.
☺ You are such a great giver.

It is amazing how accurately children and adults alike live up to the labels they acquire from society. It is easy to see why you should adopt positive labels for yourself and your family. Although labels do not guarantee the type of person you will become, they do impact your destiny in astounding ways.

YOUR GIFTS OF DESIRE AND TALENT CAN ONLY BE DEVELOPED IN YOUR DYNAMIC ZONE

Deep within you lies two marvelous gifts—your desires and your talents. Out of all the billions of people who live on this planet, you are the only one who possesses your particular combination of desires and talents. What an honor it is to be you! Nobody is capable of taking your place; you have a unique role to play in the scheme of life. But first, you must be brave enough to venture forth into your dynamic zone to develop these assets.

"To accomplish all we are capable of, we would need one hundred lifetimes."
Denis Waitley

Think about it. Nobody else could ever love your spouse the same way that you can. Nobody else could ever raise your children the same way that you are capable of raising them. Nobody else could ever provide the unique type of service that you want to provide. Nobody else could sing the song you want to sing. Even though this is true, the vast majority of people continue to die with their music still inside them. They never really step into their dynamic zone long enough to uncover their real desires and develop their natural talents.

Each one of us has an important obligation to the universe to express the unique gifts that our creator has instilled within us. No one could possibly express the gifts of another person. Take this book for example: Sean Hockensmith was the only person in the world who had the desire and talent to write this particular book. No one else in the world was capable of making my unique contribution for me. I was the only one who could have organized all of this information in the unique way that I did. I was the only one who had the vision and burning desire to see this particular book through to the end. Yes, many assisted me, yet without my own unique gifts of desire and talent, this book would have never been born. The world would have been forever without *Smashing the Wall of Fear.*

Answering the following questions will help you to recognize some of your own special gifts that lie within you eagerly waiting to be used:

- What do I love to do more than anything else in the world?

- What do I know how to do well?

- How do I want to be remembered? What kind of legacy do I want to leave?

- What would I do if I were the richest person on the planet?

- What can I do that other people either cannot do or are not willing to do?

- What activities seem natural and fun for me to do?

- How can I uniquely contribute to myself, my family, my neighborhood, my school district, my city, my county, my state, my country, my world, and/or my universe?

Look for similarities among your answers to these questions. Chances are, the answers that keep recurring are the activities that you need to focus your power upon. Also, notice which answers spark the most motivation inside you. These are the activities that will bring you the most joy. By doing this simple exercise, you will more clearly recognize your own special desires and talents.

Compare the life that you are currently living with the answers you gave to the preceding questions. Decide whether or not you are really living the kind of life that you can proudly look back upon in twenty years. Make sure you are getting your money's worth from life because this is not a dress rehearsal! Be certain that you are making good use of the unique gifts that you possess. If you have trouble looking at your own life objectively, then ask a close friend or family member to assist you. Many times a close friend or family member can help you to recognize your own personal assets better than you can yourself. Ask them to answer the preceding questions about you. It may surprise you how well a loved one may know you.

The main reason for doing this exercise is to avoid the pain of realizing that you never created the kind of life that you really wanted to experience. After all, there will come a "day of reckoning" when you will know for sure whether or not you are proud of your life. This realization usually occurs in the middle of the night when you least expect it. As you stumble toward the bathroom and turn on the light, you will see yourself in the mirror. You will feel a jolting sensation rush through your body that will cause you to spend a few extra minutes staring into the mirror. In a semiconscious state of mind you will see yourself in a way you never did before. This is the moment of truth—the moment when you will know without a doubt whether you are proud of the life you are living or whether you are embarrassed for wasting so much potential. No longer will you be able to fool yourself.

To protect yourself from this dreaded realization, you must begin today by passionately pursuing your dreams. This is the only way to prepare yourself for the moment of truth. Motivate yourself by imagining how painful it would be to never go beyond the maintenance and survival stage of life, never to really pursue your dreams. Realize that this indeed would be the ultimate pain that you could possibly experience on Earth, a pain so deep that you must take it with you when you die.

Look in the mirror today and ask yourself, "Am I proud of the life that I am living?" Then, make a game plan according to your response. Remember to focus your game plan on YOUR desires and talents. Do not look around to see what someone else has done. You would be unhappy living someone else's dreams. Get into the habit of following your own heart. Nobody could ever tell you how to live a dynamic life. A dynamic life is different for everyone. It is not determined by how many trophies you win, how many businesses you own, or how many people you know. Your life is dynamic as long as you are currently stretching yourself into a better person.

Doing the best you can do at your current level of growth is all that can be asked of you. When you give the world 100%, you will attract the assistance you need seemingly out of nowhere. The sincerest form of prayer is to give all that you can possibly give to achieve your dream and then to release the rest to the Almighty. Withholding even the slightest bit of your talent will usually cause you to fail to produce your desired results. Ironically, you will find that the little bit that you held back would have been enough to achieve your desired outcome. It is therefore vital for you to give 100% of your effort.

Giving 100% of your effort will also plainly reveal your "inner beauty" and mold you into a very uncommon type of person. Anything that is extremely rare and unique is always very beautiful and valuable. Why do you think that gold, diamonds, and other precious metals and gems are so valuable? They are nothing like the common rock. They are unique and this uniqueness is what gives them value. In a similar way, it is your uniqueness inside you that gives you value. The more of it that you can express, the more beautiful and valuable you will become.

The unique desires and talents that you possess make you different from everyone else. When you hide your unique gifts, you have nothing that separates yourself from the masses. You have no unique competitive advantage, no niche, nothing that stands out to signal your individuality. Being the same as everyone else guarantees that you have nothing of value to offer the world.

Instead of becoming another "comfort zone clone," commit yourself to becoming someone like Jaime Escalante. Escalante taught math in a very "rough" Los Angeles high school. Many of his students had the equivalent of a 7th grade education and others were altogether illiterate. Vandalism and violence plagued the school. The entire faculty lost faith in their students and believed that conditions would never change.

Despite the crime, violence, bad attitudes, low intelligence scores, lack of faculty support and the many other seemingly invincible walls, Escalante displayed his uniqueness by raising his expectations for his students. He refused to sink to their level. Instead, he made a decision that he would teach his students calculus even though many of them didn't even understand basic math. Jaime dreamed that his students would actually pass the AP Calculus test which would allow them to earn college credit while they where still in high school.

By holding fast to his dream when everyone else at the school laughed at him, Jaime began to display his individual beauty and uniqueness. He did many things that the other teachers in the high school were not willing to do. He put in extra hours, took a personal interest in his students, and fought for their best interest's. Most of all, he taught his students the importance of desire, belief, and hard work.

It was a long hard road for Jaime Escalante and his students, but in the end, the members of his class did pass the AP Calculus test and earned college credit. For each of the next five years, an increasingly greater number of students passed the AP Calculus test thanks to the unique standards set by Jaime Escalante. Jaime Escalante and his students are prime examples of people who sincerely tapped into their potentials. The beautiful story of Jaime Escalante and his students, entitled *Stand and Deliver*, can be rented at certain video stores.

It's the people like Jaime Escalante who are truly making a major difference in our world. They are the true heroes of our country. To be this type of person, you must be willing to be a little bit different, a little bit unorthodox. You must be willing to express your unique characteristics despite the walls that surround you. This is what will separate you from the masses.

It's funny how many "comfort zoners" look at others who are extremely successful and say, "They only got where they are by luck." Although this may appear to be true, the truth happens to be quite contrary to this popular misconception. People who have enjoyed tremendous success have done so by expressing their uniqueness. This is what eventually attracted the right people into their life and helped to create their "luck."

Likewise, the only way you can attract the right people into your life is by taking the risk of being yourself and expressing the unique qualities that make you different and beautiful. If you hide your genuine self, then the right people will not recognize you. They will pass you right by.

Consider how many single people you know that complain they cannot attract the right person into their life. How many of these people are really expressing their genuine self? Very few! Most people act however they think other people want them to act. They are overly concerned with what other people will think of them if they express their own unique individuality. Therefore, they never take a stand on any issue. Instead, they conform and act just like everyone else. They are wishy washy, hardly dynamic. The only chance for these people to attract the mate of their dreams is to courageously step into their dynamic zone and risk being themselves.

> *Creating a great relationship is not a matter of <u>attracting</u> the right person. It's a matter of <u>being</u> the right person.*

Aspiring to be just like everyone else is one of the greatest sins you could possibly commit. Average people do not achieve their dreams. They are merely carbon copies of the masses. Only dynamic people ever tap into their greatness.

Unfortunately, dynamic people are the exception rather than the norm in society. Even our schools and organizations seem to base their success on teaching our children to be "well adjusted" and "obedient." If we could only get the curious, energetic, fidgety, mischievous young children through our rigid, "well adjusted" school system, they would eventually illuminate the world with their energy and creativity. Instead of suppressing the energy of our youngsters, we must help them to better channel it.

In truth, we all need to learn how to better channel our energy and to tap into more of our potential. With this in mind, the following list of actions was created as a way to help you to accomplish this objective. Remember, there are many other actions you can take to tap into your unlimited potential. This list is only the tip of the iceberg:

- O Set goals in all eleven departments of your life (relationship, career, recreational, family, investment, spiritual, exploration, educational, health, time management, and contribution). Review all your goals monthly and examine your top five goals daily.
- O Read two or more nonfiction books a month.
- O Listen to educational tapes as you drive. (Contact Dynamic Life Publishing for an extensive list of fantastic educational tapes. See page 238.)
- O Attend two or more seminars or workshops a year.
- O Practice some form of prayer and meditation on a daily basis.
- O Contribute to your neighborhood and society several times a year in some meaningful way.
- O Surround yourself with dynamic people whenever possible.

o Write about the lessons you have learned, the experiences you have had, and the ideas you receive. Do so several times a week in your journal.

Taking part in habitual actions like these will allow you to tap into more of your potential. Unfortunately, most people are not willing to do these types of activities. They fear what desires and talents they may find deep within themselves. After all, if they find something great, they would be forced to leave their comfort zone and CHANGE! Instead, they choose to resist any activity that may reveal their inner greatness. This way, they will not have to do any "extra work." On the positive side, there are certain dynamic people who, despite all of the odds, take it upon themselves to do whatever it takes to make their dreams come true.

Take Les "The Motivator" Brown, for example. Les and his twin brother were adopted as infants by a single mom and lived in a low income neighborhood of Miami, Florida. His family had so little money that there were times when he wondered how he would get his next meal. Many people would say that Les Brown was a poor boy, but Les knew that he had dreams inside him that were more valuable than any amount of money. Les Brown also knew that he had the abilities to make his dreams come true. It did not matter how much money his family had.

Although Les was labeled "educable mentally retarded" as a child, flunked fifth grade, and lived in poverty for his entire childhood, he still knew that he possessed inner greatness. Even though drugs, alcohol, and crime surrounded him, Les Brown would not let himself fall prey to them. During the hard times and struggles, he focused on his dream of raising himself and his family out of poverty. Thanks to the power of his dream, the young "educable mentally retarded" poor boy rose out of poverty to become one of the greatest motivational speakers of all time. Les Brown's words are so powerful that they will send chills up your spine. To benefit from the work of Les Brown, you can read his book entitled *Live Your Dreams* or you can call 1-800-733-4226 to order some of his resources.

It is interesting to note that many of the people who grew up alongside Les Brown are now either addicted to drugs, living in poverty, and/or serving time in prison. This proves that although society may predict your future, you alone have the power to actually create your own destiny. The gifts are inside you if you will only step into your dynamic zone and develop them.

BE CAREFUL WHO YOU CHOOSE TO FOLLOW

As you prepare to step into your dynamic zone, you will have a wide variety of different people that you can choose to follow. Don't make the mistake of blindly follow just anyone. Doing so could be dangerous. Anytime you blindly follow someone, you put your fate in their hands, much like that of a dogsled team. One dog controls the direction and fate of the rest of the dogs. If the lead dog suddenly decides to run off the side of a cliff, the rest of the dogs are inclined to experience a similar outcome.

To make sure that you are not one of the people who run off the side of a cliff, you need to make one of two choices. Either decide to be your own lead dog and learn from your own experiences or be sure to follow a dog that is heading in a direction that you want to go. The best strategy is to go in your own unique direction while you remain open-minded to the advice of others along the way.

Suppose you were walking across a minefield. Wouldn't you rather duplicate the actions of someone who has already made it across safely? Isn't that much wiser than leaving your fate up to chance? The same is true in your life. Be sure that you follow only the people who have produced the kind of results that you desire to produce.

You will become like the people you associate with.

While you follow the wisdom of your role models, remember that no one will ever care as much about your life as you do. Even if someone was to dedicate her entire life to you, she could only do so much for you. Ultimately, you must take sole responsibility for your experience of life. Set a goal for yourself to live a life so dynamic that when you die the people attending your funeral will talk about your life instead of your death.

"You can lead a horse to water, but you cannot force it to drink."
An Ancient Truth

Our world can only continue to survive and thrive by developing dynamic leaders to guide us onward to greater heights. Our world was formed by courageous human beings and it will die when we cease to produce a similar quality of outstanding individuals. Start today to become someone great by stepping into your dynamic zone and modeling a wide variety of remarkable people.

YOU WILL BE CRITICIZED WHEN YOU ENTER YOUR DYNAMIC ZONE

Imagine the impact that people like Martin Luther King Jr., Winston Churchill, Christopher Columbus, and Helen Keller had in the formation of the lifestyle that we enjoy today. What separated these dynamic people from the masses? What really caused these people to achieve such high levels of greatness? It was their ability to endure criticism. They understood that in order for them to do anything great, they would have to learn how to deal with massive amounts of criticism along the way.

Anyone who desires to enter their dynamic zone and pursue a special dream that is unique, creative, uncommon, or nontraditional should be prepared for criticism. This is every bit as true today as it was hundreds of years ago. Why is this so? Shouldn't the dreamers of society be commended for their courage? Why then, does the vast majority of society reject and criticize these people for being brave enough to step into their dynamic zone?

The reason is simple. The critics are none other than the vast majority of people who have accepted for themselves a life of comfort and instant gratification, not aspiring to anything beyond mediocrity. These people are scared of their dynamic zones and the changes that accompany anything dynamic. They interpret their fear as a message to avoid any activity or experience that triggers fear. As a result, they refuse to support anyone who is interested in anything dynamic. To a "comfort zoner," change is a threat to their comfort, something that may cause them pain.

Why do you think Helen Keller was criticized? People without any handicaps were jealous that a blind and deaf person was doing much more with her life than they were with theirs. Helen Keller made the people who had full use of all of their senses look bad. She caused these people to feel jealous and uncomfortable around her. Consequently, this made it easier for them to attack and criticize her than to actually face their own fears and learn from her example. Once again, this is an example of choosing the easy way out, the path of least resistance.

What if Winston Churchill had decided to choose the path of least resistance the first time that he was criticized about his capacity to lead England? Would someone else have stepped up to the challenge of halting the wrath of Hitler and the German army? Nobody knows. All we know is that Hitler and his army were considered by many to be an "invincible wall" that was prepared to conquer the entire world. Fortunately, Winston Churchill had the audacity to step into his dynamic zone and pursue his dream of freedom despite the criticism that came along with it. By accepting the challenge, Churchill led the way to the eventual defeat of Hitler.

Martin Luther King Jr. was another wall smasher who ventured forth into his dynamic zone despite receiving various death threats. The word "criticism" does not do justice for the type of abuse he encountered while he pursued his dream of equal civil rights for all people. King was openly cursed by his peers, ridiculed by the media, and even jailed several times. Nonetheless, King persevered. Two of his most noteworthy actions included the nonviolent freedom march in Alabama that consisted of nearly a quarter of a million people, and the "March on Washington" where he delivered one of the all-time greatest speeches, his "I have a dream" speech. Eventually, King won the prestigious Nobel Peace Prize for his incredible work in the area of civil rights. Unfortunately, Martin Luther King was blatantly shot and killed one day as he was making plans with his staff. Although he never reached his 40th birthday, Martin Luther King lived one of the most dynamic lives in history.

Consider Christopher Columbus. Do you think he was criticized for believing that the world was round when everyone else said that it was flat? Imagine how tough it was to get funding for his voyage when everyone he approached believed that he would sail off the side of the Earth. This is probably why he failed seven times before he ever set sail on his great adventure. Furthermore, imagine what kind of profanity was directed toward him when he asked someone to be part of his crew. Do you think his countrymen were beating his door down to have the privilege of sailing with him? I doubt it! Even when he finally did gather up a crew to accompany him on his travels, do you think they criticized him when they encountered the first storm at sea that threatened their lives? Do you think anyone had second thoughts? The truth is that the threat of mutiny constantly surrounded Columbus, yet he endured and consequently discovered the New World. No amount of criticism could have deterred Columbus from pursuing his dream.

Although these examples consist of men and women who have become famous in the public eye, credit equally belongs to the less publicized person who also steps into her dynamic zone despite receiving massive criticism. The common individual who is willing to pursue her dream in the midst of criticism is every bit as much of a hero as is a Columbus, King, Keller, or Churchill. A hero is someone who can quit a high paying job in order to spend more of her time at home with her children even though her coworkers think she is crazy. Or the person who can give 10% of her income to a worthwhile charity even though her parents tell her that she is foolish. Or the person who has sustained devastating injuries, yet refuses to give up on the process of healing even though her doctors claim that it's hopeless. Common people like this should be applauded for displaying so much courage in the midst of criticism. They are the types of people that Theodore Roosevelt was referring to when he said:

> It is not the critic who counts, not the man who points out how the strong man stumbles or where the doer of deeds could have done them better. The credit belongs to the man who is actually in the arena, whose face is marred by dust and sweat and blood, who strives valiantly, who errs and comes short again and again because there is no effort without error and shortcomings, who knows the great devotion, who spends himself in a worthy cause, who at best knows in the end the high achievement of triumph and who at worst, if he fails while daring greatly, knows his place shall never be with those timid and cold souls who know neither victory nor defeat.

Take heed to what Roosevelt said by making a commitment to yourself to learn from those who have succeeded in spite of being criticized or harassed by others. Let their accomplishments inspire you to enter your dynamic zone and smash your walls of fear. Remember to start with yourself. Anyone who has ever made a great achievement has always attained inner greatness before they displayed outward greatness. All change must come from within before it can be outwardly expressed.

As easy as this may sound, there are still millions of people who choose to live a life of mediocrity. They consciously choose to be a carbon copy of the masses. These people duplicate the same habits as their family, friends, and neighbors without ever consulting their own heart. As a result, they end up creating a monotonous daily routine for themselves as a way to avoid criticism. Today's typical daily routine includes the following regimen:

1. Wake up at the same time each day.
2. Rush to "get ready" and grab a cup of coffee and a doughnut on the way to work.
3. Spend approximately ten hours in a mental stupor working to achieve the financial goals of someone else at a job that lacks any real fulfillment.
4. Come home and plop down in front of the TV, drink a few beers, snack on some unhealthy foods filled with sugar, fat, and caffeine, and complain about how unfair the world is.
5. Heat up a few microwave dinners for the family.
6. Spend the rest of the evening watching TV.

7. Get to bed early. After all, tomorrow is another big day.

Mix this list with a lack of exercise, low self-esteem, and a massive fear of anything dynamic and you have what has now become the typical human lifestyle. In short, most of society has become content with mediocrity. Many people have given up on the dreams they once had. What has happened to our society? Did we forget those people like Abraham Lincoln, Mahatma Gandhi, and Martin Luther King Jr. who lost their lives fighting for our freedom? Are you going to show your appreciation for our past heroes by sitting on your rocker recliner for five hours every evening watching television? Or are you going to stand up to criticism, act upon your walls of fear, and create a dynamic life for yourself, your family, and for all future generations?

Take a moment and recall how many times throughout history that people were not permitted to explore their dynamic zones. Many people were either held in slavery, restricted by a dictator, or born into the wrong class. These people did not have a choice. The only decision they had was whether to obey the laws of the land or to subject themselves to death.

Many of us forget how lucky we are to be living in a society where we have the unique opportunity to pursue our dreams without the threat of being thrown in prison, exiled, tortured, or even killed. Still, many of us disregard the dreams of our heart and settle for an average life of comfort and instant gratification, a life consisting of very little real fulfillment and joy. All of this because we are afraid of someone criticizing us for one reason or another.

Fortunately, we still have a few excellent role models to follow, people who choose to enter their dynamic zones despite receiving criticism from others. One such person is Doctor Bernie Siegel. Bernie is a renowned surgeon at Yale New Haven Hospital in Connecticut. His special gift is his ability to interact effectively with his patients and give them the best possible opportunity for healing. Despite his unique talent, he was berated by his fellow physicians for getting too close to his patients. His peers urged him to detach himself from his patients as would most traditional doctors. Their reasoning was that it would save him from feeling any emotional pain when a patient dies or does not get any better.

Regardless of the criticism, Bernie Siegel would not allow the opinions of his peers to deter the desires of his heart. He continued to interact with his patients in nontraditional, dynamic ways. Eventually, he proved beyond a doubt that his unique approach toward medical care was much more effective than the traditional approaches. Unfortunately, some of Bernie's peers continue to criticize him in spite of his proven success. After all, they perceive him as a threat to their comfort.

What if Bernie Siegel would have listened to his fellow physicians? The world would have been forever denied the wonderful education and insight that his books, tapes, and seminars have given this world. Furthermore, he would have never created ECaP, Exceptional Cancer Patients, an organization that allows cancer patients to interact with other cancer patients and explore dynamic ways to perceive their challenges. As a result of this organization, many cancer patients have learned how to better cope with their illnesses and a significant amount of them have sent their disease into remission. No one leaves the group without being affected in some positive way. And to think that ECaP would have never existed if Bernie Siegel did not exhibit the courage to shrug off the criticism that he received from his peers.

Take it upon yourself to learn from people like Bernie Siegel. Rise above the criticism you receive from your peers. Become someone who is willing to enter your dynamic zone and smash your walls of fear despite being criticized.

FOLLOWING CERTAIN RITUALS CAN LEAD TO BOREDOM

Consistently stepping into the unfamiliar territory of your dynamic zone is the only true insurance policy that can protect you from experiencing boredom in your life. Otherwise, the magnetizing pull of your comfort zone would mesmerize you into complacency. Eventually, all of your days would begin to lump together and it would seem as though you are living the same monotonous day over and over again.

Your dynamic zone is the only place that you can make your life more fulfilling and more interesting each and every day that you are alive. After all, what good is it to keep reliving the same day over and over again? Isn't life about exploring new territories, extending your boundaries, and learning new things? Isn't life about growth, change, and improvement? Stepping into your dynamic zone allows you to learn new information, meet new people, and gather new experiences. These are the things that add spice to your life. They are the only things that keep you from becoming lulled into a state of boredom. In truth, the unknown and unfamiliar is the safest place you could possibly be.

"If you want to be free, step into the unknown every second of your life, and then you will be free."
Dr. Deepak Chopra

Unfortunately, most of society has created a whole series of rituals as a way to get through certain events, activities, and experiences without feeling any discomfort in the process. A ritual is a behavior that is conducted the same way at a specific time and/or a specific place. Rituals are all around us. There are religious rituals, sexual rituals, business rituals, social rituals, and athletic rituals, to name a few. Your entire life basically consists of a bunch of rituals including shaving, eating, sleeping, brushing your teeth, and taking a shower. Holidays, religious ceremonies, customs, rules, creeds, codes, and traditions also fall into the category of rituals. Take a moment and review the following list to get a feel for a few of the most common rituals.

- Driving to work at the same time each day, taking the exact same route while listening to the same radio station playing the same songs.
- Having sex at the same time of day at the same place, beginning with the same foreplay and assuming the same positions for the same amount of time.
- Going to the same restaurant with the same people, sitting in the same booth ordering the same entree.
- Attending the same religious ceremonies at the same time each week, sitting in the same section of the church, unconsciously repeating the same memorized verses over and over.
- Spending a certain holiday with the same people at the same place, eating the same foods and talking about the same issues.
- Playing the same position in the same sport with the same people and applying the same strategy.
- Repeating the same four words (Hi, how are you?) to the same people walking the same route who reply the same way (Fine, thank you.) (By the way, do you really want to know how someone is doing or do you ask someone how they are doing as a means to avoid a deeper conversation?)

Rituals stem from the law of familiarity—whatever behavior is most familiar has the greatest chance of being repeated. Most rituals are nothing but a way for you to get through a situation without experiencing any uncomfortable emotions. Instead of inspiring you to explore your dynamic zone, rituals outline a specific way to do something. They direct you to the path of least resistance.

It is a proven fact that most college students will sit in their original seat for the entire semester even if the professor encourages them to sit in different seats. The same is true for parents. Most parents tend to raise all of their children in relatively the same way despite the obvious fact that every child is different and presents different challenges. Regardless of the situation, it is very easy to adopt a ritualistic way of dealing with any given experience.

> ### *"The ritual is designed to get a group of people through the hour without having to get close to anyone."*
> Thomas Harris

Ask yourself, "Do I really want to live my life like a preprogrammed computer software program?" I sincerely doubt it! You are a dynamic person who is meant to grow, change, and improve every day of your life. You are not obligated to take part in outdated rituals that have no special meaning to you.

Consider the ritual of blessing someone after they sneeze. What if you would rather bless someone after they burp or fart? Is that so bad? Do you really have to do what "everyone" else does? Do you really have to follow traditions solely out of obligation? Whatever happened to creating your own tradition? That's not to say that it is detrimental to your well-being if you want to follow an established tradition like blessing someone after they sneeze. Partaking in certain rituals is fine unless you give up your individual freedom in the process. Don't let your life be dictated by certain rituals. Instead, learn to recognize the patterns in your life and decide for yourself whether to continue a particular ritual or to act in your own unique, dynamic way instead.

> ### *"Making a difference is different from being different."*
> Eric J. Bowser

Blind adherence to any outdated or ineffective ritual strips you of your freedom and originality. Only growth, change, and improvement characterize a dynamic life. Therefore, you need to become consciously aware of the rituals that are holding you back from making progress in your life. But first, it may be best to recognize the positive rituals that give your life structure and promote your growth as a human being. Consider these positive rituals:

- ♣ Sleeping every night for at least six hours
- ♣ Brushing your teeth when you wake up in the morning and when you go to bed at night

♣ Kissing your spouse and children before you go to work in the morning

♣ Praying when you wake up in the morning and before you go to bed at night

♣ Reading a nonfiction book for a half-hour every morning

♣ Saying "I love you" to each of your family members before going to bed for the night

♣ Starting your morning with a glass of freshly squeezed juice

♣ Exercising for one hour immediately upon returning home from work

Once you have recognized the positive rituals in your life, proceed to make a list of your negative rituals as well. From there, eliminate the rituals that have no special meaning for you. Allow your family members to wear a baseball hat at the kitchen table if you feel that it would cause no harm. Go camping instead of attending your high school dance if that is what you really want to do. Drink water on your 21st birthday instead of forcing down "shots" of liquor (especially if you don't want to get sick and barf). What's the sense in following rituals that only bring you pain and discomfort?

Maybe your family has a ritual of coming to your house for a big Thanksgiving dinner. Perhaps you dread the thought of cooking for twenty people. Maybe you would rather go out to eat at a restaurant instead. In this case, you could still invite everyone over to your house, but instead of eating at your house, you could have your family dinner at a local restaurant. This way, you can still enjoy a delicious meal, spend time with the people you love, and most of all, rid yourself of the burdensome task of cooking for so many people.

Do this with all the rituals that you want to change. Remember, you are free to take a step outside your comfort zone any time you choose. Read through the following examples to get some ideas about how you can transform some of your meaningless rituals into dynamic experiences.

♠ Go to work early, stay late, or work a different shift at your job.

♠ Drive a different route to work and listen to an educational tape instead of the radio.

♠ Have sex in the morning if you usually do it at night. Take the process either slower or faster. Experiment with different positions.

♠ Go to a new restaurant with a different group of people. Order something you have never eaten before.

♠ Attend an "unusual" religious service. Sit in the front part of the church if you are accustomed to sitting in the back. Arrive early instead of being late. Think about what you are saying instead of unconsciously repeating a memorized verse.

♠ Invite a new friend to your holiday gathering. Prepare something untraditional to eat. Hold your party outside if you usually have it inside.

♠ Play a new sport with a different group of people. Keep changing your strategy and learn to play the different positions.

♠ Walk a different route on your lunch hour. Say something unique to the people you pass along the street.

QUESTIONS HAVE THE POWER TO TRANSFORM A RITUAL INTO A DYNAMIC EXPEREINCE

Questions are another great strategy that you can use to transform a meaningless ritual into a dynamic experience. By asking yourself the right dynamic questions, you can easily jolt yourself out of your habitual mindset. Questions also have the power to transform an experience for an entire group of people.

Let's presume you are eating dinner with your family. This particular meal is no different from any other meal. The conversation is a bit dull to say the least and everyone seems to be unconsciously going through the motions. It is apparent that no one is having a dynamic experience. In this case, by asking one simple question, you could transform a common ritual like eating dinner into a dynamic experience that your family may never forget. Consider some of the following questions:

♦ What is the meaning of life?
♦ Who was the first person you ever kissed?
♦ What has been the most joyful experience of your life?
♦ What is the funniest thing you ever did?
♦ What was the best book you have ever read? Why?
♦ Describe your dream of an ideal day?

- ♦ What do you admire most about your mother, father, brother, sister, etc.?
- ♦ What was your most embarrassing experience?

By asking one of these questions to a member of your family, you can literally transform the experience for your entire family. Instantly, everyone present will gain a new sense of energy and enthusiasm generated from a question asked so far out of context. Consistently using this strategy over time will also help you to develop a much more intimate relationship with those closest to you. In the case of your family, you could even turn it into a game. Each day a different person could create a unique question to be asked during dinner.

ORDINARY PEOPLE LIVING DYNAMIC LIVES

Choosing to venture forth into the uncharted regions of your dynamic zone entails substantial risk. Your risk may involve vulnerability, open-mindedness, time, money, commitment, and/or trust. Regardless of your specific risk, it will still involve some kind of change and, as you know, most people cringe at the sound of that word.

> *"The word risk may strike fear in your heart, but risking is the only way to grow."*
> H. Norman Wright

Nonetheless, many ordinary people still gather up enough courage to step into their dynamic zones. Consider the following people who have learned to live certain parts of their lives in very dynamic ways:

◊ Roger is a corporate executive in charge of handling millions of dollars of business every week. Despite the heavy responsibilities and countless problems that result from his demanding career, Roger still spends at least one hour a day playing with his five-year-old daughter. His commitment to his daughter is not determined by how tired he is or how many problems he encounters at work.

◊ Grandma Kopler may be a widow with a physical handicap, but she still prepares lunch for her grandchildren on Mondays and Wednesdays in the summer. During this time, she entertains them and influences their impressionable lives with unconditional love. She also tells them stories about the wonderful lessons that she learned throughout her own life. Although grandma has many walls in her life, there is not an obstacle big enough to stop her from making a difference in the world. Her love, strength, and wisdom shine forth upon all the world as her grandchildren leave her presence.

◊ Mike is a high school wrestler who wakes up an hour early every day so that he can train before going to school. He motivates himself by focusing on his dream of placing at the state tournament this year. Mike's actions are especially dynamic since most people do not expect him to make it that far. After all, he lost more matches than he won last year. At best, Mike is considered to have nothing more than average wrestling talent by most people's estimations. Nonetheless, Mike has a dream and, more importantly, Mike has the courage to pursue his dream. When he is jogging, physically he is running the streets of his neighborhood, but mentally he is winning 2-1 in overtime of the state quarter finals. He visualizes himself giving every last ounce of his being to hold on to his lead because he knows that if he advances to the next round, he will achieve his dream. In his mind, he can see the medal being placed around his neck as the sweat rolls down his face.

◊ Tom is an entrepreneur who is on the verge of bankruptcy. Although he is facing massive financial walls, he still realizes that his business success or failure does not determine his worth as a person. Despite his hardships, he still understands that his life and the lives of his family members are much more important than any number of walls he may encounter. Tom has consciously chosen to create and maintain a positive attitude regardless of what eventually happens to his enterprises. He realizes that even if he does end up going bankrupt, he still lives in a country blessed with a wonderful free enterprise system. Therefore, he can bounce back from his setbacks and continue to pursue his entrepreneurial dreams. His attitude will always be his most valuable asset.

◊ Javier is a fifteen-year-old musician from a small town in the Midwest. He has a dream of signing with a major record company and producing his own music. Once, he joined forces with the local deli and created his very own fund-raiser. He used the profits to buy his first electric guitar. On another occasion, Javier could not get a ride to a special musical event, so he rode his bicycle forty miles to attend it. Although Javier is barely a teenager, he knows more about goals and determination than do most adults. He is more than a musician. He is a dynamic person who understands the urgency of following his desires and developing his unique talents.

◊ Missy is a gorgeous seventeen-year-old high school senior who was voted Homecoming Queen by her peers. Out of the many boys who asked her to dance during the final slow song of the night, Missy chose to dance with Danny. Danny is a very special friend who happens to be handicapped. This act of kindness and compassion proved to bring a greater feeling of joy to Missy than did any popularity contest that she had ever won. At the end of the evening, it was apparent that Missy's heart was even more beautiful than her stunning physical appearance.

◊ Ben is a businessman who took a homeless person to lunch at the local diner. Ben knew that most of his friends and associates would be at the diner, yet he still had the courage to show up with his new friend. Even though he had to put up with some teasing and harassment, Ben benefited greatly from the experience. He received an abundant amount of joy and made an outstanding contribution to his society. Best of all, he accomplished all of this during his regular lunch hour.

◊ Heather is a collegiate basketball player who regularly shoots 100 free throws after practice while her teammates are in the showers. She understands that by perfecting the fundamentals of the game, eventually she will become a superstar. Heather is preparing for the day when her team is in the national finals and she is at the foul line with the score tied. There is no time left on the clock and she has an opportunity to win the national championship if she can sink her next free throw. As she releases the ball, she can sense it going through the hoop the same way it did for her so many times in practice. As the ball swishes through the net, the entire gymnasium erupts with emotion as Heather's team wins its first national championship in school history. She vividly imagines tears of joy streaking down her cheeks as she accepts the most valuable player honors.

◊ Carol is a career woman, wife, and mother of three school-age children. Each morning she wakes up an hour early to spend time with her children as they prepare for school and eat breakfast. Carol also makes sure that she inserts a special note into her husband's lunch bag as a reminder to him of her love. Although her family is not rich in financial terms, her family has a wealth that even millionaires cannot buy. They have love for each other.

◊ Jarrod is a junior high school boy who dreams about becoming a best-selling author. He wants to reach millions of people and positively influence their lives. His dream is special because he really believes that it will happen. He is taking action every day toward its achievement. Although he is only thirteen years old, he is an avid reader, writes his thoughts and ideas in his own personal journal, and has a very detailed list of goals. Jarrod also maintains excellent grades in school and participates in a wide variety of extra-curricular activities including a dynamic writing club. Jarrod works much harder than do most of his peers, but he does so because his dream is so important to him. Even though he is often tempted to take the easy way out, he motivates himself to keep moving forward by focusing on his dream.

◊　Maurice is a husband and father of four children. He may have strayed from his religious beliefs for a few years, but now he is choosing to grow in this department of his life. Maurice has begun his growth process by offering a creative prayer of thanksgiving along with his family before every meal. Although this is only one small step, Maurice understands that all momentum starts by taking one small step. He also realizes that the past is over and that he can only change his present situation.

◊　Janice is a seven-year-old girl who sings in front of hundreds of people. Her parents never forced her to do it and she doesn't even understand the concept of money. All she knows is the joy that she feels when she is singing. Although she is only seven years old, she understands the importance of doing what she loves. To her, it is only natural to pursue her dreams.

As can be seen by these examples, it is very possible for an ordinary person to make any aspect of her life dynamic by making a few key changes. Change is the only way that you can ever escape your comfort zone. Resisting change only breeds insanity, which is taking the same actions over and over and expecting a different result.

Life only begins to change once you change. No one will ever do it for you. The following list includes some additional ideas of change that you can use to make your life more dynamic:

- Take flowers to a retirement home and give them to an elderly person whom you have never met.
- Go out to a bar on a Saturday night and drink water.
- Sleep on the back porch underneath the stars.
- Make yourself a glass of carrot juice.
- Ride your bicycle to the gym.
- Volunteer a portion of your time to assist the Special Olympics in your city.
- Take your family to the city zoo.

SMASHING THE WALL OF FEAR

- Plan a surprise party for your daughter for no reason.
- Take a day off work to ride "quads" or motorcycles with your children and their friends.
- Attend a school board meeting.
- Buy a cappuccino instead of regular coffee.
- Spend thirty minutes a day reading a nonfiction book.
- Play educational tapes in your car as you ride to and from your place of work.
- Write a letter or send a card for no particular reason to someone you love.
- Forgive someone whom you swore you would hate forever.
- Genuinely compliment one of your peers for possessing a particular talent.
- Confront someone about a particular injustice instead of ignoring the situation and creating reasons in your mind to justify your inaction.
- Say your own unique prayer of thanks out loud before dinner rather than reciting the same redundant prayer you have been unconsciously repeating for years.
- Accept an invitation to be a reader at your brother's wedding.
- Send flowers to your spouse of twenty-seven years for no other reason than to proclaim your love.
- Bring home a cake for your son even if it's not his birthday.
- Sleep naked instead of wearing your pajamas.
- Donate money to someone in need even if you do not have the extra money.
- Wake up ten minutes early to write in your journal.
- Frame your life's purpose or mission statement and hang it above your desk.

EXPLORING YOUR DYNAMIC ZONE WILL GIVE YOU A CLEARER PERCEPTION OF FEAR

Becoming a dynamic person who consistently expands your comfort zone will give you a much clearer perception of fear. Perception is your current level of understanding about something. It is the mental picture you create in your mind about a particular situation. Rollo May, one of the world's most renowned psychiatrists, once explained perception by relating it to a person you see way off in the distance on a lonely, deserted road. At first, you feel frightened by the stranger since you *perceive* the stranger in your mind as an evil person who is going to harm you in some way. But, as the person gets closer to you, you realize that the person you perceived as being evil is really one of your good friends. Suddenly, your perception of the situation becomes much clearer and more accurate than it originally was. The situation did not change, only your perception of the situation changed.

Your perception of any given situation is largely responsible for determining the amount of fear that you feel in that situation. It stands to reason that the clearer you perceive any given situation, the less intense your fear will be. Coming to grips with a clear perception also makes it much easier for you to handle or even enjoy a fearful experience. On the other hand, by adopting an exaggerated mindset of a situation, you will produce tension and increase the intensity of your fears. Consequently, the experience will become less enjoyable.

For instance, if you were an actor, you could easily generate a great deal of fear by creating a ridiculous perception in your mind. You could envision yourself forgetting your lines, tripping over your shoestring, or even falling off the stage. There is virtually no limit to the ridiculous images that you could conjure up in your mind.

On the other hand, you could decrease the intensity of your fears by choosing to envision your acting experience with a clearer, more objective perception. Realize that if you forgot a line, the audience probably would not even notice. If you tripped on a shoestring, you would only be providing the audience with some additional humor. Even if you fell off the stage, you would be providing the audience with a memory of a lifetime. In fact, whatever happens to you is really no big deal. It is only a big deal if you make it one.

The single most effective shift you can make in your perception of fear is to recognize that fear is only a feeling of discomfort. It does not have the power to hurt you. Fortunately, you can come to this realization by consistently stretching yourself into your dynamic zone to take part in unfamiliar experiences. Exploring new activities will give you the confidence you need to tackle the other fears that are holding you back in your life. The more unusual experiences that you encounter, the better able you will be to handle all of your present and future fears. Even taking part in an activity that you initially interpret as being silly will often give you new eyes with which to see the rest of your world more clearly.

For example, consider the father who was willing to join his wife and children as they danced around the living room mimicking the cartoon characters from the children's movie, *The Lion King*. Even though he considered this type of behavior to be silly and weird, it still presented him with a unique opportunity to expand his comfort zone and to see the rest of his fears more clearly. By consistently making it a habit to do "silly" things like this, he found himself much more confident doing other "more important" things like developing new personal friendships and making pivotal decisions.

The same result occurred for a businessman who stepped into his dynamic zone by taking an aerobics class with a room full of women. As a result of courageously doing something that he once considered to be absurd, he began to feel much less fearful approaching business clients, making important sales calls, and speaking up at meetings. By exploring his dynamic zone, he jolted his mind out of its habitual thinking pattern into a more dynamic mindset. He realized that if he could dance around with a room full of women (something he never pictured himself doing), then he could also do other things that he was afraid to do.

Another example of gaining a clearer perception about fear is the widowed woman who displayed loads of courage by attending archery classes despite having no experience whatsoever in that field. By doing so, she suddenly realized that archery was a lot of fun. But more importantly, she also gained a newfound sense of self-confidence by successfully doing something so unusual. As a result, her perception of her remaining fears changed for the better. Suddenly, she felt truly ready to do some of the things that once seemed too scary for her to do. One of which was to finally accept an invitation for a date from a very nice man whom she had previously rejected several times.

Experiencing dynamic activities creates for yourself a brand new perception of your life as a whole. Suddenly, your old, limiting perceptions are forced to give way to new, more accurate perceptions. Even though it is impossible to arrive at a perfectly clear and accurate perception of reality while here on Earth, it is possible to keep progressing closer to its attainment.

Applying this strategy in your own life does not mean that you must force yourself to take part in an uninteresting activity. Instead, choose an unfamiliar activity that seems as if it could be fun and exciting. Be open-minded and withhold your judgment until you have actually experienced it. Life is for exploring! Our society needs more widows who take archery classes, more businessmen who take aerobics, and more fathers who dance with their family.

Review the following list of unusual and "silly" activities. Make a note of the ones that interest you. Then, go out into the world and experience them for yourself. You will expand your comfort zone and improve your perception of fear as a result:

- Go fishing in the wilderness of northern Canada at a place where you must be flown in by a helicopter.
- Take a bicycle ride to a distant campground and spend the night. Attach panniers to your bicycle in order to carry a tent, sleeping bag, clothes, food, and other supplies that you will need.
- Karaoke at a party or night club.
- Study Tae Kwon Do or some other martial art.
- Learn how to country "line" dance.
- Learn how to roller blade, ice skate, or skateboard.
- Play a game with the children of your neighborhood and follow their rules for a change.
- Go water skiing or snow skiing.
- Attend a craft show, baseball card show, or art show.
- Learn to play a musical instrument.
- Attend a play or musical.
- Go "skinny dipping" at 4:30 in the morning.
- Enroll in a special class or study group that is being offered in your community.
- Race a stock car at your local track.
- Enter a demolition derby at your county fair.

Keep in mind that there is no need to perform at any specific level when you take part in a brand new activity. In fact, it is probably best that you perform poorly at first. Poor performance allows you a lot of room for improvement. Anyway, our world needs more novice singers, more amateur writers, and more inexperienced artists. Life is not about being the best. It is about having fun and exploring the unknown.

This does not mean that you must stress yourself out to see how many "crazy" things you can do today. Nor does it mean to put yourself or anyone else in physical danger. Compulsive fanatics hurt society more than they help society and extremists are never good role models. Nature abhors extremes of any kind. Instead, have fun by safely, yet courageously, expressing your "crazy" side. Be open-minded to new and adventurous experiences.

"A dynamic life is a life full of risks, but not hazardous risks where a person takes unnecessary chances."
David Viscott, M.D.

Use your "uncommon sense" to explore new activities. Then, watch and see how differently you begin to perceive your world. Follow the guidance of your fear and you will encounter many unique experiences. As a result, you will grow, change, and improve into a more dynamic person.

CHAPTER 5

THE ESSENCE OF FEAR

"When fear is expressed, we recognize it as anger, abuse, disease, pain, greed, addiction, selfishness, obsession, corruption, violence, and war."
Shakti Gawain

As we enter the 21st Century, no longer can anybody of reasonable intelligence deny the power of emotions to both positively and negatively affect the quality of our health. Many best-selling books in this area cite loads of scientific research as proof. Best-selling authors like Deepak Chopra, Louise Hay, Ken Keyes, Joan Borysenko, Bernie Siegel, Shakti Gawain, Norman Cousins, and many others have staked their careers on the belief that emotions absolutely have the power to both kill and heal.

You create a whole realm of negative emotions when you stroll through life avoiding your fears. At some point in time, this build-up of emotional energy must find an outlet. It is no different from the engine of your car. If your engine does not have some kind of exhaust pipe to release the build-up of fumes, it would shut itself down. The following list outlines and defines some of these common negative emotions.

NEGATIVE EMOTIONS

Anger- A feeling of displeasure toward another person or toward yourself.

Anguish- A feeling of intense physical or mental torment.

Anxiety- An all encompassing feeling of fear that is created by worrying.

Apprehension- Worrying about something in the future.

Cowardice- A feeling of weakness that occurs when you do not pursue your dream.

Denial- Refusing to accept the truth.

Disappointment- Realizing that you will never accomplish your original objective.

Envy- To covet another person's skills, qualities, or possessions.

Embarrassment- A fear of exposing your genuine self.

Frustration- Feeling upset because you know that you have the talent and ability, but you are still not producing the result you desire.

Grief- Intense mental hurt over a loss.

Helplessness- Feeling as though you are powerless.

Hurt- A sensation of mental, physical, or emotional suffering.

Inadequacy- Lacking the skills to achieve your dream.

Insecurity- Feeling uncertain due to a lack of self-confidence.

Jealousy- Feeling resentful or envious of another person because you lack a similar skill, quality, or possession.

Loneliness- Feeling separated from others.

Overwhelm- Feeling out of control because you are dealing with too many things at once.

Rage- The most intense form of anger. Characterized by some type of violence.

Resentment- Feeling hostile toward another person due to a real or imagined event.

Stress- Tension that strains your mental, physical, or emotional health. Usually created by unexpressed feelings.

Terror- An overwhelming, immobilizing feeling of fear.

Uselessness (worthlessness)- Feeling as though you have no value to yourself, your family, or your society. The lowest and most dangerous of the negative emotions.

Worry- Thinking about the things you fear instead of acting upon them.

Take another moment and really look at this list of negative emotions. Notice how many of them have to do with fear. Think about it. When someone is resentful of you, isn't she just afraid of some superiority or power that you have over her? When someone feels disappointed, isn't she really afraid that she has lost an opportunity forever? When someone is in denial, isn't she really afraid of facing the truth? Fear is the one underlying emotion that exists within practically every other negative emotion. It stands to reason why it is so important for you to learn how to properly handle it. Mishandling the emotion of fear could very easily force you to pay a great price. This price might be paid in terms of your personal health.

"All negativity derives from fear."
Marianne Williamson

Did you know that when a cow is shot before it is butchered, the farmer must immediately cut off the flow of blood from the brain to the body? Otherwise, the cow's brain would send fearful chemicals throughout the rest of its body. If the farmer were to wait several hours before he cut off the blood flow, the meat of the cow would become saturated with fear. This would result in a much lower quality of meat. Anytime animals or human beings for that matter harbor excessive amounts of fear, every aspect of their life will in some way be negatively affected by it.

The same is true of a group of pigs who witness another pig getting "stuck" right in front of them. Besides the fact that this is an obvious act of animal cruelty, the other pigs who witness the event will immediately send fearful chemicals throughout their body. These chemicals will also negatively affect the quality of their meat. To guard against this natural reaction, wise farmers do all of their "sticking" away from the view of the other pigs. This way, fear will have no affect upon the quality of the meat.

Fear is always either growing or shrinking. When you ignore the guidance from your fear, you cause it to grow in intensity. The more it grows, the more it needs to find some kind of outlet. As you continue to harbor more and more fear inside your body, you create more and more negative energy until your body finally goes into an emergency state. This is the point where your body is forced to do whatever it takes to find some kind of outlet for your excess fear. Unfortunately, this outlet often results in some form of an ailment.

A great book to read on this subject is *You Can Heal Your Life* by Louise Hay. There you can discover the specific emotion(s) that is most apt to cause a certain condition to manifest itself in your body and how to reverse the effects. Another excellent book about the power of your emotions is *The Complete Guide to Your Emotions and Your Health* written by Emrika Padus.

By simply facing your walls of fear, you can give your fearful energy the proper healthy outlet. This outlet will cleanse your body and mind of its negative energy and prevent additional negative chemicals from being released.

Let's suppose you have a fear of confronting your boss about a particular comment that she directed toward you during a recent company meeting. It's been two days since the comment took place and you still feel offended by it. Instead of obeying the guidance of your fear and confronting your boss about the comment, you choose to suppress your emotions. By doing so, you force your body to find a way to discharge them. Suddenly, you start to act much more angry and critical toward your coworkers and family. Furthermore, you realize that you have not slept well since the incident, your productivity at work has slacked off significantly, and you have suffered from heartburn. In short, your suppressed emotions are eating away at your health.

After several days of ignoring the guidance of your fear, you finally decide to "do the thing you fear" and confront your boss about the comment. Oddly enough, you discover that your boss didn't even realize she offended you. In fact, she apologized over and over again and assured you that her comment was not meant to be offensive or derogatory in any way. Instantly, you feel as though a weight has been lifted off your shoulders. You feel refreshed and joyful. Suddenly, you find yourself treating people with more respect, sleeping better, being more productive, and experiencing absolutely no heartburn.

Deciding to avoid your fears negatively affects both your current and your future state of health. Avoidance is merely a prelude to a physical ailment in your body. Anytime you avoid an important situation like asking someone special for a date, applying for a much desired promotion, or telling the truth to someone you love, you make yourself more susceptible to experiencing negative side effects.

Now that you realize some of the ramifications of avoiding your fears, you are ready to direct your focus toward understanding a couple of the most common types of fear.

WORRY

Over and over again, people tell me that they are "supposed" to worry. They say things like, "I'm a parent and it's my job to worry." Or "My job requires me to worry about certain things." Or "I would not feel as though I loved my family if I did not worry about them." For one reason or another, most people feel obligated to worry.

To these people I ask, "Would you agree to quit worrying if God personally told you to do so?" Their response is usually a resounding

"Yes" until I point out to them that in the King James version of the Bible the words *fear not* (translated as "don't worry") appears over 350 times. The truth is that the words *fear not* could have been used 35,000 times in the Bible and it still would not have made a bit of difference. The bottom line is that most people are absolutely convinced that worrying is a necessary part of life.

Worrying occurs when you focus your thoughts upon a situation that you have no intention of acting upon. It's when you actually imagine that something terrible will happen, but you are unwilling to do anything about it. Instead, all you do is sit around and think about the situation until you feel helpless. The longer you sit around, the harder it becomes to ever take action. When you worry, you actually paralyze yourself in the present over some past or future situation. Worst of all, worrying totally destroys your ability to experience joy in the moment. Earl Nightingale, creator of the audiocassette program *Lead the Field* revealed the truth about worrying. He reported that:

> 40% of the things that you worry about never happen
> 30% have already happened and cannot be changed
> 12% are needless worries about your health
> 10% are petty, miscellaneous worries
> 8% are genuine worries

Even if you focus on the 8% of your worries that are genuine, you still cannot solve your problems by worrying about them. Taking action upon a problem is still the only way to solve it. Worrying provides you with absolutely no tangible or intangible benefits. It is completely useless. All it does is causes you to experience unnecessary stress in your life.

"Present dangers are less than future imaginings."
William Shakespeare

If you find yourself worrying about a certain presentation that you will be making in the future, then get up and rehearse it. Don't sit in your chair worrying about all the possible things that could go wrong. Use your feelings of fear as a sign to get yourself prepared for your upcoming presentation. Stand up and take some action. Do something to put your worries at ease.

In the case that you have already thoroughly prepared yourself for your upcoming presentation, then go outside and cut the grass or play tennis. Do something active instead of sitting around passively dwelling on what might go wrong. The more activities that you can partake of, the less time you will have to dwell upon possible misfortunes. Your mind can only focus on one thing at a time. If you can fully engage it in a fun activity, then it will not have any time to worry.

> *"Most of the time fear is due to using the mind more than the body. If you think too much and neglect action, you generate fear."*
> Dr. Robert Anthony

The only way to move beyond a certain fear in your life is by doing it. You could prepare yourself for the rest of your life for a specific presentation, but the truth remains that until you actually give the presentation, you will feel fearful. Worrying only amplifies the amount of fear that you will feel.

A great way to combat the effects of worry is to make sure that you are very sleepy when you go to bed. Bedtime is usually when you will feel most tempted to worry. To avoid this potential trap, you can implement the following strategies into your day:

♣ Take part in several strenuous activities throughout your day.

♣ Limit the amount of sugar, caffeine, and fat that you eat.

♣ Eat very light if you choose to eat anything after 9 PM.

♣ Visualize yourself performing brilliantly in challenging situations.

♣ Drink lots of water, fresh juices, and water-rich foods throughout your day.

♣ Eat two or more servings of vegetables a day.

♣ Take 10 deep breaths in a row several times during the day.

It is very wise to establish good solid habits to guard yourself against the type of environment conducive to worry. Failing to create healthy daily habits can cause worry to creep into your life little by little until it pervades your entire being. As your worries begin to overlap each other, you will experience a much more dangerous type of fear—anxiety.

ANXIETY

Anxiety is currently America's number one mental health problem. It is estimated that over 28 million people suffer from the terrible effects of anxiety. Although this number may seem high to you, my own personal belief is that it is really much higher.

Anxiety is a very dangerous form of fear. It is dangerous because it is extremely difficult for people suffering from anxiety to determine what they should do to rid themselves of their anxiety. As their worries begin to overlap each other, they no longer realize what they originally feared. These people tend to feel fearful in almost every situation that they find themselves.

Take Karen, for example. She consistently worried about meeting her boyfriend's parents. She worried about how to act around them, what to wear, how to address them, and whether or not her hair was styled the "right" way. Karen even worried about things like sweating too much under her arms or having bad breath, along with a number of other things. All of a sudden, she discovered that she had created a whole arsenal of worries.

Eventually, her worries lumped together to form one big case of general anxiety. By worrying about so many different things, Karen caused herself to feel overwhelmed with fear. She even reached the point of feeling light-headed and nauseous at certain times. In short, she lost mental control of the situation.

Instead of worrying about the situation and creating anxiety for herself, Karen could have used visualization to ease her worries. Visualization is a positive way to focus the power of your thoughts on the best possible outcome of any given situation. Visualizing actually prepares you for a situation by minimizing the amount of fear that you feel. Worry, on the other hand, is a negative way to focus your thoughts on the worst possible outcome. Worrying only paralyzes your ability to take action and increases the intensity of your fears.

Many psychiatrists believe that the average human being experiences approximately 50,000 passing thoughts a day. Fortunately, you have the distinct honor to choose what thoughts you will focus your attention upon. You can choose to focus upon the negative ones and cultivate the habit of worry or you can choose to focus on the positive ones and foster the habit of visualization. The choice is yours!

> *When you focus your thoughts upon things you do not intend to act upon, you are wasting your thoughts.*

It is important to realize that if you choose to leave your mind idle in a world as negative as ours, then it will be filled with negativity and worry as a result. If you do not believe that we live in a negative world, then turn on the news, read the newspaper, or listen to the radio. Notice how many of the stories are about crime, gossip, and defeat. Compare that to the number of stories about growth, change, and improvement.

Even our medical and scientific fields are negative. Instead of studying the habits of healthy people, most doctors and scientists search for answers by focusing their thoughts upon their sick patients. Furthermore, acclaimed psychologist Shad Helmstetter, author of *What to Say When You Talk to Yourself*, provides some additional proof of the amount of negativity in our world. He claims that by the time a child growing up in a reasonably positive home reaches age eighteen, she will have been told "No!" approximately 148,000 times. It is easy to see that only by conscious effort can you fill your mind with positive thoughts and constructive goals.

Unfortunately, most people are so addicted to familiarity in their life that they would rather cling to their ineffective habit of worry than take the risk of thinking dynamically. After all, the fear of change is usually enough to stop most people from altering their thinking patterns. Even something as simple as focusing on a positive thought instead of a negative thought is too much of a stretch for most of them. They believe that it is better for themselves to live a familiar life of misery than to risk living a dynamic life of change.

Let's suppose you are the type of person who feels compelled to lie awake in bed worrying until your teenage daughter comes home at night. In this case, you would be wise to substitute your thoughts of worry with positive thoughts. Instead of worrying, you could think about the special times that you spent with your daughter. Remember the time the two of you went trout fishing together in the spring, the time that you painted the house together, or the time that you won the basketball tournament together. This would be an active way for you to combat your worries and redirect this emotional energy in a more positive direction. After several days of practicing this strategy, you will notice that your mind will become much clearer, less fearful, and less tempted to worry.

Let's assume for a moment that one night you really did have a valid reason to be concerned for the safety of your daughter. In this case, worrying would still do you no good. After all, it has no power to change anything anyway. Instead, you should immediately take action by making phone calls to her friends, actively searching for her yourself, or even calling the police. Action is the only way to resolve a serious situation. Worrying only makes the situation more intense than it needs to be.

If you still feel compelled to worry about your daughter even if there is no logical reason to do so, it is only your fear telling you to better prepare your daughter to go out on her own. By teaching your daughter important lessons about life in advance, you can rest much easier when she leaves your sight. You can have the peace of mind that you taught her well.

The most insane aspect of worry is that most of the things you worry about don't even happen. Take a moment to prove the validity of this statement to yourself by taking part in the following exercise:

1. Make a list of your 11 greatest worries. Use some of the following examples to spark your memory.

> I worried that I'd never pass my drivers test
> I worried that I'd never learn to file my own taxes
> I worried that I'd never pass 9th grade algebra
> I worried that I'd never have a family of my own
> I worried that I'd never graduate from college
> I worried that I'd never find another dog like "Scruffy"
> I worried that I'd never find a good job
> I worried that I'd never make new friends
> I worried that I'd never get married
> I worried that I'd never finish this paper
> I worried that I'd never get rid of these zits

2. Review your list and highlight all the things that actually happened.

Chances are, you didn't do much highlighting. Think about it, did the green monster that you worried about as a child ever come out of the closet and attack you? How about the prom you worried about for two months in advance? Didn't everything turn out fine despite all the worrying you did about it? How about your son that you worried about for a week when he rode his motorcycle across the country? Didn't he arrive safely? Whatever happened to the concept of having a little bit of faith? Even faith the size of a mustard seed would be enough. Stop and think about how many of your current worries are every bit as ridiculous as the green monster that you worried about as a child.

One way to do this is by keeping a weekly list of all of your worries. Once the week is over, go back and review the items on your list. Decide for yourself which ones, if any, are worth the time and effort required to worry about them.

Worry robs you of the emotional energy that you need to smash your walls of fear. Few activities use up energy as fast as worrying does. Furthermore, it has terrible side effects. Worrying can clog up your digestion, cause ulcers, and debilitate your entire immune system. Give your body a break by having at least two sacred days in which you refuse to worry about. Make those two days yesterday and tomorrow! Vow to begin to live your life in the present moment and your worries will slowly fizzle away.

THE FEAR OF FEAR

Feeling the emotion of fear is definitely uncomfortable! There is no sense in denying this fact. Nonetheless, you must still remember that fear is an essential part of your life. If you avoid all the uncomfortable situations in your life, then you could never even take the first step toward achieving your dreams.

"Nothing is so much to be feared as fear."
Henry Thoreau

What do you fear in your life? Are you afraid of telling the truth, making a commitment, deciding upon your future, being alone, or calling an old friend? Well, the truth is, you are not really afraid of any of these things. That's right, you are not really afraid of the things you think you are. You are merely afraid of the uncomfortable feelings and sensations that you have associated with these experiences. You are basically afraid of a feeling!

Think about it. Do you really fear the telephone or are you afraid of the feelings you will feel when you call a certain person? Could the telephone actually explode? Could someone actually reach their hand through the phone and begin to strangle you? Isn't it true that the only thing you fear is the temporary feeling of discomfort associated with the phone call? Most of the things that you fear cannot possibly harm you. The only thing they can do is trigger temporary feelings of discomfort within you.

> *An unpleasant feeling is the only thing preventing you from living your dreams.*

Asking someone out on a date is another example of a common fear that poses no real threat to you. In this case, you might decide that you would rather miss out on a great opportunity than to risk feeling some temporary discomfort. This is not because you are afraid of asking someone on a date. Instead, you are afraid of fear itself. You are afraid of feeling the emotion of fear. As a result, you choose to avoid the situation that triggers the fear inside you.

When you ignore the guidance of your fear, you begin to sink further and further into the depths of your comfort zone. Soon, you will find yourself avoiding certain activities that once felt comfortable. Fear will begin to invade your comfort zone and cause it to shrink. Remember, the universal law of life is growth. If you choose not to grow, then your life will begin to shrink. Fear will eat away at your comfort zone little by little until you finally decide to act upon the message that it has to give to you.

"If we do the new thing often enough, we overcome the fear, and our comfort zone expands. If we back off and honor the 'need' to be comfortable, our comfort zone shrinks."
Peter McWilliams and John-Roger

It is impossible to hide from fear. Even if you spent the rest of your life as a hermit, fear would still find you. The only permanent way to minimize the effect of fear is to face your fears and willfully feel some discomfort along the way.

"When we try to avoid the discomfort that we call fear, our world grows smaller and smaller..."
Cheri Huber

THE FEAR OF LOSS

Ultimately, the emotion of fear breaks down to a fear of loss. Whenever you fear something, you are really afraid that you are going to experience some kind of loss. This loss could be in terms of your money, time, health, desire, luxuries, power, control or even your life.

Imagine an unarmed boy walking alone through the woods. All of a sudden, he encounters an angry grizzly bear moving directly toward him. Instantly, he is filled with fear. In this case, the boy does not fear the angry bear, but rather he fears the loss of his health or even the loss of his life if the angry bear was to attack him. But under different circumstances, it is very likely that this same boy would not experience fear. Perhaps he would not experience fear if he encountered the grizzly bear at a zoo where he was protected by shatterproof glass. Regardless of the situation, the truth remains that whenever the threat of loss is removed from any given situation, fear ceases to exist.

Consider a potentially fearful experience like running for public office. When you think about what this may entail, you may fear losing your money, your reputation, and/or your time. No matter what it is that you fear, it certainly has to do with losing something. Why do people fear public speaking? They fear that they will lose their self-confidence, their privacy, their reputation, and/or their credibility. Why do some people fear becoming rich and successful? They fear that they will lose their current friends, their humble lifestyle, or even their life if someone chooses to murder them for their money. Test this theory out for yourself. See if there is anything that you fear that does not have to do with some kind of loss.

The following list gives you a few examples of how fear breaks down to a fear of loss.

- **Fear of unemployment**- You may fear losing security for your family, losing your self-esteem, losing close friendships, and/or losing an important element of structure in your life.

- **Fear of other people's opinions**- You may fear losing the support of others, losing valued friendships, and/or losing your confidence.

- **Fear of moving to a different state**- You may fear losing close friends and family ties, losing personal property like your house and land, and/or losing a certain job or salary.

- **Fear of confronting your child about an important issue**- You may fear losing your personal privacy, losing an important relationship, and/or losing respect or trust from your child.

- **Fear of commitment**- You may fear losing your identity, losing your freedom, losing your money, and/or losing your time.

As you can see by these examples, fear basically breaks down to a fear of loss. And the one loss that encompasses all the other losses is.....**THE LOSS OF COMFORT**.

The only reason you fear the things that you do is because you are afraid you will lose your current level of comfort! This is why you are so prone to cling to your comfort zone rather than exploring your dynamic zone. Unfortunately, this also means that it will be much more difficult for you to experience genuine....JOY.

CHAPTER 6

JOY: THE SENSE OF FULFILLMENT THAT MAKES LIFE WORTH LIVING

"Joy, rather than happiness, is the goal of life, for joy is the emotion which accompanies our fulfilling our natures as human beings."
Rollo May

Joy is the natural high that you feel when you use your potential. It is a sense of fulfillment, a feeling of importance and worth. Joy is what a baby feels as she takes her first step. It's what a scientist feels as she begins to make progress toward a major discovery. It's also what the Olympic athlete feels after shaving an additional second off her time. Joy is basically what you feel when you align your actions toward a wonderful dream. It's the feeling that your life is "on purpose" and that you feel complete and whole. Joy is the greatest feeling of pleasure and happiness known to humankind.

Although genuine joy may seem like some special feeling that only a privileged few could ever experience, it is really a very simple emotion that you can learn to access on a consistent basis. Joy is the natural by-product of stepping into your dynamic zone to face your fears. The only "trick" to feeling joyous is that you must first feel some initial discomfort as you take action upon your wall of fear.

Notice the words "take action upon your wall of fear" was used in the preceding paragraph instead of "smash your wall of fear." These words were used because you do not necessarily have to smash your wall of fear in order to access genuine feelings of joy. Taking sincere action toward the achievement of your dreams is enough by itself. It is not necessary to perform at any specific level before you can feel joyous. Giving a good solid effort is all that is required.

"Without challenges, there would be no rewards."
Unknown

Consider the joy that Martin Luther King Jr. felt with each action that he took in his pursuit of equal civil rights for all people. He felt this joy long before he achieved any measurable progress. The mere process of taking action toward his dream supplied him with incredible amounts of joy. King felt these feelings of joy with every speech that he gave, every demonstration that he led, and every time he was thrown in jail for pursuing his dream. His joy came from the fact that he knew he was doing what was right. Of course, he also felt joyous when he received the Nobel Peace Prize, but he felt the same joy long before he ever won any awards.

Action is what triggers the release of joyful chemicals like interleukin and interferon throughout your entire body. These types of chemicals have been proven to be more powerful than the most potent forms of crack, cocaine, or heroine. There exists no other chemical in this world that can give you a high any greater than that of pure joy. And to think that your body already possesses the most powerful drugs in existence. All you have to do is to step into your dynamic zone and take worthwhile actions to release these powerful chemicals.

Even more important than the initial high you get from taking action is the feeling of fulfillment that you experience once the initial high subsides. You will feel as if your life is worthwhile. Without a doubt, you will know that you are an important member of society.

People __want__ money. They __need__ joy!!

Many philosophers and psychologists consider the need to feel important as the number one desire for human beings. In survey after survey, it is the one thing that people want more than anything else. Isn't this also the case in your life? Don't you want to feel important, to feel as though you make a difference in this world?

Dr. John Dewey, one of America's greatest philosophers, began teaching this principle nearly one hundred years ago. He discovered that people actually need a sense of importance in their life in order to feel fully alive. Dewey also noticed that most of the actions that people took were, in effect, ways for them to feel important. Likewise, William James, father of American psychology, agreed with Dewey. James is quoted as saying, "The deepest principle in human nature is the craving to be appreciated." In short, every man and woman has an inborn need to feel joyful.

THE WAYS TO ACCESS JOY

Although it cannot be bought or stolen, there still exist many simple ways to feel joyful. With something as powerful as joy, you will surely want to learn many different ways to access it. Review the following list for some examples of ways that you can create joy in your life:

- Create a positive attitude in your mind.
- Contribute your time, talent, or money to help someone in need.
- Learn a new skill.
- Reestablish a relationship with someone you have not communicated with in years.
- Develop a closer relationship with your creator.
- Relish the fact that you are alive.
- **Take action upon your wall of fear.**

As can be seen, the preceding list outlines a few of the many simple ways for you to bring joy into your life today. This book concentrates primarily on creating joy by facing your fears and overcoming the obstacles in your life. In truth, fear is actually an early phase in the cycle of joy. Your feelings of discomfort actually lay the groundwork so that you can feel joyful.

> *"...we find no real satisfaction or happiness in life without obstacles to conquer and goals to achieve."*
> Maxwell Maltz

Would you cherish the warmth of a beautiful summer day if you never experienced the cold of winter? Of course not. Could you appreciate the color blue if there weren't any other colors to contrast it? No! Is it possible to experience the joy of healing if you have never been separated or hurt? Absolutely not. Well, the cycle of fear and joy works in a similar way. In order for you to appreciate blissful feelings of joy, you need to experience some uncomfortable feelings of fear.

Imagine the joy a thirteen-year-old boy feels as he declines an invitation to use drugs even though "all of his friends" are using them. Initially, this boy will feel fearful about the possibility of losing his friends. However, his feelings of fear will soon become feelings of joy when he realizes how special he is for using his strength, determination, wisdom, and character to overcome peer pressure.

Any single joy can leave you feeling as though you are on top of the world. However, you need to realize that a single joy cannot keep you feeling fulfilled forever.

THE PRINCIPLE OF DECREASING MARGINAL UTILITY

Did you ever crave a milkshake so much that you actually drank five of them in a row? If you did, which one of the five tasted the best? I am sure you will agree that the first milkshake tasted the best with each one thereafter tasting a little bit less fulfilling than the one before. After the fifth, you probably found yourself despising milkshakes. This process of each subsequent "unit" being less desirable than the previous one is known in economics as the principle of decreasing marginal utility.

Consider a golf example. Larry has been an amateur golfer for eight years now. Three months ago, Larry was thrilled when he finally shot the first 79 of his career. Since that time, Larry has shot several subsequent games of 79. Each time he accomplished the feat he felt less and less of the initial thrill. Once again, the reason is due to the principle of decreasing marginal utility.

The longer you bask in your current joys without taking additional actions, the less joy you will have to feel. Eventually, you will feel bored. In order to avoid the effects of the principle of decreasing marginal utility, you need to consistently step into your dynamic zone. Each time you expand your life by doing something new and exciting, you give yourself the opportunity to feel joyful. But, like anything else, your joy will be short-lived unless you continue to stretch yourself in some way.

For instance, you may be wondering why you do not have more intimacy with someone special in your life. In this case, the chances are good that the principle of decreasing marginal utility has been the cause. You have probably developed a certain way to act around this person, certain topics to talk about, certain places to go, and certain things to do. As a result of consistently repeating the same habits and patterns, your relationship has probably grown stale from too much familiarity and not enough change. To overcome the lack of intimacy, you must be courageous enough to step forth into your dynamic zone. This might involve exploring new topics to talk about, finding new ways to express yourself, locating new places to go, and discovering new activities to experience. By doing so, you will find that your relationship that once seemed old and worn out will suddenly seem dynamic and fun.

AVOIDING YOUR FEARS MAKES IT IMPOSSIBLE TO EXPERIENCE LASTING JOY

When you choose to avoid your fears instead of facing them, you make it impossible for yourself to experience lasting joy. You need to experience fear in order to give yourself the necessary contrast that allows you to feel the bliss of joy. Without fear, you would have nothing to compare with joy. As a result, joy would become nonexistent in your life. Only by facing your fears can you ever free yourself to truly feel the emotion of joy.

Take Marissa for example. She is the healthiest person I know. When someone hurts her in any way, she politely confronts them about their particular comment or action, even though it is scary for her to do so. Instead of hiding her emotions, she accepts the fact that she will feel some initial discomfort when she challenges someone. This strategy allows her to feel the joy of life rather than the anger, envy, and jealousy that she would otherwise feel if she avoided all confrontations.

Frank, on the other hand, is an example of someone who chose to avoid a particular fear instead of facing it. Five years ago, he asked his girlfriend, whom he loved dearly, to marry him. To his surprise, she rejected his proposal and they ended up going their separate ways. As a way to avoid getting hurt by anyone else, Frank decided to avoid romantic relations with all women. During this time, Frank focused all of his extra energy on his writing career. Writing was his excuse to justify why he had no time for a romantic relationship. Although he has since become a very successful writer in the eyes of the public, he considers himself to be a failure. His unwillingness to face his fear of loving again has caused Frank to miss out on an important source of joy in his life.

"Deep in your heart, you know that you don't have more love in your life because those walls which protect you from pain also end up keeping out happiness and love."
Dr. Barbara DeAngelis

105

As can be seen from the two prior examples, the only way to keep your channel of joy open is to face your walls of fear. When you choose to avoid your walls, it is like depositing cholesterol into your arteries. Sooner or later, you will clog up your ability to experience joy in an important area of your life.

JOY CAN BE EXPRESSED THROUGH MANY DIFFERENT EMOTIONS

Just as fear expresses itself through many different negative emotions, so does joy express itself through many different positive emotions. There are literally hundreds of different emotions that can express your joy. The following list defines a small portion of these positive emotions.

POSITIVE EMOTIONS

Appreciation- Focusing your thoughts upon something or someone that you are thankful for.

Cheer- The physical expression of happiness and appreciation for life.

Curiosity- A desire to explore the unknown.

Desire- A feeling of want for something.

Discontentment- Feeling a need to experience something new.

Ecstasy- Intense feelings of pleasure without any stress.

Enthusiasm- A visible expression of excitement.

Excitement- A feeling of extreme satisfaction with life and expecting to experience more joyful experiences in the future.

Love- The highest expression of joy in which you **give** your personal best for the benefit of both yourself and others.

Motivation- A force of energy that compels you to take a certain action.

Passion- Intense feelings of excitement.

Peace of Mind- Feeling certain that you are living your life the right way.

Self-confidence- Believing and relying on your own ability to produce a desired result.

LOVE

In the highly esteemed book entitled *A Course in Miracles*, love is regarded as the natural, perfect state of being. It is a sense of oneness with yourself, with others, with nature, with your creator, and with all of life in general. Fear, on the other hand, is considered to be something that is unreal, irrational, and contrary to our natural state of being. Fear is basically regarded as an illusion of separation, something that you must overcome before you can fully experience love. Thus, your mission on this planet is to conquer your illusions of fear and to unite with your natural state of perfect love.

> *"We shall not cease from exploration*
> *And the end of all our exploring*
> *Will be to arrive where we started*
> *And know the place for the first time."*
> T. S. Eliot

The reason that fear exists is to guide you back to your original state of love. Fear is a call for more love. You need fear in your life as a guide to show you how to experience more love. It has been said that ultimately there are only two emotions—love and fear. Of which only love is real. Assuming this to be true, fear would only be a figment of your imagination. On some esoteric level, this statement may be accurate. As for now, it would be foolish to pretend that fear does not exist in our world. My advice is to recognize fear as a very real aspect of your life and to use it as an opportunity to experience more love.

Use your fear as a signal of separation from love. Whenever you feel fearful, realize that there is something you need to do, something scary you need to face. By doing so, you will feel joyously connected to the universe and your life will become more complete. Basically, you will move closer to experiencing true love.

With all this talk about love, you may be wondering, "What exactly is love anyway?" Love is the highest expression of joy. It is an emotion of **giving** your personal best to help both yourself and others. Love is the very creative substance of life. It is accessed whenever you treat another person the best way that you would treat yourself. When you actively love someone, you share your joy with that person.

> *"Love has no meaning if it isn't shared.*
> *Love has to be put into action."*
> Mother Teresa

In the case that you have very little joy within yourself, you won't have many resources with which to love other people. After all, how could you share something that you do not possess yourself? Only by smashing your walls of fear and collecting your own sense of joy will you ever be able to truly love another person. Without inner joy, you can only offer another person codependency. Codependency occurs when you live your life through someone else without making your own unique contributions to the relationship. Codependency is not love.

> *If the secret to living is giving,*
> *then love must be the secret to life.*

BALANCING THE CYCLE OF REST AND ACTION

When you feel as though you are in love with life, you can rest assured that your life is in proper balance. To get to this place of loving balance, you must first implement the right amount of both rest and action into your life. This means that you must carefully monitor your mind and body to discover how much time you need to be acting and how much time you need to be resting in order to feel balanced. At various points of your life, this formula will change. There will be times when you need large amounts of either rest or action to regain balance in your life. But, excessive amounts of either will only throw your mind and body out of balance, weaken your immune system, and decrease your ability to feel joyful.

Let's take Peter, for example. Peter grew up in an extremely wealthy family and never wanted for anything. As a result, Peter never learned what it was like to earn anything. This caused him to have a major imbalance in his life on the side of too much comfort. Soon, Peter found himself unable to appreciate all of his toys and conveniences. He began to take everything for granted.

Adults and children alike need to learn how to balance the cycle of rest (comfort zone) and action (dynamic zone) in their lives. In Peter's case, he needs to have more responsibilities around the house. He needs to take more actions like washing the dishes, mowing the lawn, trimming the bushes, taking out the garbage, carrying the groceries into the kitchen, washing vehicles, and/or doing laundry. Then, he would have a better chance of appreciating the many luxuries that are available to him.

On the other hand, it can be every bit as dangerous for you to knock your life out of balance by spending too much time taking action and not enough time resting. Take Linda, for example. Linda is a hard-driven executive obsessed with improving the success of her company and earning a higher salary for herself. Her actions are almost exclusively directed to the development of her career while all the other departments of her life are falling apart. In this case, Linda needs to balance her life by dedicating more of her time to activities that allow her body and mind to relax and recuperate. She needs to limit her work week, spend more time shopping, take more leisurely walks in the woods, cook more meals for her family, ride her bicycle more often, attend more of her children's athletic games, and have more dates with her husband. In short, Linda needs more comfort in her life.

It is always the best strategy to maintain balance in your life. Listen to the messages your body and mind are giving to you. If you feel overwhelmed, sick, or exhausted, then you probably need to take a rest. Conversely, if you feel sluggish, bored, or restless, then you probably need to take more action.

It is also very important to mention the benefits of eating the right amounts of fruits and vegetables. This will help to balance your mind and body, which will allow you to deal with the walls in your life more effectively. When you make the mistake of eating excessive amounts of foods containing surplus sugar, fat, and caffeine, you unnecessarily intensify all of your negative emotions and throw your body and mind out of balance. Then, whenever you encounter fear in your life, it seems much worse than it really is. This is a primary reason why you may feel "paralyzed" or "frozen" by many of your fears. Emotions are intense enough by themselves without your adding to their intensity by eating excessive quantities of the wrong kinds of food.

INSTANT GRATIFICATION IS NOT JOY

Simple forms of instant gratification are never enough to serve as a substitute for authentic joy. Even when you are in tremendous emotional pain and you feel as though you must change your state of mind fast, it is still a bad idea to turn to unhealthy foods, gossip, lying, gambling, and, of course, alcohol, cigarettes, and drugs. Although these forms of instant gratification often do the job of changing your state of mind in the short run, they only make you feel worse in the long run. At best, they only change the way that you feel for several hours, but when their effects wear off, you will experience much more emptiness than you originally did.

There are thousands of forms of instant gratification that can give you pleasure. Even something as simple as caressing your own skin or combing your hair can give you pleasure. The only problem is that pleasure is not necessarily joy. Yes, pleasure is absolutely necessary to your well-being as a human being and you should indulge in certain forms of pleasure, but pleasure is different from joy. Joy is an emotion of fulfillment whereas pleasure is usually a form of instant gratification.

There are no shortcuts to joy. Even the most potent drugs available cannot supply you with fulfillment. Only a consistent journey of growth, change, and improvement can supply you with lifelong joy. One of the most accurate indicators of a joyful person is someone who tells you her life's story and spends the majority of time focusing on the trials and tribulations instead of the aspects of her journey that came easily. Interestingly enough, if these types of people had to do it all over again, the vast majority of them would not trade their hardships for anything. To them, they realize that the obstacles they overcame in the process were directly responsible for molding them into the dynamic people that they are today. They realize that their journey, not their destination, was their source of joy in the past and is their source of joy in the present.

With this in mind, stop yourself the next time you feel an urge to indulge in a cheap form of instant gratification. Instead, redirect your energy upon one of your walls of fear. Even if you are shaking with fear, initiate the pivotal discussion with your children that is long overdue and notice the high you feel as you tackle your fear of intimacy. Speak out at the next meeting you attend and feel the "rush" you access the moment you face your fear of expressing yourself. Facing your fears produces a greater high than anything in the world. In addition, you will not have to concern yourself with a resulting "crash" as is the case with certain forms of instant gratification.

Gary is a prime example of a man who received a tremendous high by facing one of his greatest fears, his fear of asking a woman on a date. On this particular occasion, Gary felt attracted to a particular woman whom he had only recently met. He wanted to get to know her better and possibly date her. Instead of taking the easy route by persuading himself not to ask her out, Gary decided to face his fear. He decided that presenting her with flowers on her birthday would be a great way to express his feelings for her. The only problem was that Gary was extremely afraid to take such a bold action. It was outside his comfort zone.

Fortunately, Gary took a step into his dynamic zone and presented the flowers to this woman despite feeling a lot of fear in the process. To his amazement, the woman was unmoved by his actions and simply replied, "Thank you" and continued with her business as if nothing special had happened. As Gary walked away, instead of feeling stupid and defeated, he suddenly felt a deep sense of relief and fulfillment that penetrated his entire being. Although things did not turn out the way he had planned, he still experienced a supreme sense of satisfaction. Suddenly, his mind became totally calm and serene when only moments ago it was racing. Gary knew that he had done the right thing and as a result, he now felt totally at peace with himself.

By facing his fear even when he doubted his own ability, Gary gained the confidence to ask other women out on dates in the future. In his mind, it was as though he was once lame and now he could walk. Taking that one bold action has produced miraculous results in his level of confidence and his level of respect for himself. No form of instant gratification could have ever provided him with such deep feelings of joy.

One of my favorite examples of someone who felt immensely joyful as he slowly but surely overcame a large number of walls is a man named Morris Goodman. Morris suffered massive life threatening injuries resulting from a disastrous airplane crash. His neck was broken in both the first and second cervical vertebrae. His larynx was severely damaged beyond repair. He had permanent nerve damage throughout his body. His swallowing reflexes were practically nonexistent. His entire body was basically engulfed in intense physical pain.

Surviving the devastating crash was a miracle in itself. Even more amazing was the fact that Morris survived the original surgery. To say the least, his doctors were dumbfounded. Nonetheless, the immediate family of Morris Goodman was assured that Morris would never again walk, he would never again utter a sound out of his mouth, he would never be able to eat a piece of solid food, he wouldn't even be able to swallow a drink of water. In addition, they were informed that Morris would never again as much as breathe without the use of a respirator. The doctors admitted that it would be a blessing if Morris would just die.

The amazing part of the story is that Morris could hear the doctors and nurses talking about him. Fortunately, he chose not to believe what he heard. Instead, he made a decision to reclaim his life. He dreamed of one day walking out of that hospital on his own two feet. It did not matter to him how many walls were blocking him from achieving his dream. He would not to be denied.

Morris knew that in order to recover from his critical condition he would have to focus upon very small goals at first. He began by learning to communicate by blinking his eyes. This gave Morris a tremendous amount of joy. One of the first messages Morris signaled with his eyes was a message of thanks to his doctor. Eventually, after lying awake for hours every night in piercing pain, Morris finally learned to breathe on his own. Again, the joy that he felt was incredible. Never before would he have guessed it was possible to feel so joyous over something as simple as breathing.

Morris did not stop there. He continued to take action toward the achievement of his dream. His next step was to learn how to drink even though he could not swallow. Once again, through his tenacity, strong positive beliefs, hard work, mental visualizations, positive attitude, and lots of Zig Ziglar motivational tapes, Morris learned how to drink once again. Eventually, Morris learned how to eat. He even learned how to speak. With each step that he took along the journey to his dream, Morris felt incredible feelings of joy.

Finally, Morris came face to face with his final wall that was blocking the attainment of his dream: his physical body was still incapacitated. He wanted to walk, yet the staff at the hospital considered it to be impossible. Nonetheless, Morris demanded physical therapy. Through daily bouts of intensive, exhausting physical rehabilitation filled with excruciating pain, Morris Goodman eventually achieved his dream. He learned how to walk once again.

Nothing in the world could have given him such a feeling of accomplishment and joy as overcoming such incredible odds. As a result of his experience, Morris Goodman picked up an appropriate nickname along the way. He will be forever known as "The Miracle Man" since he overcame so many "impossible" obstacles.

Imagine the joy Morris Goodman felt as he walked out of that hospital on his own two feet. These kinds of feelings could never be experienced by indulging in cheap forms of instant gratification. Fortunately, it is not necessary for you to go through the pain and anguish of a Morris Goodman to access joy. All you need to do is to follow the guidance of your fear and act upon the most important wall in your life. This will bring you joy like you never imagined.

Morris Goodman proved once and for all what could be achieved through the power of the human spirit. He triumphed in the midst of "impossible" odds. Morris owes his recovery to the small, incremental goals he set for himself and most of all to his unwavering positive attitude. The story of Morris Goodman is available on videotape. This video will bring tears to your eyes and leave you with a memory that you will never forget. If you would like to inquire about renting or buying "The Miracle Man" video, you can call American Media Incorporated at 1-800-262-2557.

As can be seen, wall smashing is a very emotional process. Sometimes the joyful emotions that you experience will seem overwhelming, as was the case for Morris Goodman. The phrase "tears of joy" gives an accurate illustration of the flood of emotions that you may feel as you act upon the wall of fear in your own life.

112

FOCUS ON YOUR BLESSINGS

You may wonder how someone like Morris Goodman could motivate himself to achieve such an extraordinary dream in the midst of a whole series of "impossible" walls. Well, the key to this type of achievement is to focus your thoughts upon your blessings instead of your misfortunes. As for Morris Goodman, it was an immense blessing just to be alive. Regardless of how bad you think you have it, there is still something in your life that you can appreciate. You must simply expand your thinking and focus on whatever is great in your life. If you perceive nothing to be great in your life, then you are at least alive, which is plenty reason to celebrate and feel joyful!

> *"Nothing is worth more than this day."*
> Johann Wolfgang von Goethe

The truth is that you already possess many amazing qualities, talents, traits, and abilities—far more than you could ever use up, even in a one hundred year or more lifetime. Best of all, you have the opportunity at any moment to feel joyful by focusing your attention upon any one of your blessings.

Think about how many people have complimented you on any one of your outstanding personal traits. For you, it might be your beautiful hair, your attractive eyes, your astounding height, or even your overall stunning appearance? The same is true of your abilities. Chances are, you probably have full use of your body, your mind, and your five senses. Think about the eyes you are using to read this book, the fingers you have to feel the soft texture of a dolphin, the nose you have to smell the beautiful fragrance of Spring, the taste buds you have to taste a luscious Florida orange, the ears you have to listen to the beautiful sounds of nature, the body you have that houses your soul, and of course, the mind you are using to sort out and apply the knowledge you are gaining from this book. Isn't it true that you already have a wide variety of phenomenal attributes?

Even if you are someone who is severely challenged or disabled in some area of your life, you still have an abundant amount of blessings that you might not even realize you possess. Maybe you were once able to do 10,000 different things. Now, you may only be able to do 9,500 different things. The exact numbers do not matter. All that matters is that you understand that you have more blessings, more of a need to rejoice than you currently realize.

Maybe part of your problem is that you have so many blessings, you cannot keep track of them and consequently, you take them for granted.

113

Don't you live in a home where you are warm, dry, clean, and well fed? Aren't you genuinely loved by a handful of people in your life? Isn't it true that you live in a country where you can walk outside your house without the fear of being shot to death? What more could you possibly want? Maybe you lost your job. Maybe you didn't get accepted into a specific organization. Maybe you went bankrupt, got divorced, or didn't qualify for a mortgage. So what! You still have thousands of other aspects of your life that are fantastic. This should cause you to be joyful. Don't wait for some tragic experience to occur before you realize how much you have going for you.

Some time ago, there was a story about a drug dealer whom I'll call Sam. Sam was an uncaring person who infected the streets of his neighborhood with all kinds of deadly substances. Then, one day during a particular drug deal, he was shot. The outcome was tragic. Sam was paralyzed from the waist down.

As a result of this seemingly horrible experience, Sam realized how fortunate he was just to be alive. He also realized that he was ruining his life as well as the lives of others by selling drugs. So, instead of pitying himself, Sam decided to step into his dynamic zone and make better use of the blessings that he still possessed. His mission was to help the people of his city to choose religion and sports over drugs. With this in mind, Sam organized a local weight lifting gym and a church for the citizens to use. Both of the services were absolutely free of charge. He only asked that each person attend at least one ceremony at the church where he served as the minister.

Sam's only regret throughout this entire ordeal was that it took a tragic event like paralysis to get him to realize how much potential joy and contribution he had inside himself. He could only wish that he would have used enough foresight in his past to avoid his paralysis. Nonetheless, Sam willingly admits that his paralysis has been more of a blessing in his life than a curse.

As a way to avoid making similar mistakes in your own life, take the time to make a list of some of the blessings that you possess. Include things like warm showers, protection from the weather, food and drink, loving family and friends, clean clothes, heat, and many more. The longer your list, the more you will find yourself appreciating the blessings that you already possess. This in turn will cause you to attract more joy into your life. After all, one of the universal laws of life is: You will attract more of what you think about. So, be sure to think about what is great in your life!

Focusing upon what is great in your life is an important step toward harnessing the power of your....BELIEFS.

CHAPTER 7

BELIEFS: YOUR POWER TO CREATE A DYNAMIC REALITY FOR YOURSELF

"What the future could hold, and what each of us could become, is limited mainly by what we believe."
Gloria Steinem

The power of the human mind is absolutely incredible to say the least! In the book *Dare to Win*, Mark Victor Hansen and Jack Canfield are quoted as saying, "Your mind is the most powerful tool in the universe." They go on to compare the human mind to a computer by claiming that the computer would have to be the size of Texas to have equivalent power. In a similar way, L. Ron Hubbard, author of *Dianetics*, claims that the average standard memory banks would fill several libraries. Along the same lines, Dr. Wayne Dyer, author of *Your Erroneous Zones*, claims that the human brain can store an amount of information equivalent to one hundred trillion words. Other research has shown that the human brain can process 30 billion bits of information a second!

Regardless of the dispute over the specific capability and capacity of the human mind, its power is still nothing less than awesome. Even though we have unlimited access to this remarkable power, most mental health doctors claim that we have not come close to tapping into our full mental potential. Most have determined that on average, we use less

SMASHING THE WALL OF FEAR

than 10% of our mental potential while others go so far as to say that we use less than 1% of our mental powers. Once again, the controversy is not important. All that matters is for you to realize that you have unlimited power awaiting your command.

Your unlimited mental power can be harnessed through your beliefs. By adopting the proper set of beliefs, you can literally inspire yourself to smash through any wall. Even one simple change in your current beliefs could easily transform the quality of your entire life, forever. After all, beliefs are what give you stability, order, and structure in this chaotic world. Beliefs have the power to make your world a heaven or a hell and only you can determine which one it will be.

Take advantage of the awesome power of your mind by adopting empowering, supportive beliefs in place of your old, destructive, non-supportive beliefs. Fulfilling this objective will undoubtedly cause you to approach your walls in a much more effective way. Eventually, you will become like one of the many super-successful people who once started out with nothing except a dynamic belief like: "I don't care if the whole world thinks I'm crazy, I'm still going to achieve my dream!"

YOUR BELIEFS CREATE YOUR REALITY

Chances are, you have probably heard the famous quotation from Henry Ford about the power of beliefs: "Whether you think you can or think you can't, you are right." The truth of this quotation coupled with its simplicity is what has allowed it to go down in history as one of the all-time greatest quotations. Henry Ford was absolutely right; each of us really does have the power to create our own reality according to the beliefs that we choose to adopt.

Beliefs are indeed tremendously powerful. They precisely determine how you will interpret any given situation and what actions you will take to improve your situation. Nothing in your life would have any meaning without beliefs. Beliefs are the glue that holds your philosophy about life together. Look around you. What makes a particular religion different from any other religion? Isn't it the beliefs that are held to be true? How about the different parties in government? Isn't it their particular beliefs that separate them from each other? Beliefs are what separates any two groups of people from each other. The same is true at the individual level. Everyone would act like clones and experience the exact same reality if it was not for their different beliefs.

"Man is what he believes."
Anton Chekhov

Fortunately, your reality does not depend upon *what* you experience. All that matters is *what you believe* about what you experienced. If you believe that your spouse goes out of town as a means to better support you and your family, then your reality will be much different than if you believe that your spouse goes out of town to either cheat on you or to escape the burdens of raising a family. The experience didn't change, only your beliefs about the situation changed.

The physical world that you experience on a daily basis is not your reality. Rather, it is only a series of neutral events. Your reality is based upon what you choose to believe about the millions of neutral events that happen around you.

Beliefs are not right or wrong; they just are. You are free to believe whatever you want. If you want to believe that you fear public speaking, going to parties, driving over bridges, getting married, falling in love again, going to the doctor, making decisions, and/or buying a house, then you are free to do so. You are also free to believe that any one of these experiences or all of these experiences are exciting activities that bring you a greater sense of fulfillment. The choice is yours.

> *"Most of our obstacles, as a matter of fact,*
> *are mental in character."*
> Norman Vincent Peale

What greater freedom could you possibly be given than the freedom to create your very own reality, a reality independent of anybody else's in the whole world? Look at the following quotations from the Bible to gain a deeper appreciation for the power of your beliefs.

- ☐ "And all things, whatsoever ye shall ask in prayer, believing, ye shall receive." (Matthew 21:22)
- ☐ "...he will grant you your heart's requests." (Psalms 37:4)
- ☐ "If ye have faith...Nothing would be impossible for you." (Matthew 17:20)
- ☐ "If thou canst believe, all things are possible to him that believeth." (Mark 9:23)
- ☐ "Because of your faith it shall be done to you" (Matthew 9:29)

All the power that you will ever need to create a dynamic reality for yourself lies patiently within your mind waiting for you to utilize it. This power, of course, is accessed through all the wonderful beliefs you could easily choose to adopt into your life. Beliefs literally have the power to produce corresponding biochemical responses in your body.

117

Even if the entire world considered one of your beliefs to be ridiculous, but you still sincerely believed it, then it would be real to you.

To prove this truth to yourself, go back in your mind to a time when you were a young child. Remember a certain time when you felt particularly afraid of something that you now realize was imaginary. Let's say you were scared of a monster that you believed was hiding in your closet waiting to attack you. In this case, as soon as your parents tucked you into bed and turned out the lights, your mind would instantly produce fear in accordance with your beliefs. In your mind, you believed that a monster was going to get you. It didn't matter if the whole world knew that there wasn't a monster in your closet. The situation was still real to you. Your belief was your reality and every biochemical response in your body was exactly the same as if the monster was actually present in the room.

Another example of how beliefs create reality is found in the field of health care. Various studies have revealed that a significant percentage of seriously ill patients have shown remarkable improvement in their state of health simply by taking "medication" that contained absolutely no active healing ingredients. Many of these seriously ill patients have even fully recovered by taking sugar capsules or receiving injections containing nothing more than water. In the medical field, this phenomenon is known as the placebo effect.

"....statistics rarely alter deeply held beliefs."
Dr. Bernie Siegel

Other patients who took the same pills and injections began to exhibit many of the side-effects that they would have experienced had the actual medication been administered to them. In these cases where the "medicine" produced negative side effects, it was labeled a "nocebo." Regardless of how the medical field labels these studies, the bottom line is that a significant amount of the patients experienced exactly what they believed they would experience. Many of the ones who believed they would get well, got well. Similarly, many of the ones who believed they would get terrible side effects, got terrible side effects. Experiments like these have repeatedly proven that beliefs have the power to impact the health of an individual.

"Belief creates biology."
Norman Cousins

Even more remarkable is the research that Dr. Joan Borysenko presented in her book *Minding the Body, Mending the Mind.* A certain group of women who had morning sickness was asked to swallow a powerful drug called ipecac. They were told that this drug would relieve them of their morning sickness. They did not know that ipecac was actually a very potent drug that is used to induce vomiting, not to relieve nausea and morning sickness. Nonetheless, most of the women who took this drug amazingly reported that it helped to reduce their nausea. The only logical conclusion from this experiment is that the beliefs of the majority of women involved in this experiment were stronger than the actual drug itself.

William James, the father of modern-day psychology, was one of the first Americans to really reveal the power of beliefs. He became famous, in part, by making people aware that they could choose their own attitude regardless of their current circumstances. Don't let the word "attitude" throw you. Your attitude is simply how you feel about life and your beliefs are directly responsible for creating your attitude. You couldn't even have an attitude without a foundation of beliefs. Your beliefs and your attitude go hand in hand.

What kind of attitude do beliefs like "Rainy days are bad days," or "Never give any extra effort unless you are paid for it" promote in your life? Not a very good one! Wouldn't it be much wiser to adopt more positive beliefs into your life? Remember, you have the choice to interpret rain, work, or anything else in whatever way you desire. Ultimately, there is no such thing as a "bad day" or "extra effort" unless you create that type of reality with your beliefs. Some of the other beliefs you should consider changing are as follows:

- Money is the root of all evil.
- I am not smart enough to complete graduate school.
- People living in this part of the country cannot make over $17.50 an hour.
- I have a learning disability.
- I should work at one job until I retire.
- Certain people are more important than others.
- One nationality is superior to another.
- Rich people cannot enter the kingdom of Heaven.

With beliefs like these inhabiting your mind, it is no wonder why your reality might seem a bit dreary. Since everything you experience is filtered through your beliefs, it seems only logical to adopt positive, empowering beliefs. No matter what situation you encounter, the way you perceive that particular situation will be determined by your current belief system. If you have beliefs that trigger fear in a certain situation, then you will experience that situation as being fearful. Likewise, if you have beliefs that trigger joy in a certain situation, then you will experience the situation as being joyful. In the case where you have mixed beliefs, you will experience the situation according to your dominant beliefs.

Ultimately, your experiences will end up matching the beliefs you have created in your mind. This is why so many people are paralyzed by their fear. Without changing their beliefs, they can never change their reactions to the situations that produce fear in their life.

> *"The visible world is but man turned inside out*
> *that he may be revealed to himself."*
> Henry James

Later in this chapter you will learn how to change your unwanted beliefs. For now, recognize that your reality is nothing more than your beliefs!

BOTH YOUR RATIONAL AND IRRATIONAL FEARS STEM FROM YOUR BELIEFS

Since your reality is nothing more than a collection of your beliefs, it stands to reason that your fears must also derive from your beliefs. Consider the fear you feel when you accidentally do something dangerous like stepping out in front of a moving car. The only reason you feel fear when you step in front of a moving car is because you have a belief that the car would severely injure you or possibly even kill you if it were to hit you. The same is true of a hot stove. The only reason you fear touching a hot stove is because you have a belief that you will get severely burned if you do so.

Now, suppose for a moment that you placed an infant child either in the path of a moving vehicle or in the vicinity of a hot stove. In either case, the infant would not experience fear. This is true because the infant does not have any beliefs or associations about speeding cars or hot stoves that would trigger a fearful reaction. Without a belief about some type of loss, fear cannot exist. The only exception that psychologists have found to this rule is in the case of falling and loud noises, which seem to be inborn fears. Otherwise, all fears can be traced back to an individual's learned beliefs.

The fears that are healthy for you to fear, like hot stoves and speeding cars, are known as rational fears. Rational fears are fears that protect you from real danger. In the case of rational fears, there exists concrete reasons why you should continue to fear them. The following list will give you some more examples of rational fears:

- Getting too close to the blade of a chain saw
- "Messing around" with a loaded gun
- Jumping into deep water without knowing how to swim
- Walking alone at night in certain parts of the city
- Provoking dangerous animals
- Standing too close to the edge of a high cliff
- Etc...

Fearing these types of activities is what keeps you alive and healthy. It is very rational and logical to fear these things. But what would happen if you encountered these situations without having any beliefs that registered fear? If this were the case, you could cause tremendous harm to yourself.

Although your beliefs protect you by triggering rational fear responses, they can also keep you stuck in your comfort zone by triggering irrational fear responses. An irrational fear is an illogical fear, a fear of something that does not have any real power to hurt you. The following list reveals a few examples of some irrational fears:

- The fear of public speaking
- The fear of driving over bridges
- The fear of exposing your genuine self
- The fear of going to social gatherings
- The fear of asking a question in class
- The fear of loving again
- The fear of being intimate with your spouse
- The fear of applying for a job
- The fear of making a decision
- The fear of asking someone on a date
- Etc...

Your beliefs trigger these irrational fears. Fortunately, you can easily overcome these fears by changing your beliefs about them. It is impossible to fear these experiences if you only have positive beliefs about them. With only positive beliefs, you would actually feel motivated to take part in these types of activities.

> *Your negative beliefs are like quicksand. They slowly cause you to sink farther and farther into your comfort zone.*

Todd is a good example of someone who is suffering from irrational fear. He is a construction worker who deserves a raise in his salary. The only problem is that he has an intense irrational fear about approaching his boss to ask for a raise. He has beliefs like, "The boss will give me a raise when the time is right. I would probably get fired if I asked for a raise. I'm not good enough to make over $15.00 an hour. My boss won't like me if I ask for a raise." With beliefs like these, Todd instantly feels paralyzed with irrational fear the moment he even thinks about asking his boss for a raise. Until he rids his mind of these beliefs, Todd will have an extremely difficult time ever persuading himself to actually approach his boss and ask for a raise.

In your case, you might be able to ask for a raise as easily as you would make a pitcher of lemonade. For others like Todd, asking for a raise seems as difficult as performing brain surgery. This is not to say that Todd's irrational fears are not real. Irrational fears are every bit as real as rational fears. In many cases, they are even much more intense than rational fears. They simply have no logical basis to their existence.

Joan is another example of someone whose beliefs are causing her to feel irrational fear. Joan wants to become part of the upper level management team for a large telephone company, but she has beliefs like, "Only men get promoted to management positions. I couldn't handle all of the new responsibilities. My current group of friends won't like me anymore. I'm not smart enough for a management position anyway." These beliefs are responsible for generating irrational fear in her life every time she even thinks about her goal. The only way she can free herself to do her best work is to get all of her beliefs pulling her in the direction that she wants to go. It is next to impossible for her to produce a result when she has beliefs contrary to her desired outcome.

"As a man thinketh in his heart, so is he."
Proverbs 23:7

In Joan's case, she would be much wiser to adopt beliefs like, "I am well qualified for a position in upper level management. I am a fast learner. My friends like me for who I am, not the position I hold. Women are every bit as capable as men. I can handle any situation that I face. I always find a way to succeed." These types of beliefs would support her while she works toward achieving her goal. If Joan was to adopt beliefs like these, she would soon develop the confidence that she needs to pursue her dream with 100% of her effort.

HOW TO CHANGE THE INEFFECTIVE BELIEFS THAT CAUSE YOU TO FEEL IRRATIONAL FEAR

Since your negative beliefs are responsible for causing you to feel irrational fear, it is imperative for you to learn how to change them. You can accomplish this objective by adhering to the following five steps:

STEP 1: Write down the one destructive belief that you want to change.

Assuming that you are aware of the belief you want to change, take out a notebook or journal and write the belief at the top of the paper. Sometimes, it is possible to change a belief simply by realizing how silly it is once you see it on paper.

If you are unaware of the belief that you want to change, then you should brainstorm a list of all of your current beliefs that deal with your particular fear. Write down whatever beliefs happen to pop into your head regardless of what they may be. Be sure to include both your positive and your negative beliefs.

Next, go back through your list and make a note of all the beliefs that do not support the pursuit of your dreams—all of your destructive beliefs. From that list, choose the one belief that you feel is causing you to experience the largest amount of irrational fear. Begin with that particular belief.

STEP 2: Make a list of emotional reasons as to why you MUST change this ineffective belief.

Emotional reasons are simply another name for compelling reasons, reasons that are important to you and motivate you to take action. The more emotional reasons you gather, the more urgent it will become for you to change your ineffective belief. As the urgency is increased, it will become much easier for you to change your belief.

Your subconscious mind stores your beliefs. For each of your beliefs, your subconscious mind has a whole list of reasons as to why it is true. When you make any kind of decision in your life, your conscious mind first checks with your subconscious mind to see what you believe about the particular situation. In this sense, your subconscious mind is very similar to a computer. There is no judgment in your subconscious mind. It only supplies your conscious mind with information so that it can make the best possible decision in any given situation.

Your objective is to use your conscious mind to make a good solid list of emotional reasons citing all the ways that your belief has hurt you, is hurting you, and will continue to hurt you in the future. From there, your conscious mind will naturally deposit these reasons into your subconscious mind. Then, if they are emotional enough and strong enough, your subconscious mind will search for a new belief to replace the old destructive belief.

Suppose you wanted to change a belief like, "I'm not capable of starting my own business." Proceed to make a list of all the ways that this belief has caused you pain in the past, is causing you pain in the present, and will continue to cause you pain in the future. Make sure your reasons really focus on the pain associated with this limiting belief. Get as personal and intimate as you possibly can. List a wide variety of reasons and make sure they provoke as much emotion as possible. In this case, your reasons may include some of the following:

- ♠ I have worked as an employee for my entire life and I'm fed up with following orders from my boss.
- ♠ I have worked hard for this company for many years and I still do not feel appreciated.
- ♠ Someone other than myself is currently in control of my financial future and I do not like that.
- ♠ I am not currently being paid what I am really worth.
- ♠ I do not enjoy my present job.
- ♠ I do not like the hours of my present job.
- ♠ If I do not make some changes, I will die without ever pursuing my real desires and developing my natural talents.
- ♠ If I continue to work at this job, I will have to tell my grandchildren that I gave up the pursuit of my dreams.
- ♠ I will never be financially independent if I continue to work at my present job.
- ♠ If I do not take a risk, I will have to live with the pain that I honored my comfort zone more than my dreams.

Keep in mind that your most personal reasons will be the ones that motivate you the most to change a particular belief. Denis Waitley, one of America's top peak performance counselors, developed an audiocassette program focused on in-depth studies of what motivates human beings. In his program entitled *The Psychology of Human Motivation,* Waitley consistently reiterates the fact that internal motivation (intrinsic motivation) is a much more effective means of motivation than is external motivation (extrinsic motivation). This means that you will be more motivated to do something out of your inner passion than you will be to do something out of obligation.

Emotion is the fuel of life. The entire human race runs on emotions. Emotions are what makes life real. Therefore, collect as many emotional reasons as you can and use them to trigger your own personal motivation to change your unwanted beliefs.

STEP 3: Make a list of new beliefs that you can substitute for your old, limiting belief.

Now that you have created doubt in your subconscious mind, there is a void where your old limiting belief used to reside. Therefore, it is a prime time to fill this void with new empowering beliefs, beliefs that will inspire you to take the necessary actions to achieve your dreams and to have fun in the process. Be sure to take this step quickly because a vacuum will not exist for long in your mind. Some type of belief will soon fill the void. You might as well choose a belief that will support you instead of leaving it to chance.

If you are unsure about the specific beliefs you need to achieve a certain dream, then ask one of your role models for some advice. Discovering the beliefs of your role models is not difficult. Maybe you live or work with your role models and you can simply ask them about their beliefs. In the case that a certain role model is not readily available to you, you can either make a phone call to this person, talk to someone who knows her, go see her speak, read her book, listen to her tapes, or watch her on TV. Even if this person does not come out and actually express her specific beliefs, you will get a very good feel for what she believes by spending only a few moments with her. All you need to do is to ask some creative questions and you will discover a lot about her. There is nothing more effective than learning from someone who has already overcome many of the obstacles that you are facing.

In the case of our ongoing example about changing the belief, "I'm not capable of starting my own business," you may choose to create some new beliefs like the following:

◊ If I can dream it, I can achieve it.
◊ I have unlimited potential inside me waiting for me to tap into it.
◊ If I am committed to do something, then I will find a way to make it happen.
◊ Whatever I am passionate about, I can accomplish.
◊ If somebody else did it, then I can do it too.

STEP 4: Make a separate list of emotional reasons as to why your subconscious mind should accept your new dynamic beliefs in place of your old limiting belief.

As long as you can come up with a bunch of emotional reasons to back up your new beliefs, your subconscious mind will accept the new beliefs into your existing belief system. Keep in mind, this means that you must convince your subconscious mind that your new beliefs will be more pleasurable than your old belief. Once again, you need to remember that your mind is motivated by emotions. So, get as emotional as possible with your list of reasons.

Remember that this procedure of gathering reasons must be an intrinsic process. Don't listen to reasons from other people. Reasons are no good if YOU are not personally motivated by them. The whole world could be motivated by a particular reason, but if the reason does not spark your own personal emotions, then it is worthless to you.

The most effective reasons to create lasting change are usually actual experiences that you have had in your past. Think about the special honors you've received, the great achievements you've made, and the courageous actions you've taken. Remember the many dynamic experiences you have had. Chances are, you have forgotten how many terrific things you have already done in your life.

In order to spark your memory, you might make a list of all the special moments of your past. From that list, you can proceed to look at each one of your accomplishments to determine if it would be an appropriate reason to support the adoption of your new beliefs. I personally keep an ongoing list of all of the special moments in my life, which includes a wide variety of experiences that were special to me in one way or another. My list includes notes of special camping experiences, long bicycle rides, special relationships, personal accomplishments, intimate conversations, speaking engagements, exciting vacations, special contributions, funny jokes, parties, counseling sessions, special ceremonies, holiday fun, unique seminar experiences, and any other dynamic experience that I want to remember. This way, I can refer to this list whenever I need some additional reasons to change one of my ineffective beliefs.

Gather as many reasons as you possibly can. Do so until your list of emotional reasons looks irresistible to your subconscious mind. Every reason you create will increase your investment in your new dynamic beliefs. Anytime you have a lot of energy and time invested in something, you feel much more reluctant to change it. This is why people have such a hard time getting out of their comfort zone. They have invested so much of their life in it that they feel guilty whenever they even consider the possibility of leaving.

Let's refer back to our original example of changing the belief "I'm not capable of starting my own business." In the preceding step, we listed several new beliefs you could choose to adopt in place of your old limiting belief. In this step, you need to create a list of emotional reasons to support your new beliefs. Consider some of the following reasons:

- There are many books, tapes, and seminars that can teach me how to start my own business.
- In the past, I have learned how to do my own taxes. Surely, I can also learn how to start my own business.
- I know many successful business owners who would gladly give me some advise on starting my own business.
- During my senior year in high school, I was voted "most likely to succeed."
- I have a burning desire in my heart telling me that I can do this. And my inspirations are genuine because they are connected to and originate from my creator.
- Several of my most trusted friends keep assuring me that I have what it takes to create a wonderful business.

Another alternative way for you to create emotional reasons is to gather up enough courage to do something you thought you could never do. Tony Robbins, one of America's foremost success coaches, created an entire seminar focused on giving people real life references to help convince their subconscious minds of their unlimited power and potential. One of the strategies that Robbins uses is to have the seminar attendees walk over burning hot coals. The whole idea behind this unique ritual is that if these people can walk across fire, then they will believe that they can do almost anything.

Although the "firewalk" experience is a great reason to change many of your limiting beliefs, you do not necessarily have to go to such extremes. You could do something as simple as telling a joke to a group of people, standing up and asking a question in a meeting, or denying an unreasonable request from your boss. All that matters is that you do something dynamic, something unfamiliar to you. This will give you an additional real life reference that can serve as another reason why you should adopt your new beliefs.

Sometimes, you can give yourself a reason to adopt a new belief simply by reading an account or listening to a story about someone who overcame obstacles similar to yours and still achieved her dream. After all, if someone else did something, then you should be able to do it too. I personally listen to tapes or read books in the *Chicken Soup for the Soul* series by Jack Canfield and Mark Victor Hansen when I feel a bit down and in need of some encouragement. These books and tapes provide me with real life examples of people who have overcome tremendous obstacles and still achieved their dreams. Deep in my heart, I know that if they did it, then it's also possible for me to do it. You can take advantage of this strategy by buying these books in your local bookstore or ordering the audiocassette tapes by calling 1-800-441-5569.

Emotional reasons are indeed the key to changing your limiting beliefs into dynamic beliefs. They are the secret ingredient that makes the difference between what motivational expert Zig Ziglar calls positive believing and positive thinking. Ziglar teaches that positive believers are much more effective than positive thinkers since their enthusiasm stems from solid reasons instead of abstract thoughts.

STEP 5: Use your new beliefs on a consistent basis.

Begin today by creating one situation where you implement your new beliefs. Consistently taking action is what cements your new beliefs into your existing belief system. Acting out your new beliefs creates an awareness in your subconscious mind that your beliefs are real. Then, the next time your conscious mind checks with your subconscious mind before it makes a decision, your subconscious mind will retrieve one of your new dynamic beliefs instead of your old limiting belief. This will also cause you to feel much less fearful when you decide to act dynamically. Furthermore, when your new beliefs become part of your belief system, they will serve as part of the filter that all of your experiences must pass through.

Remember, your reality merely consists of your beliefs. Change your beliefs and you change your reality.

> *"It can be reasonably said that belief is the most*
> *powerful force in the world."*
> Dr. Robert Anthony

Let's refer back to our example about starting your own business. One action that you can take today would be to go to your local bookstore and buy a book on the particular business of your interest. More importantly, you should invest some of your time in actually reading the book and highlighting the key areas. Another action could be to make an appointment to speak with a member from your local chamber of commerce. This person might be able to answer many of your questions and guide you in the right direction.

Whatever you do, make sure you take some type of action today that is in alignment with your new beliefs. Otherwise, your new beliefs will not have enough strength to stick in your subconscious mind and to survive the pivotal probation period.

By aligning more of your beliefs in one common, positive direction, you will begin to feel a power surge in your life. All of a sudden, you will be backed by a belief system that supports you. You will have created a strong foundation for yourself that will support you in all of your wall smashing adventures.

CHANGE YOUR OLD LIMITING BELIEFS OR ELSE YOU WILL EXPERIENCE COGNITIVE DISSONANCE

Cognitive dissonance is a psychological term referring to a conflict between your beliefs and your actions. It occurs when you prepare to take action contrary to your existing beliefs. Inevitably, when this is the case, you will experience a significant amount of discomfort, which is symbolic of cognitive dissonance. As a result, you must either modify your behavior to match your beliefs or change your beliefs to match your behavior. These are the only two options that will relieve you of the discomfort. Unfortunately, it is usually the behavior that is modified since it is the newer and less stable of the two.

Suppose you attend a dieting seminar and you get all excited about the possibility of losing thirty pounds. In this case, you will feel excited about your new dream until you get home from the seminar and settle back into "reality." At this point, your excitement will wear off and your negative beliefs will remind you that it is impossible for you to lose that much weight. You will experience dissonance between your actions (following a plan to lose the weight) and your beliefs (I am not capable of losing the weight. It would be too painful to lose the weight. I am meant to be fat anyway.) One of the two has to go. Since your old limiting beliefs are more familiar, they tend to win the battle while your dream of losing the extra weight gets "flushed down the toilet."

Cognitive dissonance hinges on the law of familiarity: Whatever is most familiar to your mind will be repeated and whatever is unfamiliar will be avoided. Ask yourself the following questions to get a general idea of what effect the law of familiarity has on your own life:

⇒ Do you sleep on the same side of the bed night after night?
⇒ Do you drive the same route to work in the mornings?
⇒ Do you eat the same foods and drink the same beverages every morning for breakfast?
⇒ Do you talk to the same people about the same issues?
⇒ Do you go to the same "hangouts?"
⇒ Do you complain about the same problems?
⇒ Do you vacation at the same place each year?
⇒ Do you tell the same jokes?

It is relatively easy to notice how quickly human beings can be drawn to comfort and familiarity. So, instead of fighting the law of familiarity, you should learn how to get it to work for you. To do so, you need to change those old, familiar, limiting beliefs that keep you stuck in the rut of your comfort zone. Replace them with new, dynamic beliefs and then, let the law of familiarity work with your new beliefs the same way it used to work with your old, limiting beliefs.

"Choose your rut carefully, you'll be in it for the next forty miles!"
A sign on an old country road

Remember, make sure that your beliefs support the pursuit of your dreams. If your beliefs do not support the pursuit of your dreams, then you are in for a tremendous struggle with cognitive dissonance when you act in opposition to them.

BEWARE OF OTHER PEOPLE'S OPINIONS

Forming your beliefs around other people's opinions is extremely dangerous. You must be very careful to disregard comments like "You're too young. You're too old. You could never accomplish that kind of dream. You should get a real job. You're not smart enough." Accepting these types of comments from other people as your own personal beliefs can easily create additional, unnecessary obstacles in your life.

In the same respect, you must not close your ears to everything that people tell you. There will be certain people who will offer you their advice. Note that someone's *advice* is totally different from their *opinion*. People who offer you their advice genuinely want to help you to achieve your dreams. On the other hand, people who give you their opinions are the ones who either consciously or unconsciously want to discourage you from pursuing your dream.

One way to guard yourself against other people's negative opinions is to act like the person you most want to become. Politely disregard the opinions of others and commit yourself to becoming something more than you are currently showing. By doing this, you will eventually become the type of person you have been acting out. You will actually reach a point where it will become harder for you NOT to be the type of person you have been pretending to be. At this time, you will know you have made a lasting change in yourself.

Charles Givens, the author of several financial bestsellers and *Super Self* has developed a strategy known as "TTR," Taking Total Responsibility. In his early days as an entrepreneur, he had nine businesses that eventually went broke. During that time, he could have easily blamed his failures on his insurance company, his family, his education, his experience, or his consultants. But Givens never blamed another person for his personal downfalls nor did he accept their negativity into his mind. Instead, Givens always assumed total responsibility for his own life. This key strategy is what eventually permitted him to succeed in a grand way. Charles Givens is now one of the richest and most joyful persons in America. He is also the proud founder of The Charles Givens Organization, which is the largest nonprofit financial organization in America. It is dedicated to assisting over 400,000 members to achieve financial independence.

Likewise, you must also assume full responsibility for your own life. You must guard your mind to ensure that other people's negativity does not seep into your belief system. For one reason or another, most people either consciously or unconsciously discourage you from pursuing your dreams. Thus, you must cling to your own positive beliefs and disregard the lethal opinions of society if you are to achieve your dreams.

Let's suppose you were craving chocolate-covered cherries. Would you walk into a candy store and let the sales clerk persuade you into buying peanut butter meltaways? Of course not! Well, life outside the candy store should be no different. If you want to align your arsenal of beliefs toward the achievement of a dream that is special to you, then you should never let the opinions of others sabotage your belief system.

As long as you know in your heart that you are doing what is right, then you have no obligation whatsoever to concern yourself with other people's opinions. When someone disagrees with your actions, it's not your problem, it's their problem. These people do not pay your bills, raise your children, deal with your boss, or take any of your responsibility in life. Why then, should you concern yourself with their negative opinions about your life?

> *Six billion people live in this world. What an honor it is for this person to choose my life to criticize!*

When you step outside your comfort zone, you are going to get bombarded with negativity. People will do their best to infect you with their negativity and inaccurate opinions. You will feel like a crab who is crawling out of a bucket, but is being held back by all the other crabs because they do not want you to leave the comfort zone. They do not want you to "show them up." This is the point when you must be strong enough to hold tight to your positive beliefs without giving in to the negativity that surrounds you.

> *Your creator made you stronger than a million words of discouragement.*

Life is challenging enough without the added burden of concerning yourself with the opinions of your brother-in-law Barry. Your only logical course of action is to follow the desires of your heart. Let other people think whatever they want about you. Remember, opinions are given out for free and that is exactly what they are worth!

By resolving to create your own positive beliefs in the midst of a negative world, you are on your way to....HANDLING THE FEAR IN YOUR LIFE.

CHAPTER 8

HANDLING THE FEAR IN YOUR LIFE

"...security is not having things; it's handling things."
Dr. Susan Jeffers

As you know, fear is meant to be a positive force in your life. In order to take advantage of this positive force, you must first learn how to effectively handle it without feeling overwhelmed and losing control whenever you feel it. You can do this by following three simple steps: 1. Welcoming fear into your life. 2. Laughing during fearful situations. 3. Feeling your fear.

WELCOME YOUR FEAR

The first step to effectively handling your fears is to welcome fear into your life. It stands to reason that it is only natural to welcome such an awesome source of protection and guidance into your life. After all, fear brings you information that you cannot get elsewhere. The least you can do is to have enough courtesy to accept these vital messages from your friend. Stop and really feel what your fear is directing you to do next in your life. It will always guide you to do what is most important. You must simply be strong enough to look into the eye of fear to receive its message.

It is never wise to deny the presence of fear. If you enter a formal social function affirming, "I'm not afraid. I'm not afraid," this form of preparation does you much more harm than good. Resisting fear only causes it to intensify. Many times denial will bring about the very situation that you want to avoid. Instead, you should welcome fear into your life by saying, "Wow, I sure feel afraid. This is new to me. I must have a lot to learn from this situation. Please continue to guide me as to what I should do."

The best way to handle a fearful situation is to openly admit to yourself and to the people close to you that you are indeed feeling fearful. It's okay to be afraid, but it's not okay to deny the fear that you feel. Admitting your fear makes it easier for you to deal with it. Of course, this does not mean that it is necessary for you to wallow in your fear. It only means to accept fear as an important part of your life and resolve to learn from it. Let your fear know that you are willing to face it. Welcome fear into your life.

> *Life is a process in which fear guides you along a journey to become yourself.*

LAUGHING IN THE MIDST OF FEAR

The second step in successfully handling your fear is to laugh in the midst of a fearful situation. Laughter has an almost miraculous way of putting your mental and physical life back into balance. It is an immediate way to ensure that you are perceiving a situation with a clear mind.

In his book, *Anatomy of an Illness*, Norman Cousins explains how laughter put his life back into balance and actually saved him from a life-threatening illness. Cousins was suffering from severe arthritis throughout his body. It was so severe that he could barely turn over in bed and his jaws were practically locked together. When he asked his doctors about his chances of survival, they admitted at the time that they had never witnessed anyone who recovered from such a comprehensive condition.

Nonetheless, Norman Cousins believed that by consistently indulging in short episodes of laughter, he could eventually restore balance in his mind and body. In a desperate act to save his life, he discharged himself from the gloomy hospital and stayed at a nearby hotel. There, he watched funny movies and entertaining shows that caused him to laugh. By following this strategy, Norman Cousins successfully sent his crippling disease into remission. Since that time, Cousins has publicly proclaimed that he actually laughed himself back into perfect health.

Laughter is such a great gift. Think about it. What are the only "animals" that can laugh at themselves? Human beings. Therefore, learn to make good use of this awesome gift. Begin by taking a lighter approach to life. There does not exist one shred of evidence that proves life to be a serious event anyway. Why then, would you choose to tense your body and fill your mind with fear when you could choose to relax your body and mind with frequent episodes of laughter? Even if you are stuck in a "terrible" problem, you can still choose to laugh.

I distinctly remember a time, not so long ago when my motor home broke down alongside a dark highway in the middle of the night. I was stranded all by myself. Fortunately, I had a cellular phone that I used to make all the necessary phone calls to solve my problem. Nonetheless, I was still left alone and feeling a bit fearful. At that point, I had a decision to make. I could either curse the situation, tense my body, and produce fear or I could laugh at the situation, relax my body, and produce joy. Wisely, I decided to laugh about the situation. I didn't even have a rational reason to laugh, but by forcing myself to go through the physical motions required to produce laughter, I actually began to feel quite a bit less fearful than I originally had. In a short amount of time, I actually felt a sense of calm and peace within myself. Soon after, the situation was resolved and I continued on my way.

Another great quality about laughter is the way that it can remind you that your personal fears are only a speck of dust when compared to the much larger realm of fears facing society. As a society, we are faced with seemingly insurmountable walls like crime, disease, starvation, racial hatred, religious cults, terrorism, gangs, illiteracy, alcoholism, drugs, and war. Considering the magnitude of all of these problems, your fear of asking a question in the middle of class, making an important phone call, or changing your eating habits, seems trivial to say the least.

Laughter also tends to reverse the very characteristics that fear thrives upon. As you know, fear feeds on tension and avoidance. Since laughter is a form of release and acceptance, it tends to neutralize the effects of your fear. Laughter allows the muscles in your body to relax. In his book *Psycho-Cybernetics*, Maxwell Maltz reveals that scientific experiments have proven it to be impossible to feel fear or any other negative emotion while the muscles of your body are kept perfectly relaxed.

Ask yourself the question, "Can I laugh about this?" when you are faced with a challenge in your life. Answering "Yes" to this question means that you are still capable of controlling your fear. Answering "No" means that your fear is controlling you. Laughter is a sure-fire test to determine whether you are looking at a particular situation with a clear mind. If you cannot free yourself to perceive a situation with an objective mind, then you have very little chance of properly handling it.

As you can see, laughter is very capable of giving you relief from your fears. It drains the tension and stress out of your body and leaves you feeling calm and in control. The high school boxer who can laugh about his upcoming match with the returning state champion has positioned himself to have the best opportunity to beat his opponent. Yes, he will still have to fight the match of his life to win, but now he at least has a reasonable chance of success.

Many top-notch athletes, public speakers, and performers alike have adopted this kind of "laughing attitude." At the most crucial moments when all the "pressure" is on them, you can see a sense of calm control engulf them. Some will even exhibit a faint smile. It's as if their entire body is saying, "This is the moment I've been waiting for. Now is my time to shine!" It's the kind of "Watch this!" attitude displayed by American Mary Lou Retton in the 1984 Olympics when she delivered a perfect "10" routine under extreme pressure to win the gold medal in gymnastics.

It is not imperative that you physically laugh, although it is fine to do so. Laughing is more of an attitude or mindset. It is a way to interact with the environment around you. Why would you choose to act tense and restrictive when you could choose to act loose and carefree? Laughter is a way to open yourself up and let life pour itself in. It gives you the opportunity to interpret any fearful situation with a clear mind.

One way to successfully access this attitude of laughter prior to or during a fearful situation is to visualize the fearful situation as a ridiculous cartoon. Feature yourself as the main character in the cartoon and make sure that you poke lots of fun at the most fearful aspects of the situation. Create all kinds of funny images in your mind. Add silly music to your visualization to make it even more comical. Remember, the reality you create in your mind does not have to be "realistic." In fact, the more "unrealistic" your visualization, the more effective it will be.

Once you have created your own unique visualization, run it backwards and forwards in your mind. This will help to destroy the original image you had in your mind that was causing you to feel fearful. By destroying the mental image that was triggering the fearful response in your body, you will feel much more calm and in control of the once feared situation.

For example, you may be one of the millions of people who fear public speaking more than you fear death, itself. In this case, it would be wise for you to create an attitude of laughter in your mind. You can do this by visualizing yourself speaking in front of a group of people who have big silly grins pasted all over their faces. Imagine your audience wearing large funny hats on their heads coordinated with bright cheerful colored clothing. If you choose, you can go a step further and visualize certain people in your audience picking their nose or scratching their rear ends. There is no limit to the humor that you can poke at any given situation in your mind.

Then, when the day finally comes and you approach the microphone to speak, you will certainly remember your amusing visualization. Of course, you will still feel some fear, but it will be much less than if you had chosen to focus your thoughts on a serious, fearful visualization where you imagined yourself performing poorly. This strategy allows you to speak with the right state of mind. Instead of acting rigid and afraid, you will act loose and confident. Regardless of whatever type of scenario you choose to visualize, make sure you have fun with your mind.

Perhaps you fear interacting with the members of management at the annual summer picnic. In this case, close your eyes and create a mental image of the picnic. See the members of management as being ten times more afraid of you than you are of them. Make yourself out to be much larger and much brighter than the others at the picnic. See the president spilling her entire plate of food all over herself as she speaks to you. Picture the vice-president hiding behind a garbage can hoping not to be seen by you. Hear the voice of the office manager quiver and see her arms and legs shake as she speaks to you. Conjure up a totally outrageous mental image of this event. Then, when the time comes to experience the summer picnic, you will feel much more at ease interacting with the members of management. Your perception of that experience and your self-image will be changed forever.

One of the keys to using this strategy is to use real people, real places, and real objects in your visualization whenever you can. This will attach your feelings of merriment to specific stimuli. As a result, your mind will be programmed to experience feelings of amusement instead of feelings of fear whenever you encounter the particular experience. Consequently, you will act much more calm and natural as a result of your unique preparation.

Consider Michele, an underpaid, overworked secretary who has a desktop full of papers, a list of thirty people to call, five people waiting in line to speak with her, and a phone that is ringing off the hook. Most people in her situation would allow these kinds of working conditions to cause them stress, but this is not the case with Michele. Michele controls her stress levels by joking and laughing with everyone who comes into the office. At home, she laughs as she tells her family about the way her boss expects her to do the work of three secretaries.

Michele's unique attitude allows her to tolerate her job until she finds a different source of income. You can bet that someone like Michele will not be working as an underpaid secretary for long. With an attitude like hers, someone will soon pay her closer to what she is really worth.

FEEL YOUR FEAR

The third step in handling your fear is simply to feel it. Fear, like all emotions, is meant to be felt. After all, how else could you receive fear's message? You cannot see, hear, taste, smell, or touch fear. The only way left for fear to make you aware of its presence is through feelings.

Whenever you fail to admit that you are feeling fearful and that you need to take a particular action, you infect your life the same way a splinter eventually infects your finger. The only way to go beyond your fears is to feel them until there is no more fear to feel. Of course, doing so means that you will experience some physiological changes in your body. The following list includes many of these changes:

- A loss of warmth in your extremities (cold hands or cold feet)
- Increased heart rate
- Excessive sweating (usually your underarms)
- Tightness in your neck, back, chest or stomach
- Heartburn
- Chills up and down your spine
- "Butterflies" in your stomach
- Headache
- Shallow breathing pattern
- Hot flashes
- Quiver or cracking in your voice (stuttered words)
- Dryness of the mouth
- Shakiness
- A "lump" in your throat

Tensing your body in an effort to avoid these physiological changes will only serve to amplify them. Instead, learn to appreciate the keen sense of awareness that your emotions provide you. Feel your fear. Soak it up the same way that a paper towel soaks up a spilled glass of water. By doing so, you will eventually be left with nothing but joy.

Sarah is a great example of a young woman who recently experienced a significant amount of fear. Her fear stemmed from the fact that she was afraid to admit to her friends that she was "stood up" on a very important date. Sarah felt particularly fearful since she had already openly expressed her excitement about this particular date to her friends.

Sarah was faced with a decision. She could either opt to lie about the fact that she was "stood up" or she could choose to face the issue and feel the fear associated with it. By lying to her friends and telling them that her date went fine, Sarah would have saved herself from experiencing some temporary feelings of discomfort. The only problem is that she would have been living a lie.

Fortunately, Sarah chose to expose her genuine self by telling her friends the truth about her date. She knew that this would give them a chance to tease her about the situation. She also knew that some of them might even talk about her when she was not around. Nonetheless, Sarah decided to stand there and to feel all the painful emotions that were linked to the situation. To her amazement, she discovered that her friends were actually very supportive of her. They were not interested in embarrassing her or making her feel bad. Many of her friendships even became stronger as a result of her courage and honesty.

> *"First you have to live through it. Wisdom comes later. Just have to stand there like a jackass in a hailstorm and take it."*
> Robert Fulghum

The emotion of fear is much like a fill/hold/release mechanism. When you encounter a fearful situation, your body begins to **fill** itself with fear. Next, your body **holds** the fear inside you. Finally, it is **released** when you permit yourself to feel it in its entirety. This process is very similar to the one used by your bladder. Surely, you can imagine what it would be like if you did not release the liquid in your bladder. Therefore, do yourself a favor and complete the natural cycle of fear by allowing yourself to feel your fear until the intensity is gone.

Use the following letter to remind yourself about the three steps involved with successfully handling your fears.

Dear Fear,

Welcome to my life! I know you have come to give me an opportunity to improve the quality of my life and to tap into more of my potential. I rejoice over the opportunity of spending time with you. You are truly a good friend.

Although you make me feel uncomfortable for short periods of time, I will not allow you to overwhelm me. Instead, I will maintain the distinct ability to **laugh** during any fearful situation that arises in my life regardless of how bad it seems to be. I know that laughing puts me into the best state of mind to most effectively act upon the walls in my life.

Even though you look really scary right now, I am still prepared to **feel** every bit of your intensity. I can hardly wait to feel your passion pulsating through every cell of my being. Your energy is truly awesome and I realize that it is merely a prelude to joy. You provide a valuable service to my life and I am looking forward to a wonderful transforming process with you.

Thank you!

Your Friend,

Sean

Although these three steps to handling your fears are extremely effective, they are absolutely powerless unless you apply one additional quality. This indispensable quality is courage.

COURAGE

Courage is your ability to take action in the presence of fear. It is the only way you can overcome your current fears. Without courage, you could not possibly gain access to your dynamic zone. A coward simply cannot live dynamically.

"Do it trembling if you must, but do it."
Emmett Fox

The Pilgrims would have surely never found the New World without the courage to leave their homeland. Of course they were scared, but more importantly, they were armed with a picture of a better life firmly implanted within their minds. Their dream is what motivated them to set sail into uncharted, treacherous waters. This brave group of men and women took action despite the presence of their fears. They actually risked their lives and the lives of their children when they entered their dynamic zones. What uncommon courage!

"All our dreams can come true if we have the courage to pursue them."
Walt Disney

Don't worry, you aren't being asked to risk your life by setting sail on the stormy seas with minimal food and supplies like the Pilgrims once did. Instead, you are being prompted to merely risk feeling a bit of emotional discomfort by acting upon the wall in your life. Even by doing something as simple as saying, "Hello" to someone that you fear can be a mark of courage. As long as the element of fear is present and your intentions are good, then you have the opportunity to act courageously right now.

"Be strong and courageous."
Joshua 1:6

Courage is needed in every department of your life. The following list outlines a few of the ways that you can apply courage to the different departments of your life.

- ♦ Career courage (Contact a few key people who can assist you in getting the type of job that you really desire.)
- ♦ Contribution courage (Visit an elderly care facility and spend time with an elderly person that you have never met.)
- ♦ Educational courage (Attend a motivational or educational seminar.)
- ♦ Exploration courage (Visit a third world country.)
- ♦ Family courage (Buy your eleven-year-old son a good reference book about sex and spend time answering his questions.)

141

- Health courage (Exercise four times a week.)
- Investment courage (Put 10% of your "take home" pay into a mutual fund investment.)
- Recreational courage (Play a sport that you never played before.)
- Relationship courage (Initiate a discussion about an intimate topic.)
- Spiritual courage (Attend a different religious service.)
- Time management courage (Carry a small piece of paper in your purse or wallet noting the five most important things you have to do today.)

The time to start being courageous is right now. The moment the repairman charges you $12.00 more than you agreed to fix your furnace is the moment you should act courageously. Immediately confront the person about the mistake. Demand to pay no more than the agreed-upon price for the contracted work. If you do not first act courageously upon the small daily walls in your life, then you will never be courageous enough to handle much larger issues.

> *Everyone is born with an overflowing amount of ability. Rare is the person with the courage to use that ability.*

Smaller walls, like being overcharged on a repair, confronting someone about a particular comment, or having to deal with uncharacteristic weather, serve in part to strengthen you. They prepare you to handle bigger walls, like having insufficient funds to pay your bills, suffering a severe injury, or dealing with the death of a loved one. Smaller walls strengthen your muscles so that you are capable of handling much greater challenges in the future.

Muscles only get stronger with use and wall smashing muscles are no different. You cannot expect your wall smashing muscles to be strong for the rest of your life after only one workout. Would you go into a gym and expect to bench 300 pounds if you have never benched before? Of course not. First, you must begin with smaller weights and gradually work your way up to heavier weights. The same is true with courage. First, you must use your "muscles" to act courageously upon your smaller walls until you become strong enough to act courageously upon your larger walls.

"God did not give us a spirit of timidity."
2nd Timothy 1:7

Consider "the wall of slavery." Would Abraham Lincoln have been strong enough to smash such an immense wall without first smashing other smaller walls? Of course not! Before he could make definite progress toward the abolition of slavery, first, he had to overcome "smaller" challenges like childhood poverty, tragic deaths of people he loved, business failure, a nervous breakdown, and countless political defeats. Only by successfully dealing with these smaller issues did he develop the courage and strength to take on such a colossal issue like that of the abolition of slavery.

"Courage is the capacity to go from failure to failure without losing enthusiasm."
Winston Churchill

It is a well-known fact that a turtle cannot move without sticking its neck outside its shell. Likewise, only by sticking your "neck" outside your comfort zone can you make progress toward the attainment of your dreams.

FEAR CANNOT PHYSICALLY STOP YOU FROM TAKING ACTION

As you courageously take action toward the attainment of your dreams, there will be times when you will feel paralyzed by fear. You will freeze. Even the thought of taking action will cause you to tremble. At this point, you must realize that you still possess the distinct ability to take action. Ask yourself, "If I were offered ten million dollars to take this action, could I do it?" Of course you could! Even your most intense feelings of fear could not physically grab hold of you and keep you from taking action. The truth is that you are free to take action regardless of how much fear you are feeling at any given moment.

Suppose you feel deep feelings of fear when you even think about calling an old friend. In this case, stop and ask yourself these questions, "Can I still move my arm to pick up the telephone? Can I still say my name? Am I still breathing?" If you answer these questions honestly, you will prove to yourself that the only thing stopping you from taking action is a feeling inside your body that you choose to label as fear. So often, it is merely a little feeling of discomfort that stops you from pursuing your dreams. In truth, it does not matter how scared you are to

143

take a certain action, you still have the physical ability to do it. In the case of our telephone example, you can still pick up the phone, dial the number, and make the phone call. It really doesn't matter how scared you are.

> *"Weak is he who permits his thoughts to control his actions; strong is he who forces his actions to control his thoughts."*
> Og Mandino

Fear is an integral part of life. I happen to be feeling fear right now as I write this paragraph. I am fearing that I may not effectively communicate my message to you. I am fearing that I may accidentally delete or lose all the work that I did today. I fear that I may get "writer's block." I fear that I may get "burned out." My point is that regardless of how much fear I am feeling, I still retain the physical and mental ability to write this book. Even the times when I feel most fearful, my feelings of fear cannot physically stop me from taking….DYNAMIC ACTION.

CHAPTER 9

DYNAMIC ACTION: THE MOST EFFECTIVE TYPE OF ACTION

"Life affords no higher pleasure than that of surmounting difficulties..."
Samuel Johnson

SMART ACTION

Before you can overcome any obstacle in your life, you must take *smart* action, which is the first ingredient in the recipe for dynamic action. Anytime you contemplate taking an action, it is best to first determine if the action is for the highest good of all who will be affected by it. Make it a point to do what is right for both you and for all humankind. Ask yourself, "Will taking this action be in my best interest and the best interest of my society?" Commit yourself to examining the consequences of your actions before you actually take them.

When you are feeling really motivated, it is very easy to rush into a certain endeavor without thinking about all of the consequences involved. I have personally fallen into this trap in the area of real estate. As a teenager, I was so motivated to take action and buy some rental properties that I forgot to ask some very important questions like, "Are there any problems with the foundation of this building? What are other comparable properties selling for in this area? Will I be able to rent these apartments and houses for enough money to cover my expenses?"

As you can see, these are pretty important questions to "forget" to ask. My foolish actions caused me to lose a significant amount of money in the area of real estate.

As it turned out, my real estate experiences were not quite enough to teach me about the importance of taking smart action. Within a short period of time, I found myself purchasing vending machines from a company who promised me that vending machines are "easy money." Once again, I neglected to ask some very important questions like, "Will I be able to find locations for these machines? Will this product sell in my community? Who fixes the machines when they break down? Can I return these machines if I am not pleased with them?" As a result of my foolish actions, my finances suffered once again. Ever since this particular experience, I have become much more conscious of the need to take smart actions.

"For every thousand hacking at the leaves of evil, there is one striking at the root."
Henry Thoreau

For many people in our society, it seems as if they will never learn to correct their foolish actions. Did you ever wonder why drunks continue to drive their cars while they are intoxicated even though the newspapers, radios, and television are full of tragic accounts about drunk drivers? Or why overeaters continue to pack their body with fats and sugar despite their obvious lack of energy and poor self-image? Or why smokers continue to smoke cigarettes when scientists have proved that each cigarette takes 14 minutes off their life span?

The answer to these questions is that most of us believe that tragedy always happens to someone else. Despite the reports splattered all over our newspapers, radios, and televisions, many of us continue to do things that are bad for us, bad for our children, and bad for society. Part of the problem is that we never had any real life experiences to serve as references to teach us how costly our foolish actions can be.

Real life experiences are the absolute best way to learn a lesson once and for all. The only drawback is that real life experiences can be very costly in terms of your health, money, relationships, career, or even your life. Therefore, it much wiser to learn your lessons from simulations of an actual event or situation.

For example, as a child, I had the opportunity to view a horrifying film about the dangers of drug use. This particular film was a grueling account of a young woman who virtually ruined her entire life as a result of drug abuse. She became so addicted to a certain drug that she would do anything to get her "fix," including prostitution, theft, and other crimes.

By the time her parents intervened, this young woman had lost all control of her life. The only option left for her parents was to take her to a nearby drug clinic where she would either die, go crazy, or break free of her addiction. Upon arriving at the drug clinic, the staff locked the young woman in a padded room. I remember it taking five full-grown men to accomplish this task. From there, nutrients were injected into her veins in hope of sustaining her. Her hair was even shaved off to prevent her from strangling herself.

Even at this very moment, I can still vividly recall this young woman bouncing herself off the padded walls as she screamed at the top of her lungs that she wanted to die. She acted like an enraged animal. It was a horrible sight to see. After what seemed like forever, the young woman finally collapsed out of complete exhaustion. There she lay, a pile of skin and bones. She looked as though she had aged twenty years.

As a result of that one film, I gained a very real reference point that ensured that I would never even experiment with drugs. Basically, I learned to fear the consequences of drug use. Prior to this film, I had heard many stories and read many accounts about the harmful effects of drugs, but nothing impacted me nearly as much as this one vivid experience. Only by actually witnessing the graphic horrors of this film did I ever become passionate about never ever using drugs.

The closer you can get to actually experiencing a tragedy, the more you will be impacted by it. In my case, I felt as though I was actually in the room, as the drug addict insanely bounced herself off the walls. This is much more effective than passively reading the newspaper, watching the news, or listening to radio accounts about a tragic event.

Sometimes, you can even go somewhere or do something that would allow you to feel what it would be like to actually experience a certain tragedy. It is wise to expose both yourself and your family to a wide variety of experiences so that you will actually experience some of the consequences of taking foolish actions. This will help to ensure that you and your loved ones make the right choices in the future. The following list includes a short summary of a few such experiences:

◊ Visit the ghetto to see what it would be like to be so poor that you had to live in a rat infested shack. Feel how crowded it would be if your entire family was forced to live in a single room no larger than your bedroom. Imagine what it would be like not to have any heat in the freezing cold winters or to live in a room that reeks of urine.

147

(Maybe this experience would motivate you to save 10% of your paycheck, create an IRA, or get a better education.)

◊ Take a tour through a maximum security prison. Notice the lifeless expressions upon the faces of the inmates. See how the guards treat them. Get a good feel for what it would be like to spend time there. Then, as you step foot outside the prison grounds, take a deep breath. You can actually smell the freedom. (This experience could motivate you to follow the law, better appreciate your freedom, or to take some important actions.)

◊ Go on a church mission to a devastated third world country and see for yourself the scores of little children who are suffering from malnutrition and other deadly diseases. Notice how frail and fragile they appear and how easy their bones break. Compare the size of your arm to one of their legs. Take note of their expressions as they sit helplessly watching their family members die one by one. (This experience could motivate you to contribute more of your time, talents, skills, and/or money to worthwhile organizations, improve upon your daily health habits, or better appreciate the complex food distribution system that serves your needs.)

◊ Visit the junk yard to see what a car looks like after being mangled from a drunk driving accident. Notice how much blood is splattered throughout the hunk of metal that hardly resembles a car. Smell the putrid odor of death that reeks from the vehicle. Imagine how fast someone's dreams were shattered. (This experience could motivate you to quit drinking alcohol, appreciate the time you spend with your family, or stop a friend from driving while intoxicated.)

By going out into the world and gaining some real life references like those mentioned above, you can show yourself and your family the real consequences of taking foolish actions. Vivid experiences like these will stick in their minds for a long time to come. You can rest assured that they will think twice in the future before they act foolishly.

As a human being, you possess a limited amount of time and energy. This is why it becomes vital to use your time and energy wisely. Make sure your actions are those that are most important to you. Use your mind and take smart actions. Every foolish action you take robs you of the energy you could have used to pursue your dreams.

Remember, you are never obligated to take action at the expense of your happiness. Nothing is worth the price if you must forfeit your happiness in the process. Be smart enough to pursue only those things that you are passionate about. This means that you should not be working at a job that you hate for any longer than is absolutely necessary. Doing so is one of the most dangerous things you could possibly do. After all, a week consists of only 168 hours. If you spend 40-50 hours every week doing something you hate, then you are wasting away a large chunk of your life.

Learn to follow your passions and, while doing so, avoid taking any foolish actions. As a result, you will have successfully completed the first step of dynamic action.

SMALL ACTION

Taking small actions is the second ingredient in the recipe for dynamic action. It is important to realize that you are not required to conquer the world in a day. In fact, drastic actions can be quite dangerous. Instead, all you really need to do is consistently improve your life in small increments.

When you are preparing to take action, think of a highly skilled mountain climber. Experienced mountain climbers do not focus on climbing the entire mountain at once. Rather, they focus 100% of their attention on their very next step. They are well aware that their chances of a mistake increase significantly when they focus on more than one step at a time.

> *"You never conquer the mountain.*
> *You only conquer yourself."*
> Jim Whittaker

Small actions are easy to take and can quickly add up to significant progress toward the attainment of your dreams. You will also save yourself the painful burden of having to take drastic actions to make up for all the times that you neglected to take small actions. Drastic actions are a bad idea since they often cause you to feel overwhelmed by your fears. This, of course, could be enough to cause you to retreat back into your comfort zone. There is truth in the saying, "It's hard by the yard, but it's a cinch by the inch." Be sure to keep this idea foremost in your mind as you contemplate your next action.

The basic theory behind taking small actions is that they can easily and consistently be taken in the presence of fear. Your mind will not fight nearly as hard against you when you prepare to take little steps as opposed to when you plan to take giant steps. When you contemplate the possibility of taking big steps, you cause your mind to send off signals of panic. Although it is possible to be successful by using this approach, small steps are still the best insurance to keep you from feeling overwhelmed.

Even the greatest achievements in the world all began with one very small step. It doesn't matter if it was Neil Armstrong landing on the moon, the Wright brothers flying the first airplane, or Benjamin Franklin inventing the lightning rod. One simple step marks the beginning of all great achievements.

Take Bill for instance. Bill is a 54-year-old man who has been ninety pounds overweight for twenty years. During that time, he feared the consequences of what would eventually result from carrying around so much extra weight. Instead of making minor changes to his eating habits so that he would lose as little as two ounces a day for two years, he planned to lose all the weight within a few weeks. Unfortunately, none of his diets ever worked. In fact, after each of his diets, Bill went on an eating frenzy and ended up regaining all of his original weight along with a few extra pounds. Bill soon learned that willpower alone is not enough to make lasting change.

As a result of his poor strategy, Bill is currently in the hospital recovering from his first heart attack. He only wishes that he could turn back the clock and have the opportunity to take those small effective actions that would have preserved his good health. He could have made very simple changes like drinking skim milk instead of whole milk, eating meat no more than once a day, snacking on fruit instead of candy bars, and exercising for 45 minutes three times a week. Unfortunately, Bill overlooked these types of small actions and now, he is forced to make massive changes to his eating habits just to stay alive. Bill could have saved himself a lot of pain had he chosen to make small changes in his eating habits twenty years ago.

The primary problem with taking massive actions as opposed to taking small actions is a lack of strength. This occurs when you spend too much time in your comfort zone. Long periods of inactivity tend to drain most of the strength you once had. Then, the moment you act boldly, you find that you do not have the necessary strength to accomplish your objective. Wall smashing muscles are no different from your physical muscles. The longer they go without use, the weaker they get.

Imagine how ridiculous it would be for someone who has been physically inactive for ten years to wake up one day and run a marathon. As silly as this sounds, you probably act the same way in many aspects of your life. It is so easy to overlook how many small actions actually go into the preparation of any major accomplishment. In the case of the marathon runner, she must spend months or even years in training before obtaining the endurance to run a marathon. The same is true with every facet of life. In order to create the kind of foundation that will support you when you aspire to greater heights, you must use the same strategy as that of a successful marathon runner.

No matter what level of success you aspire to attain, one truth remains the same, *you must start where you are!* There are marathon runners who have confessed that their initial day of training involved running from their front porch to their mailbox on the street. Although a small action like this may seem insignificant, it still can be your beginning mark of a major achievement. It can become your foundation to build your future success upon.

Suppose you were totally lost, so lost that you didn't even know the general vicinity of your whereabouts. In this case, even if you had the best map available, you still could not find your way back on course. Your only hope of ever getting back on course is to figure out exactly where you are so that you can determine which way to go. This truth applies to all of life. You must begin where you are. Only then can you take action to improve your situation.

Action marks the beginning of everything. When you take a small action, you have set a cause in motion. One simple, little action is the secret to creating the momentum it takes to finish a large project. A writer could sit and stare at the computer screen all day, but until she starts typing, she has no power. If she waited until she knew exactly what she was going to write, she would never write a book or article. She may have an idea, but until she begins the process of typing, the idea will never completely unfold. Often, the best advice for her is to start typing something until she discovers what she has to write. Her initial small actions are usually enough to get the momentum rolling.

There is magic in taking action. Even if your action is flawed in some way, it still decreases the gravitational pull of your comfort zone and makes it easier for you to take the next step. Ask any good performer and she will tell you that action is the number one antidote to stage-fright. There is simply no better way to overcome your fears. With this in mind, take Nike's advice and "Just do it!"

"Beginning is half done."
Dr. Robert Schuller

The sooner you can take action, the less fear you will have to feel. Walls only become tougher to deal with the longer you delay your actions. Suppose you have been hurt by something your spouse said to you. In this case, your best course of action would be to confront your spouse immediately about what was said. The longer you wait, the harder it becomes to take the necessary action to dispel your hurt. Your best strategy is always to attack your walls when they are the weakest.

If you want to take off some extra weight from your body, then you cannot wait until after the holidays to start. Instead, you must make minor changes in your eating pattern today. If one of your changes is that you will no longer eat cake, then you must spit the cake out of your mouth at this very instant. The same is true if you want to begin a savings program. In this case, you must immediately go to the bank, open a savings account, and deposit something into your account right now. Even if you have to borrow a quarter from someone on the street, you still must take some small action today. Otherwise, you will be left right where you started and you still will not have broken through the inertia of your comfort zone and actually begun the process.

"The beginning is the most important part of work."
Plato

Although it seems logical to wait until all the walls are out of your way before you begin to take action, the truth is that you would end up waiting forever. If this were the case, you could never get married, have children, go back to school, or get your driver's license. Walls are here to stay. They are a vital part of your evolution as a dynamic human being. You might as well get used to taking action in spite of your walls rather than waiting for the "perfect time."

Let's suppose that you are a novice real estate investor. As a novice real estate investor, you have an incredible amount of walls that you must smash before you can make big profits. You need to avoid pitfalls like buying properties in the wrong part of the city, renting properties to tenants who destroy them, overpaying for the properties, buying defective properties, or violating city ordinances.

The only way to start the process of smashing these walls is by taking some kind of small, initial action. You could buy a real estate audiocassette program, attend a real estate seminar, make a list of the best neighborhoods to buy real estate, cut out information on mortgage lenders, read the first chapter from a real estate book, or call a real estate agent or broker in your city. As long as you take some type of small, worthwhile action, you will have successfully completed the second step of dynamic action.

CONSISTENT ACTION

Consistent action is the third and final ingredient in the recipe for dynamic action. When you apply consistent action along with the first two ingredients of smart action and small action, you assure yourself that you will eventually succeed. Consistent action always wins out in the end. It does not matter about the strength or the size of the wall facing you. As long as you keep plugging away, eventually the wall will crumble to the ground.

Suppose you want to read over 50 books this year. How could you accomplish such a large goal when you already have so little time? You could do so by consistently reading 27 pages a day. What if you wanted to create a multi-million dollar law firm? You could accomplish this objective by consistently gaining one new client a week until you achieve your dream. No matter what your dream is, it is possible for you to achieve it as long as you consistently take action toward its attainment.

Along the way, you may find that your primary adversary is laziness. Laziness makes all the rest of your dynamic qualities useless. You could be healthy, smart, good-looking, kind, strong, and highly educated, but if you are lazy, the rest of your personal assets are useless. Laziness negates every good quality that you possess.

Suppose you possess skill as an auto mechanic and you chose not to use this skill to earn money for your family when you were laid off from your job. How would your knowledge and ability have benefited you? Likewise, if you possess reading skill, yet choose not to read, what good is your skill? If your skills are not put to use, you might as well not even have them.

> *Talent + Knowledge + Experience + Good Contacts + Positive Attitude + University Degree +* *LAZINESS* = ***FAILURE***

Laziness is one of the primary reasons why so many professional and collegiate athletes are unsuccessful in the other areas of their life outside their sport. Instead of applying the same desire and work ethic that they use to excel in their particular sport, they decide to be lazy. For some reason, many athletes believe that life outside sports has a different set of rules. What most athletes fail to realize is that sports are merely a form of preparation for real life.

Take Jackie, who was a superstar basketball player. In the off-season, she would practice for hours every day to refine her basketball skills. She would shoot free throws, practice lay-ups, and work on her outside shooting. She would also play in basketball tournaments, lift weights, run, take aerobic classes, and use visualization techniques.

Jackie was absolutely committed to becoming the best basketball player that she could possibly be. And she was willing to pay the price.

Unfortunately, Jackie did not apply this same sense of consistency and hard work when she applied for a job following her sports career. Instead, she became lazy and quit looking for a job after she was rejected on her first job interview. Jackie wrongly assumed that life outside sports was easy. She failed to realize that every aspect of life requires the same kind of consistent action as does the world of sports.

Regardless of your current situation, go out and consistently give everything that you have in all that you do. Combine your smart, small, and consistent actions together into one force of dynamic action and use your dynamic actions to smash through your walls of fear. But, along the way, be sure to guard yourself against the trap of.... PROCRASTINATION.

CONGRATULATIONS!!!!

You have proven to be one of the ten percent or less who actually read past the first chapter of a nonfiction book. Your habit of taking dynamic action is probably already rewarding you with big results in your life. You are the kind of person who has what it takes to live a dynamic life. Continue to plunge ahead into the remainder of this book and remember to apply this knowledge in your life today.

CHAPTER 10

PROCRASTINATION: THE ULTIMATE DREAM STEALER

"Life is the most exciting game in town.
I'm surprised there aren't more players!"
Sean Hockensmith

Take a moment and go back into your past to relive your latest high school class reunion. How did the members of your class regard the element of time? Did most of your classmates think that time went by quickly between graduation and the reunion or did they claim that it went by slowly? How about yourself? Does it really seem like it has been 5, 10, 25, or even 50 years since you graduated from high school?

If you are like most people, then you will agree that time has passed by very quickly indeed. Many of your high school memories might seem as if they only took place yesterday. This is probably true for all aspects of your life, not only your high school graduation and other significant events. Even the times of your life that seemed as if they would never end, now seem like they barely lasted a moment. Indeed, few people can account for all the years that have gone by, all the time that has expired.

Dr. Paul Pearsall, author of the best-selling Nightingale-Conant audiocassette program *The Pleasure Principle* shrinks all of the history of the world into one theoretical year. By doing so, he found that all of human history would take place in the last minute. This proves that human beings are newcomers to this world. Compared to the millions of years that the Earth has existed, any given lifetime is nothing more than a blink of an eye. With respect to the limited amount of time you have to spend on this planet, you cannot afford to spend another moment postponing an important action.

> *A twenty-year old is really not much younger than a seventy-year old.*

When your fear guides you to act upon a certain wall and you choose to "put off" taking the necessary action, then you are procrastinating. Procrastination is a method used to avoid taking certain actions in your life. Each time you delay taking an important action, you are creating a negative habit for yourself. The longer you strengthen this habit, the harder it will become for you to step outside your comfort zone and pursue your dreams.

"Most men die at age 25, but aren't buried until age 67."
Benjamin Franklin

Every time you put off doing something that needs to be done, you intensify your fear. Issues only become harder to deal with the longer you wait to confront them. This is not to say that you should not plan to take certain actions in the future. Planning is totally different from procrastinating. Planning is a strategy where you designate a specific time in the future that will enable you to take the best course of action. Procrastination, on the other hand, is a strategy where you indefinitely avoid taking action.

A prime example of procrastination is the mother who puts off talking to her daughter about the important issues that revolve around sex. In this case, the mother will feel increasingly more fearful the longer she avoids facing this wall. At some point in the future, she might even give up on the idea altogether. This would obviously force her daughter to find out about sex from either her peers or though personal experience. Either way, the mother will have failed her daughter by avoiding this vital wall.

The negative effects derived from habitual procrastination quite often appear as one big lump of overwhelming depression. The common "mid-life crisis" is nothing more than the debt of years of procrastination becoming due and payable. This is no different from the way a bank will "call" a loan due and payable when it goes too far into delinquent status. The only difference is the severity of the penalty. With a bank, you are only losing your money. With procrastination, you are losing your dreams!

The only way to avoid this tragedy is by taking action upon your wall of fear in this very moment. Otherwise, you might wake up one day and realize that your life is more than half over and you haven't even started to live. Taking action today is all that can save you. It is so easy to say, "I'll do it tomorrow." The tragedy is that tomorrow does not exist. Tomorrow is a figment of your imagination. It's all a scandal and a lie. Anything that you put off till tomorrow will never get done. The present moment is all that you have.

> ### *"A life lived for tomorrow will always be just a day away from being realized."*
> Leo Buscaglia

It is impossible for you to escape the here and now. You can load your body with drugs, skydive into the Grand Canyon, race your Porsche down the interstate at 150 miles per hour, have sex with all of your fantasy partners, indulge in every type of virtual reality technology available, practice every form of hypnosis and meditation in existence, and pray until your knees are stiff, but in the end, you will always come back to the present moment. You are trapped! And the only way to escape is by consciously smashing the walls that are holding you prisoner.

Tomorrow is now all over again.

Since you are forever bound to the present moment, you must learn to take action in this very moment. If you do not take action right now, then you don't really want the things that you claim to want for yourself and your family. If you want financial independence and you are not reading a financial book and applying financial strategies to your life, then you don't really want financial independence. Likewise, if you want to have a "washboard stomach" and you are not doing some kind of stomach workout today, then you don't really want a "washboard stomach." Your consistent daily actions alone prove what you really want in your life.

The reason you avoid pursuing the things that you claim you really "want" is simply due to a fear of pain. You fear that the actions involved with pursuing your dream would be too painful. In your mind, you believe that it would be more pleasurable to put off the action to some indefinite time in the future when you fantasize that the action will be easier to take. Thus, you choose to procrastinate.

Sigmund Freud first made this discovery many years ago when he noticed that the behavior of all living creatures is determined by an inborn desire to minimize pain and maximize pleasure. Thanks to Freud, we now realize that the only reason we procrastinate is because we believe that procrastinating will be more pleasurable than taking action. Review the following list and consider how pleasurable procrastination appears to be in the short-term.

THE SHORT-TERM PLEASURE OF PROCRASTINATION

* I can avoid the initial discomfort of facing my fears.
* I won't draw much attention to myself, which means that very few people will criticize me.
* I will fit in and be well accepted by other people who also hide in their comfort zones.
* There will be no pressure on me because no one will be counting on me for anything.
* I will have more time to watch television and to indulge in other similar activities.

As you can see, procrastination seems pretty tempting in the short-term. It is totally logical why you would choose to procrastinate. The main problem is that you usually neglect to consider the long-term pain of procrastinating. Take a few moments to review the following list and really feel the pain of long-term procrastination.

THE LONG-TERM PAIN OF PROCRASTINATION

- I will never achieve my dreams.
- My life will be boring.
- I will lack any real feelings of fulfillment in my life.
- I will have to explain to my children that I am a coward.
- My comfort zone will begin to shrink.
- I will not be able to face myself in the mirror.
- I will have to face my creator when I die and explain that I wasted away the priceless gift of life.

As you can tell, procrastination is a terrible choice once you consider the long-term consequences. Remember, life is a long-term project that needs consistent long-term planning. A short-term approach to life only guarantees yourself a future that consists of boredom and a lack of fulfillment. By choosing to take action on the other hand, you may cause yourself to feel a bit uncomfortable in the short-term, but the long-term benefits will prove to be nothing less than remarkable.

As Robert Ringer writes in his book *Million Dollar Habits*, "Conditions are never right at the right time; the timing is always wrong." Realize that there is no sense in waiting to pursue your dreams. The person who waits for ideal conditions is nothing but a coward. A coward leaves at the first sign of fear. Cowardice is the opposite of courage. The only thing the two words have in common is their beginning letter. There could not be two more extreme opposites. Cowardice is like an ice cube and courage is like the sun.

> ***"One man with courage makes a majority."***
> Andrew Jackson

It is impossible for you to display courage and cowardice in the same moment. One or the other has to give way. Friedrich Nietzsche, a famous German philosopher, warned us over one hundred years ago about the dangers of cowardice. He is quoted as saying, "Error is cowardice!" Nietzsche understood that many people possessed the skills to achieve their dreams, but there was one essential ingredient that these people were missing. They lacked the courage to apply their skills toward the attainment of their dreams. Without action, their skills became worthless.

TRIVIAL ACTIONS

Sometimes procrastination can be very difficult to detect. You may have become so skilled at procrastination that you can even fool yourself at times. Instead of avoiding certain actions by doing nothing, you may choose to immerse yourself in a bunch of trivial actions. Trivial actions are a deceptive form of procrastination where you focus your attention upon petty, insignificant issues and activities as a way to avoid taking other, more important actions. It is a form of procrastination that distracts yourself from facing your fears.

For example, some people will clean their house even though it is not dirty, iron clothes that are not wrinkled, wax a car that is already shiny, cut the grass that is already too short, or spend hours on the phone gossiping. Anytime you engage in a meaningless activity as a way to avoid doing something much more important, you are using a high-level form of procrastination.

By distracting your mind and focusing your attention upon something trivial and petty, you can gain some temporary relief from your fears. After all, you cannot feel fearful if your mind is totally occupied with another activity. The problem is that this approach only works for a very short period of time. Eventually, your original fears will return with more intensity than ever.

Sam is a prime example of someone who used trivial actions to avoid facing key issues in his life. He and his wife had lost their sense of partnership, lost their passion, and they no longer communicated beyond a superficial level. The dynamic way to handle the walls in his life would have been to confront them head on by speaking to his wife about their marital problems. Then, they could have sought counseling, read books on communication, and possibly attended a relationship seminar together.

Instead, Sam chose to ignore his problems by engaging in trivial activities like working excessive amounts of overtime and sitting on a corner bar stool at the local tavern. That way, he could at least pretend that everything was fine with his marriage. Although Sam would have desired a dynamic marriage, he felt overwhelmed when he thought about confronting all the different issues with his wife. In Sam's mind, it was less painful to spend time away from his wife than it was to endure the short-term pain of confronting their problems.

When Sam finally came home at the end of each day, he would only spend a few moments exchanging meaningless small talk with his wife before he went to bed. Neither Sam nor his wife said anything more than was necessary to each other. In short, Sam's excessive overtime and frequent bar visits were merely an avoidance and procrastination ploy to sidestep the problems he really should have been addressing.

This is a prime example of the modern-day marriage where two "adults" have chosen to live a life of independent trivial actions. Neither of them are really contributing any kind of love to the relationship. They are merely conducting their daily affairs as if nothing were wrong. It is no wonder they are having problems. They have both given up on their dreams of ever having a dynamic marriage. All they want is to make it through another day.

CODEPENDENCY

Codependency is another discreet type of procrastination. Codependency occurs when one person desires to live her life through someone else as a way to avoid certain issues in her own life. This can occur in a friendship, marriage, partnership, or any other type of relationship.

A father may desire to live his life through his daughter in order to avoid facing certain issues in his own life. He may immerse himself into her world by doing things like coaching her little league baseball team, driving her to and from school every day, and attending all of her extra-curricular events and practices. He might not even enjoy many of these activities, but by doing them, he successfully avoids certain fearful issues in his own life. He believes that if he can only distract himself long enough with his daughter, all of his problems and fears will magically disappear.

This is not to say that parents should not participate in the lives of their children. Rather, it is to remind parents, business partners, lovers, spouses, and siblings alike that they must still allot enough time to face the important issues that arise in their own personal lives. It is not enough to be immersed in someone else's life.

HOW TO ENJOY TAKING ACTION

Even if you are courageous enough to overcome the temptations of procrastination, you may still find it difficult to enjoy certain tasks. Maybe for you it is cutting the grass, doing the dishes, washing the car, or cleaning the house. In any case, you can easily solve these problems by hiring someone else to do these things for you. Then, you can spend more of your time doing the things that are most important to you. Even if you think you cannot afford to pay for these services, you may find that with a little contacting and some creativity on your part, you may find the right person at the right price who would be happy to help you.

A good financial rule to follow is the one taught by Marshall Sylver in his audiocassette program, *Passion, Profit, and Power.* He teaches that you should analyze your own life to determine how much your time is worth in terms of an actual per-hour dollar amount. From there, Sylver advocates that you should pay other people to do all of your work that can be done for less money per hour than you are worth. This strategy will ensure that you are spending your time doing only those activities that you must do from a financial standpoint.

For instance, spend $800.00 on a good dishwasher that will save you a half hour or more of your time per day. Spend $50.00 every third week to have a housekeeper come into your home and dust and run the sweeper for you. Pay a company $25.00 to cut your grass once a week instead of spending your own time doing it. Of course, if you thoroughly enjoy performing any one of these activities, then by all means, do it yourself.

Although it would be ideal to spend a portion of your money paying other people to do all of your undesirable tasks, it is possible that you might not be earning quite enough money as of today to do so. In this case, you would have to do many of these tasks yourself for the time being. Fortunately, there is a way that you can learn to enjoy yourself in the process.

The key to enjoying "undesirable activities" is to focus your thoughts upon the benefits derived from them instead of all the other things that you would rather be doing. For instance, when you are preparing supper, focus on the wonderful food that will nourish the body and mind of you and your family rather than the book you would rather be reading. When you run the sweeper, think about how fortunate you are to have a family to clean up after. By focusing on the benefits that created the dusty carpets, you will feel a much deeper sense of enjoyment from doing the necessary work. It only stands to reason that if you decide to do something, you should also decide to enjoy it.

The same principle can be applied when you are washing dishes. There are many benefits that are derived from dirty dishes. Consider some of the following:

◊ The food that nourished your body
◊ Hot water to clean the dishes
◊ Your physical and mental ability to wash dishes
◊ The money you have to buy nice dishes
◊ The house you live in
◊ The family you have the honor to feed
◊ The privilege to live in this free country
◊ The extensive food distribution system that you have access to

And the list goes on and on. There is no end to the benefits and blessings in which you can direct your focus. You could even focus upon things like the air that you breathe, the wonderful aroma in the kitchen, or your ability to laugh. The only limit is determined by your own willingness to think creatively. This strategy can literally transform your daily chores into daily joys.

The next time you feel upset about having to maintain your yard, focus your thoughts on your yard being the place where you throw the baseball with your son, picnic with your family, and play with your dogs. Notice all the beautiful trees and shrubs in your yard and appreciate your own physical gifts that enable you to maintain your yard. There are certainly many less fortunate people who are not able to do yard work because of some sort of physical or mental incapacity. Whatever it is that you decide to do, focus on the joy that is present before you. It is so easy to miss the simple joys in life by wrongly focusing your attention on the "downside" of a certain activity.

Consider Martin, a low-paid janitor at a public utility company. Despite the fact that he has a job with very little social prestige, he always has a smile on his face. No matter what he does, he finds a way to enjoy it. He even smiles when he cleans the toilets. Compare this kind of attitude with that of Nancy, who is a high-powered executive of the same company. Nancy makes a salary ten times larger than that of Martin. Unfortunately, Nancy always appears to be stressed and rarely does she ever find joy in any of her activities. She works solely out of obligation as a means to bring home a large paycheck. In this comparison, both Nancy and Martin have successfully overcome procrastination, but only Martin has truly succeeded in enjoying the work that he does. The only way for Nancy to reverse this process is with a willingness to change, the proper knowledge, and lots of....DETERMINATION.

WHAT IS YOUR FEAR TELLING YOU TO DO NEXT?

CHAPTER 11

DETERMINATION: THE UNDERLYING KEY TO YOUR SUCCESS

"Press on. Nothing can take the place of persistence. Talent will not; the world is full of unsuccessful people with talent. Genius will not; unrewarded genius is almost a proverb. Education alone will not; the world is full of educated derelicts. Persistence and determination alone are omnipotent."
Calvin Coolidge

If there is one "secret" to success, it is undoubtedly determination. Determination is the one quality that guarantees the effectiveness of every strategy presented in this book. When applied alongside dynamic action, it is the one trait that makes your wall smashing skills invincible. You can rest assured that you will not fail for long when you apply the power of determination. With determination, even the dreams you once considered to be impossible can become real.

Ponder for a moment over the ancient fable of the tortoise and the hare. Who would have ever thought the tortoise would defeat the hare in a race? After all, the hare had every conceivable advantage over the tortoise except one—determination. But that one quality proved to be the only advantage that the tortoise needed to win the race. It did not matter that the hare had more speed and talent than the tortoise. Determination alone proved to be the most valuable asset.

And so it is with all of life. You can be gifted with talent, time, education, support, and money, but if you lack the determination to apply these assets, then you are destined to fail. The achievement of your dreams basically boils down to creating a burning sense of determination that pulsates throughout your veins and drives you forward on your journey through your dynamic zone.

THE DECISION

The best way to tell if you are determined is whether or not you can make a courageous decision to plunge ahead while you are in the midst of a crisis. There is simply no greater way to test your determination. Take a moment and ask yourself the following questions:

⇒ Can I keep plugging away even if I have to go through twenty-five "No's" to get a "Yes?"

⇒ Can I bounce back from the tragic death of a loved one?

⇒ Can I continue to pursue my personal goals even if the love of my life abandons me?

⇒ Can I maintain a positive attitude toward all of humanity even if a certain individual commits a terrible crime against my family?

⇒ Can I continue to have fun even if I lose every time that I play the game?

If you can honestly answer "yes" to these types of questions, then you are well on your way to creating a burning sense of determination within yourself. Even if you answered "No" to many of these questions, you can still learn to be determined.

One such example of a person who learned to be determined is a man named Mark Victor Hansen. Mark was a successful executive in the geodesic dome business until the first Arab oil embargo occurred and made it impossible for him to get the materials he needed to continue building domes. Suddenly, Mark found himself in court declaring bankruptcy. At one moment, he was on top of the world and the next moment, he felt as though he had lost it all. Walls surrounded him on every side.

At that point in his life, Hansen was faced with a decision. He could either choose to adopt an attitude of determination and step back into his dynamic zone to regain his fortune or he could settle for a low-paying job and compromise his entrepreneurial dreams. For a while,

Mark slept excessively, moped around, and basically, pitied himself. He even accepted a job that consisted of unloading toilet paper from a railroad car. Mark truly felt as though he had hit rock bottom.

Fortunately for Mark, he realized that since he had already hit rock bottom, the only way he could go was up. Wisely, he made a decision to use his determination to rise up from his despair and to pursue his entrepreneurial dreams once again. From that point, Mark never looked back. He has since regained his wealth and become a prominent entrepreneur, speaker, and co-author of the best-selling *Chicken Soup for the Soul* series.

The success of Mark Victor Hansen can be traced back to the decisions that he made during the days, weeks, and months that followed his bankruptcy. Instead of permanently retreating into his comfort zone, Mark slowly resolved to read positive books, spend time with positive people, and learn more about business success. Eventually, he decided that one failure was not going to cause him to be a failure in his life. From there, he proceeded to create a dynamic reality for himself.

Likewise, you create your personal destiny during your most intense moments of crisis, when you are filled with fear. The decisions you make when you are down and out create the kind of person you become. When you feel as though you have lost it all, you must somehow find the courage to make a decision to continue pursing your dreams.

> *Make sure you never fail the last time you do something!*

In order to make sure that you have enough courage to make a committed decision when the time calls for it, you must strengthen your decision-making muscles. Begin by making small decisions and work your way up to larger decisions. You can initiate this process by doing something as simple as making a firm decision as to what clothes you will wear tomorrow. Lay tomorrow's clothes out before you go to bed, and when you wake up, stick to your decision regardless of what happens in the meantime. You can even expand upon this exercise and begin to decide in advance exactly when you will do certain chores around your house, whom you will call on the phone, and what you will prepare for dinner. The key is to teach yourself how to make firm decisions and how to stick to them regardless of the present circumstances.

Once you create a strong foundation of decision-making habits, you will more easily be able to make a committed decision over a much more important issue like getting married, changing careers, or having children. The key, once again, is to start where you are. If you have trouble deciding what to wear or what you want to eat, then you will certainly have trouble deciding whether or not you should accept a job in a different state, buy a particular house, or run for public office.

A real decision is not an option! A decision is *a definite commitment to produce a certain result.* Whether or not you take committed action toward your objective is the only true test of an authentic decision. Giving up on a decision during challenging times only indicates that it never was a real decision in the first place. Real decisions remain standing when all the dust and smoke are cleared from the battlefield.

I personally know of an athlete who made a real decision while she was still a youngster in high school. She decided that after she graduated from college, she was going to play on the Olympic volleyball team. It didn't matter that she was only five foot three inches tall and considered significantly too short to play at that level. Her decision was final. There was no turning back.

In the years to follow, she trained diligently and excelled at volleyball throughout high school. Despite her success in high school, she did not receive any type of athletic scholarship. In fact, several college coaches blatantly told her that she didn't even have a chance of making a good collegiate volleyball team, lead alone the Olympic team. Instead of giving up on her dream and taking the easy way out, she chose to focus on her decision to play on the Olympic volleyball team. As a result of her determination, she not only "walked on" and made a highly regarded collegiate volleyball team, but she also cracked the starting lineup as a freshman. During each of her four years in college, she led her team to national championship contention.

As her senior year in college came to a close, she realized that it was now time to make her dream come true. Her next step was to attend an Olympic tryout. After driving hundreds of miles to the tryout and giving 100% of her efforts, the coaches told her exactly what she had heard all along. They said that she was a great volleyball player, but that she was too short to be selected for the team. She felt devastated! However, she still held fast to her decision and she continued to work on improving her volleyball skills. She knew that there was still one more tryout that she could attend—one more chance to achieve her dream.

The only problem was that the tryout was being held clear across the country and she did not have enough money to purchase an airline ticket. After all, her college tuition was very expensive and she was already tens of thousands of dollars in debt. To further complicate matters, her friends and family urged her to give up on her dream. They told her not to waste her money just to get "heartbroken" again. They told her that her actions were in vain and that she was being ridiculous.

Nonetheless, her decision was final and no one could stop her from getting to that tryout.

So, with no support and no money, she decided to use a credit card to finance the expenses involved with her trip across the country. On the day that her flight was scheduled to depart, a major winter storm blanketed the highways with ice and snow. There were wrecks everywhere. Radio stations were urging people to stay off the roads. But this young woman would not be denied. Although it took her over four hours to get to the airport, she managed to arrive before her flight was scheduled to leave.

But to her astonishment, she discovered that all of the departing flights were put on delay because of the wicked storm. Worse yet, there was no indication of any kind as to when her flight would receive permission to take off. Instantly, she began to panic. She wondered if she would even get to her tryout on time. She felt totally helpless. All she could do is put her head down and pray that the storm would soon subside.

As fate would have it, the weather cleared up after a few hours and she was finally permitted to board the plane. Fortunately, in her planning, she allotted some extra time for delays. As a result, she still had enough time to get to the tryout before it started. However, when the plane landed, she ran down to the baggage claims area and waited for her luggage. After quite some time, she discovered that all of her luggage had been lost. By this point, she was really pressed to get to the gymnasium on time.

Courageously, she left all of her luggage behind and quickly hopped into a cab. When she told the cab driver where she wanted to go, he informed her that the gymnasium was about a fifty minute drive from the airport—thirty minutes longer than she had originally planned. Tears began to stream down her face. She felt as though her entire world was crumbling upon her. She realized that she was in very serious danger of missing part of the tryout. Fortunately, the driver felt her desperation and he responded by doing everything in his power to get her there on time.

Amazingly, she arrived at the gymnasium six minutes before it was scheduled to start. She ran out of the cab, registered herself at the front office, and proceeded to borrow some clothes from a few girls that she had never met. Finally, she was prepared to play. And play she did! She was awesome! But to her dismay, she was once again rejected on account of her height.

Several years later, I spoke with this woman. With passion in her eyes, she convincingly told me that she did not regret her decision to become a member of the Olympic team. Even though she didn't make the team, she was still extremely proud of herself. I could literally feel her satisfaction and joy as I spoke with her. Although she was deeply hurt by what she felt was an obvious injustice, she told me, "The pain I felt from not making the team was nothing compared to the pain I would have felt if I didn't pursue my dream." She went on to say, "I didn't care if the whole world was against me. I made a decision and no one could have stopped me from pursuing its attainment.

To this day, she is still paying on her credit card that financed the pursuit of her dream. Frankly, she wouldn't have it any other way. Although she failed to achieve her dream, she can look back and say, "I gave it everything I had." She held fast to her decision. As a result, she is now at peace with herself. She is satisfied that she did everything in her power to make her dream come true. And as long as she continues to pursue her dreams, she will forever remain at peace with herself.

People who make firm decisions to pursue their dreams despite the walls that are in their way rarely, if ever, regret their decision. Test this theory out for yourself. Go up to someone and ask her what was the easiest thing that she ever did. You will find that this person will have a hard time answering you. Next, ask the person what was the hardest thing she ever did and she will tell you a long joyful story about the obstacles she overcame along her journey. It will be apparent to you that this person is very proud of her story and wouldn't trade it for anything.

> *Deciding does not guarantee success,*
> *but NOT deciding guarantees failure.*

The worst mistake you could possibly make is to decline the opportunity to make a firm decision. Use your courage to make an important decision. As long as your decision does not harm you or anyone else, the decision cannot be wrong. Oftentimes, one decision is no better than any other decision, only different.

Steven Spielberg made a decision while he was still in his teens that he would make movies. At the age of seventeen, he took massive action upon his decision. Without permission, he dressed up in a suit and tie and proceeded to occupy a desk in an empty room at Universal Studios. From there, he began to learn all about the "ins and outs" of the film business. The rest is history. Steven Spielberg is now considered to be one of the greatest filmmakers of all-time. He is responsible for creating *E.T. the Extra-Terrestrial*, *Indiana Jones and the Last Crusade*, *Jurassic Park*, and many other blockbuster movies.

All of the world's peak performers, outstanding athletes, and great leaders can trace their success back to the time when they made a definite decision in their life. Consider how the decisions of the following people have impacted our world:

- ◆ Abraham Lincoln made a *decision* to help America to grow, change, and improve by abolishing slavery.
- ◆ Mahatma Gandhi made a *decision* to free the Indian people from British control.
- ◆ Martin Luther King Jr. made a *decision* to obtain civil rights for all people in the United States.

Would you be where you are today had it not been for the decisions made by these courageous souls? Isn't it true that all great achievements are first marked by a firm decision? Therefore, use your decision-making ability to forecast your future accomplishments. Then, all that you will have left is the actual journey to unite with the type of future that you have decided upon.

Some people argue that there are actually two separate decisions involved in a real decision. First, there is the decision to achieve a specific desired outcome. Second, there is the decision to actually take the necessary actions required to achieve the desired outcome. Anyone can make the first decision, but only a courageous person can make the second decision.

For instance, many people buy nonfiction books with the intent to gain knowledge that they can apply to their life. Their first decision is great, but the problem occurs with their second decision. Research has indicated that only one out of ten people will read a nonfiction book past the first chapter. In this case, 90% of the people fail to commit to the decision. Remember, a decision is not a true decision unless it is carried out to the end.

THE "TRY" MENTALITY IS NOT ENOUGH TO ACHIEVE YOUR DREAMS

As you begin to make pivotal decisions in your life, you will soon realize that there will not be room for a "try" mentality. Trying to do something is not the same as doing something. *Trying* and *doing* have two totally different meanings. When you *try* to do something, you are merely going through the motions without seriously committing yourself to achieve a certain objective. On the other hand, when you *do* something, you give 100% of your effort to attain your desired result.

Trying presupposes that you will fail.

Let's suppose you are a chef. Would you try to make your famous German chocolate cake or would you simply make it? What would you do if you wanted to pick up a fifty dollar bill lying in the middle of a sidewalk? Would you bend over and pick up the fifty dollar bill or would you try to pick it up? Picking something up is totally different from trying to pick something up.

Trying to do something is nothing more than a fancy excuse to disguise a lack of effort. When you say that you are going to try something, your mind immediately associates the word "try" to something that is destined to fail. As a result, it becomes impossible for you to give your best effort. After all, why would your mind allow you to give 100% of your effort to something that isn't going to work anyway? Only when you commit to *doing* something, will your mind allow you to give 100% of your effort.

I have personally taught people of all ages to water-ski. The most successful beginners are the ones who jump into the water and say, "I will do this!" They may fall a great number of times, but their attitude of certainty eventually allows them to learn how to water-ski. On the other hand, there are other beginners who jump into the water and try to water-ski. They are the ones who half-heartedly go through the motions once or twice and then say, "Oh well, I tried. I guess I'm not meant to do this." These people are the ones who are not committed to water-skiing. They merely go through the motions to give others the impression that they did their best.

In the case of water-skiing and certain other activities, it is perfectly fine for you to perform at a very average level. You do not have to be the absolute best in everything. You don't even have to give 100% of your effort toward everything that you do. There is absolutely nothing wrong with taking a casual walk, playing an easy game of basketball, or taking a relaxing fishing trip.

But in the case of your dreams, it is not enough to merely try. Dreams are challenging and they require 100% of your effort. A "try" mentality is not enough to achieve your dreams!

GIVE 100% OF YOUR EFFORT TO THE THINGS THAT ARE MOST IMPORTANT TO YOU

Your dreams are the most precious commodities that you possess as a human being. It only stands to reason that you should give 100% of your effort toward smashing the walls that are preventing you from achieving them. Every time you take action upon your walls, you inch closer and closer to achieving your dreams. Each action that you take builds upon your foundation of previous actions and simultaneously weakens the wall that you are facing.

Unfortunately, there will still be times when you give 100% of your effort and it will not be enough. For instance, is the runner-up in Olympic diving a loser? Does it mean that she didn't give 100% of her effort? Of course not! As long as you can go to sleep at night knowing that you did your best, there is nothing more you could ask of yourself. Even if you "lose" while giving 100%, you still win because giving 100% of your effort is all that is important anyway.

> ### *"Throw your heart over the bar and your body will follow."*
> Norman Vincent Peale

Whatever dream you discover within yourself, pursue it with passion. Don't hold anything back. Today is all that you have. Make the most of it! Remember the words of George Bernard Shaw,

> I want to be thoroughly used up when I die. For the harder I work the more I live. I rejoice in life for its own sake. Life is no brief candle to me. It's a sort of splendid torch which I've got to hold up for the moment and I want to make it burn as brightly as possible before handing it on to future generations.

What a noble way to die! There are few sins greater than the sin of dying without ever having pursued your dreams. To avoid committing this mortal sin, go out and give 100% of your effort toward the things that are most important to you.

ENERGY

One of the greatest benefits about giving 100% of your effort is the energy that you will generate in the process. By taking committed action, your body will naturally supply you with a rush of adrenaline which will give you the energy that you need to perform at your best.

Have you ever felt a bit sluggish after a long day and found yourself considering the possibility of skipping your daily exercise routine? Let's suppose that despite the temptation to skip your workout, you decide to exercise anyway. In this case, you probably amazed yourself with all the energy you accessed once you began your workout. It's almost as if the very process of taking action summoned the appropriate amount of energy into your life.

> ## *"Do the thing and you will have the power."*
> Ralph Waldo Emerson

Energy has a way of rising to the call of duty. It rushes to your aid as soon as you face your fear and initiate some type of action. The moment you stretch yourself into your dynamic zone, your body will naturally give you the energy that you need to do your best.

PAYING THE PRICE

The only way you can ever achieve your dreams is if you are willing to pay the price. Smashing your walls of fear is hard work! You are going to feel dumb, embarrassed, rejected, and exhausted at times. Furthermore, there are no discounts, no coupons, no bargains, and no sales of any kind in wall smashing. You will never pay anything but full price. The truth is, if your dream is worthwhile, then you can count on the process of wall smashing to be hard.

> *Everyone must pay a price. Would you rather pay the price for a life of determination or a life of mediocrity?*

There is no way to determine how long it will take, how many obstacles you must overcome, or how much fear you must endure before you achieve your dreams. The only meaningful decision you can make is to commit yourself to taking action until you achieve the results you are seeking. As long as your dream is worth it, it should not matter how long it takes. After all, you are doing what you have to do—you are following your heart's desire.

Along your journey, you will be knocked down many times. People will tell you to quit. Your walls will seem insurmountable. You will feel as though you have exhausted every possibility. At these points, there is only one logical question to ask yourself: "Will I get back on my feet?" True success is getting back on your feet one more time after you fall.

> ## *"The glory is not in never failing, but in rising every time you fail."*
> Chinese proverb

The sport of amateur wrestling provides a great example of this type of resiliency. Each year, thousands of young children join this challenging sport without realizing just how tough it is both physically and mentally. Many of them are overwhelmed from the physical exertion that the sport requires. Others discover that they are afraid to wrestle an opponent all by themselves in front of many fans. To make matters worse, most of the beginners lose the majority of their matches. A high percentage of the wrestlers end their initial season feeling very discouraged, to say the least.

As a result of all the losses they suffered, their fear of wrestling all by themselves, and the intense physical and mental disciplines involved, there is usually a very noticeable decline in the number of wrestlers who return for a second season. Usually, it is only the most talented children who end up returning. The other children who quit usually do so because they are not willing to pay the price to be successful in this sport. Instead, they opt for a sport that is less physically and mentally demanding, a sport where they can rely on other team members.

Along with the talented children who return for a second wrestling season, there is usually a handful of less talented children who also return. Out of this small group of less talented wrestlers, there is usually one or two children who lost every single match in their rookie season. They were the ones that were "sure bets" to give up on wrestling. Yet, for some mysterious reason, they returned. These are the special children who love the sport and who are willing to pay the price to be successful. They realize that the law of averages guarantees that sooner or later, they will begin to win some matches.

"Dreams do come true...You can have anything in life if you will sacrifice everything else for it."
Sir James Barrie

Oftentimes, it takes these special wrestlers several years of consistently losing all of their matches until they finally win a match. Nevertheless, little by little, they transform themselves into skilled wrestlers. By the time they reach high school, many of these wrestlers become highly regarded athletes. Some even contend for various wrestling awards in their district, region, or state. It's almost as if these wrestlers had to first lose a certain number of matches before they earned the privilege of winning. More important than the fact that they learned how to win is the fact that they learned how to pay the price to achieve something that was special to them.

Sports are great activities for children and adults alike, but there is much more to life than just sports. A truly dynamic life cannot be attained solely from athletic pursuits. Athletes must learn to apply the same determination that they use in sports to the other areas of their lives. Only then will they feel genuinely fulfilled.

Joe was one of those rare people who had very little natural athletic ability, yet possessed a huge amount of determination. As a result of his determination, he molded himself into a skilled athlete in several sports. Then, several years after his participation in sports, he had a dream of opening his own consulting firm. He knew it would be tough, yet he also knew that he had what it took to make it work. During this pivotal time in his life, he reminisced about how much hard work and determination it took for him to succeed in sports. As a result, Joe decided to transfer that same kind of determination into the business world.

Courageously, Joe resigned from a well-paying job in exchange for the opportunity to chase his dream. Even though his first eight bids were rejected, Joe continued to pay the price. He was determined to do whatever it took to create the kind of company he dreamed of creating. It did not matter how many "No's" he got in the process. Joe knew that the "Yeses" were on the way. After a few more rejections and some more growing, changing, and improving, Joe finally landed his first contract and then his second, and then his third, and so forth. Joe's choice to be determined ended up making him more money in his first two years in his own business than he would have made in five years had he stayed at his previous job. In addition, he thoroughly enjoyed his journey and, most importantly, he became a more dynamic person in the process. Joe owes a lot of his success to the determination that he first learned in sports.

"Where there is a will, there is a way."
An old wise man

The great French philosopher Voltaire is another example of someone who had to pay a great price as he pursued his dream of spreading his philosophy throughout the land. Along his journey, he was thrown into jail, exiled, and publicly humiliated while every one of his books was suppressed by the church and state. All of this occurred because the king and the pope did not approve of his philosophy. In the midst of all the adversity, it would have been easy for Voltaire to quit.

Instead, Voltaire chose to be determined. He willingly accepted the humiliation and abuse that were dished out by his compatriots. Little by little, his philosophy spread until it eventually pervaded all of his society. There even came a time when kings and queens hung on his every word. As a result of his determination and resiliency, Voltaire allowed himself to become one of the most influential writers to ever walk the face of the Earth.

People with Voltaire's determination do not ask, "How long will it take to smash this wall?" Instead, they realize that they must persistently pursue their dreams regardless of how long it takes. That's not to say that they do not set specific goals with plans to achieve them, it only means that if their initial plan does not work, then they discover a plan that does work. They do not care how long it takes to smash their walls because they know in their heart that they are smashing the right walls.

> *"When the dream is big enough, the facts don't count."*
> Dexter Yager

Rare is the person who is determined enough to pay whatever price it takes to achieve her dream. This person should never be judged by the statistics for average people. Determination always outperforms statistics. If a mother of three children is sincerely *determined* to find a way to return to college and get her doctorate degree, then she cannot be accurately compared to another mother of three children who is merely *interested* in getting her doctorate degree. The reason is quite simple. The first mother is not average. Her determination qualifies her as an exceptional human being. Mere statistics do not apply for her.

The problem with statistics is that they are only valid for the average person. My business experiences have proven this to me time and time again. I have repeatedly obtained business contracts in which my statistical chance of receiving them was less than 1 out of 100. Why is this so? The answer is simple. I was much more determined than were my fellow business colleagues. My passion and determination melted the hearts of those with the power to give me the contract I wanted. Consequently, the standard statistics proved to be inaccurate for me.

USE YOUR ANGER FROM REJECTION TO FUEL YOUR DETERMINATION

Regardless of how much action you take or how determined you are, there will still be times when you will be rejected. Rejection is a natural part of life that you must learn to accept, especially if you choose to live dynamically. There is simply no way to avoid it. The next best thing is to learn to use it to your advantage. Use it as an opportunity to prove your strength and resiliency both to yourself and to those who rejected you. Develop an attitude like, "I'll show you that it was a big mistake to reject me!" Use your anger to fuel your determination. Get stronger with every rejection that you encounter. This will transform your rejections into a catalyst for your success.

Lee Iacocca is a prime example of a person who used rejection to fuel his determination. On July 13, 1978, he was fired from Ford Motor Company after nearly 32 years of loyal service. As a result, Lee became extremely angry and wanted to prove to Ford the magnitude of their mistake. So, on October 30, 1978, Lee accepted the position of president for Chrysler Corporation, a rival of Ford Motor Company.

The amazing part of Iacocca's story is that on the same day that he accepted the position, Chrysler reported its largest quarterly loss in history. It was obvious to the "experts" that Chrysler was on the verge of bankruptcy. Iacocca became the brunt of jokes all across the nation. Many people openly called him a fool for even dreaming that he could possibly turn Chrysler around. Nonetheless, Lee had faith in his ability to make Chrysler a success.

Iacocca knew that the only way to save Chrysler was to make massive changes. He began by instituting drastic reform in both the structure and the personnel of the company. From there, he went to work on the attitudes of the remaining people. Lee understood that it was necessary for all the employees of Chrysler to believe in themselves, to believe in him, and to believe in the potential of the company. In less than five years, the Chrysler Corporation announced first quarter earnings of $172.1 million—its largest quarterly profit in history. Lee Iacocca's leadership brought about a modern-day miracle.

"Chrysler will be the biggest and the best."
Lee Iacocca

It is safe to say that Chrysler would not exist today was it not for the anger that Lee Iacocca used to fuel his determination. Fortunately, you can use the same formula to produce measurable results in your own life as well. Your anger can easily serve as a strong source of motivation in your efforts to achieve your dreams. The key is to develop enough discipline within yourself that you don't release your anger in ineffective ways like taking revenge on someone, sitting around pouting, gossiping to your friends about how you have been wronged, or worst of all—quitting.

> *Your greatest growth usually occurs when you are hurting the most.*

The famous rock band, the Beatles, is a great example of how a group of people used their anger from being rejected to ignite their determination. After hundreds and thousands of hours of preparing and refining their music, several record companies initially declined an opportunity to record their songs. Although the members of the band felt personally rejected and angry, they chose to use their emotional energy as added fuel to find a record company who was willing to record their music. Deep down, the Beatles wanted to prove to the world the magnitude of mistake that those original record companies made when they refused to record their music. As you know, the Beatles did just that. Eventually, they became one of the most popular bands in history.

Imagine for a moment how many other bands gave up when they encountered rejection. Instead of using rejection as a springboard to greater success, they chose to quit. In truth, some of those bands who misused their anger and quit were quite likely even more talented than the Beatles; they only lacked an equivalent amount of determination.

Put yourself in a similar situation. Wouldn't you be angry if someone rejected your "masterpiece" after you spent eight, ten, or twelve hours a day for many years writing, composing, painting, or drawing it? Of course you would! The only question is, "What would you do with your anger?" You could use your anger as a reason to quit or you could use it as a reason to propel yourself to even greater heights. The choice is yours!

DETERMINATION + CHANGE = PEACE OF MIND

If you are determined to achieve a worthwhile goal and you are willing to make some changes in the process, then you will create peace of mind for yourself. Peace of mind is a blissful feeling that you get when you know that you are living your life in the right way. Peace of mind occurs when you can look upon your life and say, "Even if this was my last day on Earth, I still wouldn't live it any differently."

Although this strategy sounds simple, you must remember that the basis of this principle involves change and change is something that most people resist. But, without the willingness to change, you would be no different from a fly that repeatedly bounces itself off the glass of a closed window even though there is an open door across the room. Although a fly may be determined, it must change its actions if it is to successfully get outside.

Taking the same ineffective actions over and over is a form of insanity. If you already know that something is not working, what sense does it make to continue to duplicate your actions? Instead, you should take action, notice what's not working, and make the necessary changes. You can have all the determination in the world, but if you are not open-minded enough to change your ineffective actions, then you will never truly experience peace of mind.

Suppose you wanted to be the most efficient person in math, but you refused to use a calculator or computer. In this case, you would never surpass the efficiency of someone who does. The same is true if you wanted to drive five hundred miles to the beach for a vacation. Could you truly have peace of mind that you will arrive at your destination if you were not willing to stop for gas along the way? No! Peace of mind will continue to elude you until you finally incorporate a willingness to change into your determined actions.

Even if you have been going in the wrong direction all of your life. You still have the ability to make a change and go in the right direction. Think of your life as an airplane that is off-course 90% of the time. If the pilot keeps correcting her errors in direction, then she will eventually arrive at her desired destination. But if the pilot is stubborn and unwilling to make the necessary changes, then she will never reach her destination. Similarly, if you want to reach your destination of peace of mind, then you must have the wisdom to make the necessary changes to your thoughts and your behaviors.

The worst thing that you can do when you get off-course in your journey through life is to....RETREAT!

CHAPTER 12

RETREAT: THE TRUTH ABOUT WHY YOU ARE TEMPTED TO GIVE UP

"The world breaks everyone and afterward many are strong at the broken places."
Ernest Hemingway

By this point in the book, you have surely grown to the level where you are now prepared to receive the absolute truth about wall smashing. You deserve to know what you are getting yourself into by becoming a wall smasher. This chapter will not pull any punches and nothing will be held back. Nor will any information be sugar-coated or intentionally left out. Prepare yourself to receive the hard facts about what it takes to achieve your dreams.

This chapter was intentionally placed toward the end of the book so that you would be better prepared to handle it. Up to this point, most of this book has been written to present you with the benefits of wall smashing. However, it is now time to make you aware of the pitfalls as well.

STAY IN YOUR COMFORT ZONE UNTIL YOU HAVE FINISHED READING THIS CHAPTER!!!

As of now, you are probably not quite ready to leave your comfort zone. That's right! You should stay in your comfort zone until you have finished reading this chapter. Maybe you are a person who has spent your entire life in your comfort zone. If this is the case, I congratulate you. Although this may sound contradictory to the entire theme of this book, you are nonetheless very intelligent for making this particular decision. By staying in your comfort zone, you have saved yourself from experiencing tremendous pain, pain that you were not prepared to endure. Stepping into your dynamic zone without realizing the actual ramifications could generate enough pain to cause you to retreat into your comfort zone forever.

A retreat occurs when you quit taking action upon a certain wall in your life. The most common reason for a retreat is because you expected your dynamic zone to be easy and you found out that it wasn't. Unfortunately, many motivational speakers and authors paint too nice of a picture of your dynamic zone. They make it out to be a place where everything goes smoothly as long as you follow their "secret success formula." Well, I am here to tell you that your dynamic zone is not easy! Your dynamic zone is actually the most challenging place in the whole universe. If you enter your dynamic zone expecting it to be easy, then you will only be disappointed and sink further into your comfort zone. That's why you must understand the complications of your dynamic zone before you decide to pursue your dreams.

LIFE IS HARD

The first thing you need to understand is that life is hard! Life is especially hard if you decide to become a dynamic wall smasher. Make no mistake about it, you will be overwhelmed at times. Other times, you will be disappointed. The people who love you the most will also hurt you the most. On top of that, you will fail repeatedly before you ever achieve a significant level of progress. Basically, your patience, determination, compassion, resiliency, and positive attitude will all be pushed well beyond their limits.

Soon, you will become a believer in Murphy's Law—whatever can go wrong will go wrong and it will happen at the worst possible moment. You will not get the job you desperately need, even though you were interviewed on four separate occasions. When you decide to get back together with your spouse whom you are separated from, you will discover that your spouse has already found someone else and is no longer interested in you. As soon as you fire your long-time therapist, you will encounter your greatest psychological challenge. When you quit your job of ten years to open your own business, you won't even get one customer to walk in your door on opening day.

These types of situations and experiences are the real truth about life. Do not believe the pretty picture that others paint for you. Achieving your dreams is an ugly process. Your worst nightmares won't even prepare you for the roadblocks that lie ahead.

> *Circumstances will get worse*
> *before they get better!!!*

Maybe your dream is to raise six children, write a best-selling book, create a multimillion dollar company, become governor of your state, or win a national championship. Whatever your dream is, you can be sure that life will be hard on you. Life will eat you up. It will step on you and squash you like a grape. Life will kick your butt. The following list will provide you with an accurate description of the types of adversity that you will likely have to endure.

- Your family and friends will not support you. They will urge you to quit. Some will curse you and intentionally hurt you as well.

- You may or may not go bankrupt, but you will undoubtedly feel as though you have gone bankrupt five times.

- Statistics will tell you that it is highly unlikely for you to achieve your dream.

- When you think your troubles are over, your situation will get worse than you ever imagined.

- You will be severely criticized.

- You will go backward before you are permitted to go forward. And when you finally do go forward, you will be knocked backward further than when you started.

Welcome to life! As you can see, stepping into your dynamic zone to become a wall smasher is not easy. Walls are everywhere. And your walls will not budge an inch. Furthermore, life is totally unfair.

Consider Hurricane Andrew. Was it fair to the people who lived in Homestead, Florida to lose their cars, their homes, their clothes, and their memorabilia? Did all those people really deserve to experience such a disaster? Was it fair to them? How about the animal kingdom: Is it fair to zebras when lions eat them? Consider the relationship between human beings and animals. Is it really fair for human beings to hunt game animals and to butcher farm animals? What did they ever do to us? Ponder for a moment about the area of employment. Was it really fair that the boss's brother's best friend got the promotion over you? I doubt it! But life is not fair and you should not expect it to be.

Drill this fact into your head. Life is not fair! Why do you continue to believe that life is fair when you have already encountered hundreds of situations in your life that have proved the contrary to be true? Wake up and understand that when you step into your dynamic zone, you will be treated unfairly. In fact, unfairly is not a strong enough word. What I mean to say is that when you step into your dynamic zone, it will seem as if the entire world is against you. Don't expect to be spared any pain.

Even if you are the ultimate role model of society, life does not care. It will still knock you down. You have no choice in the matter. The only thing fair about life is that everyone gets knocked down. Yes, everyone! There are no exceptions. Nobody is exempt from life's thrashing.

Amidst all of this grim truth about wall smashing, there really does exist one genuine fundamental "secret" that will allow you to defy the odds and to achieve your greatest dreams. Don't get too excited because you already know this "secret." The secret happens to be long, hard work.

OVERWHELM

Who knows? Maybe you are one of the few people who are willing to work really hard in pursuit of your dreams. Even if this is the case, you probably still find yourself doing too many things at once. This is a sign that you are neglecting to work smart before you work hard. Instead of taking smart, small, consistent actions, you probably choose to take illogical, exhausting, random actions. As a result, you end up feeling overwhelmed, which is the first of the four major reasons that will tempt you to retreat into your comfort zone.

Take a moment and really imagine how silly it would be to expect to accomplish any of the following achievements in the stated amount of time:

∇ Grow a harvest in a week
∇ Win the state championship after only a few practices
∇ Write a book in one day
∇ Run a marathon after being physically inactive for seven years

∇ Teach your children everything about sex during one weekend visit
∇ Build a skyscraper without making any plans
∇ Become a celebrity after one performance
∇ Lose twenty pounds in a day

Although these examples are ridiculous, you probably expect to produce equivalent results in certain areas of your life. Whether you realize it or not, you probably step into your dynamic zone and expect miracles to happen instantly. Well, they don't! The only miracle that you are going to create is the one that results from your own hard work. Ludicrous expectations will sink your ship faster than you can jump overboard.

Aiming too high all at once causes your mind to send your body false signals of fatigue. Your mind is programmed to discourage you from doing anything it deems to be impossible. It will only support you when it believes that it can reasonably achieve what you demand of it.

Suppose you want to do one hundred pushups. By focusing on doing chunks of ten pushups at a time, you will increase your chances of successfully completing your goal. In this case, your mind believes that you can do what you ask of it. After all, ten pushups is not an unreasonable number of pushups. On the other hand, if you tell your mind that you must do all one hundred pushups during one interval, your mind would sound an alarm and go into a state of overwhelm. This would actually weaken your physical muscles. As a result, your goal would become much more difficult to achieve.

Your mind will always urge you to do nothing before it allows you to act upon too many things at once. It will always seek the path that it perceives to lead to the most pleasure. And you can rest assured that your mind does not associate overwhelm with pleasure. In fact, your mind will "shut down" when it feels you are putting too many painful demands on it.

The challenge with living is that lifetimes are so short, yet we have so much that we want to do. The irony is that we usually become overwhelmed and end up doing nothing. This is why it is wise to focus your power upon taking one action at a time.

As you know, there are exceptions to every rule. Perhaps you know someone who has accomplished a wide variety of goals "overnight." Although this is possible, it is a dangerous mindset to adopt. There is no need for you to set out on an obsessive rampage to bull your way to your dreams. The purpose of life is not so much for achievement, but rather for the enjoyment that accompanies your journey. Life is about progress, not destination. The wisest wall smasher is always the one who enjoys the process.

Another way that you can be overwhelmed is to have all of your emotions riding on the outcome of any single event. Suppose you have been searching for the ideal home to buy for your family. Finally, you come upon your "dream house." Everything is perfect and you desperately want to purchase it. The only problem is that several other families also want to buy the house. All you can do is submit your bid and wait to see if it is chosen.

A situation like this can be dangerous if you have all of your emotions riding on the attainment of this particular house. In this case, you will feel overwhelmed long before you even submit your bid. Your thinking will become blurred and you will not be capable of seeing the many alternatives that you have. You will be unable to make the best possible decision for your family.

The best way to guard against experiencing overwhelm is to prepare yourself for the fact that life is hard and that living dynamically is incredibly hard. Having unreasonable expectations about everything unfolding perfectly will only give you a rude awakening when you finally encounter reality.

For instance, a young man once accepted a door-to-door sales position. He expected everyone to be friendly and to buy something from him. Unfortunately, he ended up feeling overwhelmed because he was not prepared for the truth of door-to-door sales. He found out that he was not only denied sales, but he was also ignored, verbally abused, and outright rejected. The truth is that he could have been better prepared if he were not convinced that door-to-door selling would be easy.

When you do not prepare for something to be difficult, you put yourself in a dangerous position. Suddenly, you have a much greater tendency to fall back into your old habits regardless of how ineffective they may be. Your mind always chooses the most familiar way to deal with overwhelm even if that means for you to act in some irrational or immature way. This is why many ex-smokers find themselves smoking again whenever they feel overwhelmed by a certain crisis.

The ex-smoker who reaches for a cigarette during a time of overwhelm should realize that she only needs to prepare herself better in the future. She is not a failure for cracking under pressure. Nor does this necessarily mean that she is a smoker again. She simply must realize that life is hard and that it is best to focus on doing one thing at a time.

DISAPPOINTMENT

The second major reason that will tempt you to retreat into your comfort zone is disappointment. Disappointment is the pain you feel when you realize that your expectations will never be met. This empty feeling often occurs when you abandon your plans and seek some kind of shortcut.

Look back upon your own life. Wasn't there a time when you really became excited about some "get rich quick" plan that you received in the mail? Most people, including me, certainly have. The problem is that these "opportunities" are never as easy as the brochure would have you assume and some are merely scams to get your money. In any case, you probably got your hopes up in anticipation of easily achieving your financial dreams. Unfortunately, you probably ended up feeling disappointed when things did not work out as you envisioned.

To avoid disappointing situations, you must become involved only with products, services, businesses, organizations, etc., that are in alignment with your own personal dreams. It is foolish to invest your time and money in "shortcuts" or false opportunities that are not in proper alignment with your personal dreams. Before you act on any "opportunity," first, you need to make sure that you are passionate about your undertaking. Don't waste your time sending "chain letters" through the mail if your real dream is to become a physical therapist. Pursue a dream that is meaningful to you. Then, when you get "slammed" by life, you will still have enough passion and genuine excitement to bounce back from your setbacks.

Furthermore, realize that there exists no product or service that can achieve your dreams for you. It doesn't matter if the product is priced $9.95, $99.95, or even $995.95. Although many self-improvement products are fantastic, they can only be effective if you do the necessary work. Many of these companies fail to mention that without your committed personal effort, their product or service cannot help you.

It's no wonder that the general population has become so skeptical. We are basically overwhelmed with opportunities, services, businesses, seminars, computers, books, tapes, bills, commitments, loans, obligations, warranties, mail, faxes, rebates, sales, memos, discounts, taxes and information in general. Our modern day "high-tech" society is changing at such a frantic pace that no single person could possibly stay up-to-date in even one field. We are inundated with so much information that we no longer know what to believe or whom to trust. This is why it is so tempting to believe a cunning salesperson, a sly advisor, a dishonest organization, or a deceptive special interest group when they promise you some kind of shortcut in your life. Unfortunately, these so-called "shortcuts" usually lead to disappointment.

Even if you do manage to avoid the many distractions and stay focused on your particular dream, you will still encounter disappointment along the way. The key is to never allow your feelings of disappointment to cause you to retreat into your comfort zone. Instead, simply recognize disappointment as one of the major hurdles that you must clear on your way toward achieving your dreams.

One example of a person who made a very wise decision to bounce back from disappointment is a man named Dale. Dale is a 38-year-old father who decided to pursue an undergraduate degree in accounting even though it had been twenty years since he had any formal schooling. Unfortunately, he wrongly expected the whole process to be easy. This type of attitude set himself up to feel very disappointed when his application for admission was denied. Wisely, Dale quickly realized that his expectations were only a fantasy and that the process leading to the achievement of his dream would indeed require quite a bit of work. As a result, Dale met with certain key people, wrote letters, and gathered valuable references that eventually allowed him to be accepted as a student.

In Dale's case, it would have been easy for him to retreat into his comfort zone. After all, he felt disappointed because the whole process was much more involved than he had originally expected. Fortunately, Dale was smart enough to soak up his feelings of disappointment and to struggle through his initial adversity. Dale never realized the magnitude of his decision until four years later, on graduation day, when he finally received his undergraduate degree. At that moment, he clearly understood how important it was for him to keep taking action in the face of disappointment. He realized that the long-term pain of retreat would have been much greater than the short-term pain of disappointment.

Adversity has a way of forcing you to become a stronger person. Did you know that the strongest trees are the ones that are exposed to the most treacherous weather? They are the ones that encounter the most adversity from nature. When a tree encounters high winds, heavy rains, intense heat, snow, ice, and blistering cold temperatures, it is forced either to become stronger or to die. The same is true with human beings. The one who can handle the most adversity will eventually become the strongest person.

"The greatest satisfactions come from the pursuit of the difficult, which makes men strong, rather than from the pursuit of easy things, which makes men weak."
George Romney

It is also important for you to permit your children to experience some adversity early in their lives so that they may become strong too. Give them the freedom to step into their dynamic zones and pursue their dreams. Encourage them to take part in dynamic activities such as joining clubs, participating in sports, making new friends, saving money, learning new skills, starting part-time businesses, organizing parties, planning vacations, and initiating conversations. These types of activities will expose your children to various amounts of difficulties which will better prepare them for the obstacles they will face as adults.

> *Human beings have a tremendous ability to handle much more than we are willing to admit.*

The sixteen-year-old girl who dreams about starting her own lawn care business should be encouraged to take on such a challenge. Surely, such an endeavor will give her the opportunity to encounter some early success as well as some healthy disappointment. Although she will earn some money, learn to manage her time more effectively, and learn how to delegate certain tasks, she will also encounter rude customers, people who refuse to pay, equipment that doesn't work properly, vehicle problems, and scheduling conflicts.

Her experiences will naturally make her into a better person as long as she bounces back from each of her disappointments. In fact, the more adversity that she faces, the stronger she will become. She may or may not make lawn care her career, but that is not important. The fact that she is learning to explore her dynamic zone at such an early age is one of the most valuable gifts she could ever receive. It doesn't even matter if her business fails or succeeds. As long as she gives the business 100% of her effort, she will reap a lifetime of rewards.

DISCOURAGEMENT

The third major factor that will tempt you to retreat into your comfort zone is discouragement. Even if you have somehow found a way to overcome the first two major causes of retreat, discouragement will almost certainly cause you to wonder if your dream is really worth pursuing. The reason is simple. The people whom you deeply love and respect are often the same people who will discourage you the most. Worst of all, they will discourage you at the very moments when you most need them to support you. You can rest assured that when the heat is on and you are being pushed to your limits, your loved ones will urge you to quit.

> *Let someone steal your car, your house and your money, but never let anyone steal your dreams!!!*

The reason your loved ones discourage you is not because they don't love you. Your friends and family really do love you and they truly want you to succeed, but they do not want to watch you pay the price. They don't want to see you get hurt. Therefore, it becomes much easier for them to discourage you from exploring your dynamic zone than it is for them to support you.

"Measure a man by how much opposition it takes to discourage him."
Unknown

Another reason why your loved ones will discourage you with such conviction is because they fear that when you step into your dynamic zone to pursue your dreams, you will consequently force them to step into their dynamic zones to rescue you. This, of course, would disrupt their comfortable lives.

> *Discouragement is really an opportunity for you to show the world how much courage you possess.*

Furthermore, when you do something dynamic and "rock the boat," you make those who are closest to you very uncomfortable. You force them to change the way that they think about you and the way that they interact with you. Since most people resist change with every fiber of their being, it becomes easier for your loved ones to discourage you than to change their beliefs about you.

FAILURE 101: YOUR FIRST SERIES OF TESTS FROM LIFE

Once you learn to handle overwhelm, disappointment, and discouragement, you will encounter failure, which is the fourth major reason that will tempt you to retreat into your comfort zone. Before you are permitted to achieve your dream, you must first go through a whole series of tests from life itself to see whether or not you are worthy. The first series of tests will come soon after you discover your dream and begin taking action toward its achievement. In order to pass these tests, you must bounce back from your failures and continue your quest to your dreams.

As you know, smashing your walls and achieving your dreams is not easy! It will surely be the most difficult thing you will ever do. The most precious things in life are always the most challenging. They are saved for those special souls who are willing to pay the astronomically high price that is required to receive them. Dreams could not exist if they were easy. They would be esteemed too lightly. This is why you *need* failure in your life.

"Success is failure turned inside out."
Bradley Tyler

Look at the lives of many millionaires and you will notice that many of them have gone bankrupt at least once before they became strong enough and wise enough to succeed. Henry Ford is one of the obvious examples that comes to mind. Everyone knows that he created a massive automobile empire, but most people do not realize that he went broke five times in the process. Another prime example is Winston Churchill, the person who was most instrumental in saving the world from the terrors of Adolf Hitler and the German army. Do most people remember his success or do they focus on the fact that he failed sixth grade? The common denominator shared by all of the great men and woman in history is that they did not allow any one or more failures to stop them from achieving their dreams.

As the saying goes, "The path to success is paved with failure." Failure occurs when your actions do not produce the result that you desire. Thomas Edison once defined failure as "one more way not to do something." Failure is simply a sign that success is close at hand. After all, success is merely a numbers game. Sooner or later, your "failures" have to lead you to success.

The only variable is how long it will take you to achieve your dreams. Some people will fail five times, others will fail fifteen times, and still others will fail one hundred and fifty times. The only thing you can know for sure is that if you never fail, you will be the one who ultimately fails the most in the game of life. Life is not about perfection. It is about consistently pursuing your dreams despite any amount of failure that you encounter along the way.

In my own life, I nearly gave up my dream of becoming an entrepreneur because I had a very hard time bouncing back from even the smallest of failures. On one occasion, I distinctly remember being on the verge of quitting what has since become a lucrative gourmet coffee concession business because my brand new $3,000.00 cappuccino machine was malfunctioning and I did not know how to fix it. Since the majority of my business revolved around my cappuccino machine, I felt helpless when it stopped working. Instead of searching for the cause of the malfunction, I started beating the machine and yelling at it. From my initial reaction to the situation, you would have thought that I was a crazy man.

The only reason I didn't choose to quit right then and there was because I was out of money. It was imperative for me to find a way to get my cappuccino machine up and running so that I could make enough money to pay my bills. As a result, I swallowed my pride and began to make some phone calls to figure out how to fix it. The problem ended up being nothing more than a loose wire at a connection point. To think that my entrepreneurial dreams were almost shattered over something as insignificant as a ten-cent wire.

As a reminder to myself about the importance of persevering through times of failure, I hung a beautiful framed poster above my desk that reads, "The race is not always to the swift...But to those who keep on running." This poster reminds me that I must keep "running" even when I encounter failure.

Your failures are what give your successes meaning. Failure actually allows you to appreciate your successes. Without experiencing the pain of failure, you would have nothing to contrast your successes. Eventually, your successes would become meaningless.

> *"...every failure brings with it the seed of an*
> *equivalent success."*
> Napoleon Hill

Life knocks everyone down as a way to determine who is most qualified to achieve their dreams. That's how things work on this planet. Before life permits you to succeed, it tests you to make sure that you can first handle failure.

Collegiate freshmen are often the recipients of life's first series of tests. Many of them enter their first semester with dreams of graduating with a distinguished degree. Unfortunately, many of these students quickly give up on their dreams and change their major field of study before the end of the first semester. The reason is because their professors make their introductory classes so hard that it forces many of the students to fail or to come close to failing. This technique weeds out all of the students who are not willing to bounce back from their failures. That's why so many freshmen drop out of the more challenging fields of study and decide to pursue a field that is less challenging.

This strategy is a great way to weed out the students who are merely interested in achieving their dreams from those who are committed to achieving their dreams. A *committed* student would rise to the occasion after an initial failure and find a way to succeed. She would meet with the teacher, study differently, spend more time reading, and pay closer attention in class. An *interested* student, on the other hand, would give up after an initial failure. She would not be willing to make the necessary changes and rise to the occasion like a committed student. Instead, she would run to the dean's office, drop the class, and change her major.

The amount of failure that you can endure is probably the greatest single indicator of your level of commitment to your dream. Without a significant amount of commitment, you would not be motivated to keep taking action when times get tough. In fact, you would be no different from the collegiate freshman who runs to the dean and changes her major as soon as she realizes that her classes are hard.

"Calamity is man's true touchstone."
Francis Beaumont and John Fletcher

The way that you handle failure in your life proves whether you are a weed or a flower in the garden of life. If you prove to be a weed in the garden of life, then life will rip out your roots and throw you outside the garden until you become capable of dealing with failure. On the other hand, if you can endure life's series of tests, then you will be permitted to remain in the garden of life and grow into a beautiful flower. Life is a prudent gardener who takes considerable amounts of time to rid her garden of the invasion of any weeds. After all, weeds can ruin the rest of the garden if they are not removed.

The garden of life is symbolic of your dynamic zone. Only those who pass the tests can remain there. If you do not pass, then you are weeded out and thrown back into your comfort zone. In that respect, the first series of tests from life is a lot like a weeding process.

FAILURE 102: YOUR SECOND SERIES OF TESTS FROM LIFE

Let's suppose that you do successfully bounce back from your initial failures. In this case, you will probably be reaping some great rewards from all of the resiliency that you have displayed. Who knows, you might even consider yourself to be a skilled wall smasher. After all, it may seem as if there is nothing left to stop you from living your dreams.

Then, out of nowhere, life will begin to administer its second series of tests to you. In a moment, life will place several totally unexpected walls in your path that will cause you to lose everything you have worked so hard to attain. These tests will be many times more challenging than your original tests of failure. In fact, life's second series of tests will undoubtedly be the single-most powerful walls you have ever faced. Emotionally, you will be crushed. It will feel as though your life is over! All of your confidence will evaporate in an instant. Even if you do not end up losing everything, it will feel as though you have. Your dreams will appear to be shattered.

> *When the going gets tough,*
> *most people retreat to their comfort zone.*

At this point, you will be faced with one of the most pivotal decisions of your life. You can either retreat into your comfort zone or you can bounce back like a true champion and continue your quest for excellence. The rest of your life is at stake in this very moment. You have the power. What will you do?

If you choose to retreat into your comfort zone, then you will forever have to live with the fear of knowing that you might have stopped one step short of achieving your dreams. On the other hand, if you choose once again to plunge into your dynamic zone, then you will prove to life that you are indeed worthy of achieving your dreams. All of a sudden, people will appear out of nowhere to help you. Permissions will be granted. Contracts will be signed. Deliveries will be made. Communication will be understood and help will emerge from every direction. At this point, life will know that you are indeed worthy of living the most dynamic life imaginable.

Tony Robbins is one such person. Currently, he enjoys owning one of the greatest personal development organizations in the world— Robbins Research International. Although he has achieved many of his original dreams, he did not get to the place where he is now until he proved to life that he was worthy.

Early in his career, Robbins was smashing walls and making tremendous progress in his business. He could feel himself on the verge of living his dreams. Then, one day, as he returned home exhausted from a seminar tour, he found that one of his employees had embezzled a significant amount of money and put his company $758,000.00 in debt. Little did he know that while he was giving of himself to help others, his own financial dreams were being destroyed by someone in his own company.

"...there's no such thing as failure.
There are only results."
Tony Robbins

Despite the fact that everyone close to him, including his accountant, urged him to file for bankruptcy, Tony chose to rise to the occasion. He made a decision to take his company to a whole new level in the midst of his failures. Through the realization that failure was only another step toward the attainment of his dreams, he was able to motivate himself to take the necessary actions to turn his business around. In a short period of time, Robbins not only saved his business from bankruptcy, but he also took his company to a whole new level of success. By passing this test, he proved beyond a doubt that he was worthy of achieving his dreams. As a result, you and I can go to the bookstore and benefit from the books by Tony Robbins or we can order his other fine products by calling 1-800-445-8183.

When things are going smoothly and you are progressing at a steady rate, it is important to realize that life is only playing a trick on you. Life is setting you up so that you will feel what it is like to hit rock bottom. Hitting bottom can occur in many different ways. Maybe the passing of a federal law will cause your product to be banned from all stores. You may hit bottom if you were to discover that one of your children has been experimenting with illegal drugs. Hitting bottom might even occur if you were forced to deal with an unexpected lawsuit that has been filed against you. Whatever the case, you will feel as though you have lost everything.

The advantage of hitting bottom is that you can push off the bottom much like a swimmer would push off the bottom of a pool to propel herself to the surface. A swimmer wouldn't get nearly the same kind of momentum if she didn't use the bottom of the pool to spark her momentum upward. The same is true with your life. When you use the bottom as a springboard, you can easily launch yourself back into your dynamic zone.

If you think about it, once you hit the bottom, you cannot lose anything more. This is why so many people have gone from "rags to riches." Once they realize they have nothing left to lose, they no longer fear failure. In their minds, there is nothing left that they cannot handle. After all, they have already hit rock bottom and proved that they can deal with it. Thus, they go on to achieve massive success.

"The darkest hour occurs just before the dawn."
An age-old truth

To be a skilled wall smasher, you do not have to be invincible, you must only be willing to rise to the occasion when the situation calls for it. Are you this kind of person? Will you rise to the challenge or will you retreat to your comfort zone? Your answers to the following scenarios should reveal whether or not you have what it takes to pass life's tests:

⌒ It is fourth down and goal at the three yard line with one second left in the game. Your team is losing by five points. A touchdown would win the game and allow your team to advance to the next round of playoffs. The roar of the crowd is deafening. The fate of your football team relies on the next play. Do you want the ball?

⌒ For the past 18 years of your life, you have worked at the local steel mill. The industry is no longer what is used to be. The company begins to close most of their divisions so that they can move outside the country to find cheaper labor. In the process, you lose your job. Do you choose to mope around cursing your employers and looking for sympathy or do you choose to look at the situation as a prime opportunity to embark upon another career?

⌒ For eleven years you have upheld your vow of silence toward your sister. After all, she should have never treated you the way that she did. Then, one day you come home from work and notice a message on your answering machine. It's from your sister and she wants to make amends. Your stomach gets tight and you hands get cold and sweaty. Do you call her back or do you stick to your vow of silence?

⌒ It's late at night. You are sharing a hotel room with a business acquaintance to cut down on some travel expenses. You are both ready for bed. As you approach your bed, your mind begins to race and your heart beats frantically. Although you want to kneel down and say your prayers, you fear what your friend may think of your actions. You are tempted to slide into bed and avoid this potentially awkward situation. At this point, you are faced with a decision. What will you do?

THE DANGERS OF RETREAT

As you can tell, this chapter isn't anything like the "typical chapter" from a self-help book. Critics may call this chapter negative, but regardless of how it is labeled, it is still the truth. Now that you are aware of the pitfalls that accompany wall smashing, you also need to be reminded about the dangers of retreating from your walls.

Choosing to retreat into your comfort zone is like burying yourself alive. The only reason that life is so hard is to make sure that quitters never achieve their dreams. In one sense, life is fair—fair in the way that it forces all great achievers to overcome massive adversity before they succeed. To put it simply, quitters cannot enter the dynamic zone. If they were, the dynamic zone would cease to be dynamic.

"Adversity is the first path to truth."
Lord Byron

Quitting is totally different from failing. Quitting occurs when you stop taking action upon your dream and consequently retreat into your comfort zone. Failing, on the other hand, is when you take action, but you do not produce your desired results. The difference between the two is that nothing can be done for a quitter. A quitter has no chance of achieving her dreams while someone who merely fails can always take additional actions to make her dreams come true. Along your journey through life, you will "fail" many times, but you will never be defeated unless you choose to quit.

Quitting was a word that Ludwig van Beethoven did not have in his vocabulary. Beethoven faced many walls in his life, walls that caused many other musicians of his time to quit. Even though Beethoven was a musical genius, his greatest attribute was not his musical talent. His most important asset was his commitment to wall smashing. He was not deterred from pursuing his dream even though his teacher called him "hopeless" as a musician. Nor did he quit when members of the public urged him to play music that was more traditional to their day. Even during the time when Beethoven was slowly growing deaf, he still would not allow himself to quit composing music. Quitting simply was not an option for Beethoven! That's what really allowed Beethoven to become one of the greatest musicians of all time.

"It's not whether you get knocked down.
It's whether you get up again."
Vince Lombardi

Can you imagine the consequences that Beethoven would have had to pay for repressing his natural musical talents? Music was his life. It was who he was. Even though he had many walls in his way, he still was better off in music than in anything else. Without music, there would have been a massive void in Beethoven's life.

Once you know in your heart what you are inspired to do, go out into the world and do it! Don't ask your peers for their approval. Don't check statistics to see if it is possible. Don't even consider how many walls are in your way. None of this matters. Just run with your inspiration.

If you choose to retreat in spite of your inspiration, you will sap the passion right out of your life. You will throw your entire life out of balance and leave yourself with an overwhelming sense of boredom.

"Running away solves nothing; eventually the same
problems show up further down the road."
Harville Hendrix

The way to prevent this tragedy is to follow the guidance of your fear. Whenever you fear an obstacle in your life, step into your dynamic zone and take action on it. Be willing to feel some short-term pain. It will hurt much less than the pain you would feel if you woke up one day and realized that you neglected to live the kind of life you really wanted to live.

> *It's a shame how many people die*
> *without ever having lived.*

If the fear of dying before you ever really lived is not enough motivation to get you to live a dynamic life, then think about the terrible example you are setting for your children when you retreat from the challenges in your life. Without even saying a word, you give your children complete permission to retreat from their challenges as well. In this sense, your habit of retreating becomes hereditary and your cowardice is passed along to your next generation.

RETREATING CAN EASILY BECOME A LIFELONG HABIT

Anytime you decide to quit taking action upon an important wall in your life, you run the risk of creating a lifelong habit of retreat for yourself. The first time you quit will be the hardest. You will feel as though you let yourself down. Then, each subsequent time will become easier and easier. Pretty soon, you will accept quitting as a habitual part of your life.

"We first make our habits, and then our habits make us."
John Dryden

The instant comfort that accompanies retreating is very appealing. Initially, you will experience much less stress, enjoy more free time, and have less burdens to deal with. It will feel as though a weight has been lifted off your shoulders. This will cause you to become more apt to retreat again in the future.

Retreating from life occurs as a natural by-product for someone who has formed the habit of consistently retreating from her walls. This can happen so easily that you may not even be aware of it. All of a sudden, retreating can become part of your being. To determine whether or not the habit of retreat is slowly creeping into your life, proceed to answer the following questions:

Ω   Do you value other people's opinions more than your own?

Ω   Have you stopped setting goals for yourself?

Ω   Do you work only to be paid rather than to increase the value of the company that you are serving?

Ω   Do you watch more than three hours of television a day?

Ω   Do you rely on substances like drugs, alcohol, or food to change your state of mind?

Ω   Do you always have a hard time getting out of bed in the morning?

Ω   Do you ignore obvious problems with your spouse and children?

Ω   Do you slack in the area of personal hygiene?

Ω   Have you closed your eyes to an obvious injustice in your church, organization, neighborhood, or family?

Ω   Do you sleep more than eight hours a day?

Ω   Do fail to exercise at least three times a week?

Answering "Yes" to any one or more of these questions is a signal that the habit of retreat may be slowly creeping into your life. To avoid this type of disaster, you need to determine what is most important in your life, and then, you must go out and take action in order to achieve it. The following questions will help you to motivate yourself to take the necessary actions:

1. What would I lose if I quit?
2. What do I think of myself when I look in the mirror?
3. Do I want to teach my children to act like me?
4. Does this behavior move me closer to achieving my dreams?
5. Am I a quitter?

Use these questions or develop some soul-searching questions of your own that motivate you to take action. Make sure your questions focus on the excruciating pain you would feel if you decided to retreat. Imagine how painful it would be to stick a knife through the heart of your dreams. Your questions may save you from falling prey to your comfort zone.

> *Either your dreams or your nightmares will come true; the choice is up to you.*

Close your eyes and visualize yourself lying in a hospital bed unsure whether or not you will even survive. Imagine what it would be like to realize that your spirit really died many years ago when you gave up the pursuit of your dreams. How would you to feel? Would you be proud of the fact that you quit the game of life before you ever really started? What would it be like to die and have to stand before your creator and return the gift of life unused?

"What man needs is not a tensionless state, but rather the striving and struggling of some goal worthy of him."
Viktor Frankl

Retreating from life creates a permanent aching pain inside you. It is unlike the pain felt from a bruise or a broken bone. The pain of retreat is a much deeper pain, a pain resulting from a lack of fulfillment in your life. It is a pain that will not go away. Unlike a bruise or broken bone that heals naturally, the pain of retreat will remain with you forever.

ARE YOU A WALL SMASHER?

Now that the facts have been laid upon the table, it is time for you to determine your own destiny. Are you willing to pay the price to become a wall smasher? Or would you rather take the easy road and retreat into your comfort zone? The choice is yours!

Although life is hard, it is also every bit as fulfilling as it is hard. The only catch is that you must first learn to handle adversity before you receive the rewards.

"But if the task is difficult, the reward is great."
Edward W. Brooke

Once you learn to deal with overwhelm, disappointment, discouragement, and failure, something magical happens. Suddenly, you will forget how hard it was to smash your walls. It will be much like the mother who forgets the pains of childbirth as she holds her newborn baby in her arms. The same feelings of fear that once seemed unbearable will become a faded memory. It will seem as though your fears were a figment of your imagination, mere illusions. The resulting joy will diminish the memory of all of the pain that you had to endure along the way.

Now that you have chosen to become a wall smasher, you need to understand the power of....PROGRESS.

ARE YOU WILLING TO LIVE UNTIL THE DAY THAT YOU DIE?

CHAPTER 13

PROGRESS: THE KEY TO CREATING LIFELONG JOY

*"If one advances confidently in the direction of his
dreams, and endeavors to live the life which
he has imagined, he will meet with success
unexpected in common hours."*
Henry David Thoreau

Just as the Earth is divided into different sections called continents, so
is your life divided into different sections called departments. These
departments represent the eleven major divisions in your life. When all
of your individual departments are growing, changing, and improving,
your life as a whole becomes much more joyful. When any one of your
departments is stagnant, complacent, or inactive, your life as a whole
becomes much more painful. The following list outlines these eleven
departments:

- ◆ Career (business, occupation, profession, job)
- ◆ Contribution (wisely giving of your money, your time, and/or
  your skill to help others)
- ◆ Education (tapes, books, seminars, modeling others, formal
  schooling)
- ◆ Exploration (doing new things and visiting new places)
- ◆ Family (spouse, children, parents, siblings, etc.)
- ◆ Health (food choices, personal habits, exercise)

- Investment (mutual funds, IRA, annuities, real estate, etc.)
- Recreation (sports, hobbies, organizations, entertainment)
- Relationship (friends, acquaintances, dating partners, business associates, environment)
- Spiritual (religion, meditation, prayer, study groups)
- Time Management (personal, family, career)

As you can see, these eleven departments encompass your entire life. Everything that you do can be classified in at least one of these departments. Some of your activities can even be classified into multiple categories.

In order to live a balanced life, it is essential for you to consistently expand and explore each one of your life departments. The good news is that each of your departments has an unlimited number of walls for you to smash. There is literally an endless amount of opportunities for you to make progress in each one of your departments.

"Success is never final."
Winston Churchill

Once again, it is best to follow the guidance of your fear as to what department you most need to direct your actions at any given time. Choosing to avoid walls in any one or more of your departments will only create a void in that area of your life. In turn, it will actually throw your entire life out of balance until you finally take the necessary actions.

Consider the married couple who concerns themselves only with their career department. Each one of them works over 60 hours a week while the rest of their life departments are falling apart. No longer do they attend church on Sundays. They are each about thirty pounds overweight. They have very few friends outside their business acquaintances. Having kids is totally out of the question and they feel as though they never have any time for themselves. In this case, it is easy to see that their lives are severely out of balance.

Anytime you build your entire world around one department of your life, it drastically reduces the total amount of joy that you can experience. The same is true for any type of dependency regardless of whether it's a job, relationship, sport, religion, organization or anything else. Limiting your participation primarily to any one department sets you up for a big fall.

Think about the people in your life. Don't you have a friend or two who consistently talks about the "great high school years" or the "outrageous college years" even though this person may have been out of high school or college for five, ten, twenty or more years? This is an example of someone who has forgotten the fundamental element of progress in her life. A person like this is living in her past while her present life is passing her by.

> *"The good of man is a working of the soul in the way of excellence in a complete life;...for as it is not one swallow or one fine day that makes a spring, so it is not one day or a short time that makes a man blessed and happy."*
> Aristotle

Although memories do have their place, life is not solely about reliving the past. It is about living in the present moment and creating a fantastic future for yourself and your loved ones. It's a shame how many people become dependent on retaining their identity as the star football player, the homecoming queen, or the class president. These people are simply afraid to step into their dynamic zones to expand their identity.

Another good example is doctors. Many doctors tend to forget that they are merely human beings who practice medicine. Instead, many regard themselves solely as doctors and are offended when referred to in any other way. For many, they would be appalled if you ever called them by their first name.

Regardless of whether you are a doctor, lawyer, banker, veterinarian, teacher, or entrepreneur, you must see yourself as being more than your identity or title. You must realize that you are a dynamic human being who is multi-faceted. Don't limit the amount of joy you can experience in your life by excessively clinging to a single identity, label, position, or title. Doing so would only result in your becoming a very unhappy, lopsided person. Avoid this trap by consistently expanding your identity in every department of your life.

Life is constantly changing and in order to keep pace with it you must continue to change as well. It is wise to enjoy your special talents, abilities, honors, awards, and accomplishments as long as you realize that you must build on your successes instead of resting upon them. Strive each day to become a better friend, a more knowledgeable associate, a more loving parent, a more compassionate spouse, a more curious explorer, a more helpful volunteer, a more effective organizer, a more diverse investor, a more competent teacher, a more open-minded worshipper, and a harder working student.

Begin the process of improving every phase of your life by getting a small notebook and placing each of the department names at the top of a separate page. Proceed to make notes of all the dreams you have in each of your departments. Once you have finished making these lists, make another list of all the special accomplishments you have already had in each one. Update your lists periodically so that you know exactly where you are in your life. Then, use your lists as an ongoing way to measure your progress in each of your life departments.

THE JOURNEY IS ALL THAT MATTERS

As long as you are still living on planet Earth, you can be sure that you have not arrived at your final destination. If you are alive, then you are expected to be growing, changing, and improving. Growth, change, and improvement are the essence of life.

Proof of this truth can be found in every great movie that was ever made. Ponder for a moment about some of your favorite movies. Aren't they all about the journey of a particular hero who overcomes tremendous obstacles and finally achieves her dream? Of course! Well, what if the hero didn't have any obstacles and she achieved her dreams without a fight? Would you pay to see this kind of movie? Of course you wouldn't! Without the journey, movies would be boring.

"The road is better than the end."
Cervantes

Look at your own life. What kind of "movie" are you living? Would people pay their hard-earned money to watch a movie of your wall smashing adventures or would they demand a refund? Only you know the answer to this question. Life has done its part by presenting you with everything you need to produce a great movie. The walls are all in place. All you have to do is follow the guidance of your fear and take the necessary actions to allow your journey to unfold. Remember, whatever you fear is what you need to do next!

Without walls, you would have no resistance in your life. There would be no such thing as your dynamic zone. No longer would you be able to feel joyful emotions like excitement, passion, curiosity, adventure, and suspense. Everything would be comfortable and you would soon become listless. Walls make sure that you always have new frontiers to explore along your life's journey. They also give you the distinct opportunity to mold yourself into a more complete person.

THE MASTER PLAN FOR PROGRESS

1. *Enter your dynamic zone and take action upon your wall of fear.*
2. *Rest in your comfort zone to regain balance and to evaluate your actions.*
3. *Keep taking action and evaluating your actions until your wall is smashed.*
4. *Go back to number 1 and continue your progress.*

Every wall that you ever encounter will force you to grow and growth is the law of life. Growth is what distinguishes life from death. If a plant is not growing, then it is dying. The same is true for human beings. You are either growing or dying. Even though it is scary to step into your dynamic zone and grow, growing pains are much less agonizing in the long run than are the pains that result from complacency.

One way to guard against complacency is by focusing on one simple question, "How can I make my life and/or the life of someone else a little bit better today?" This question will remind you each day about your need for progress. Write this question on a small piece of paper and place it somewhere that you will see it several times a day.

> *The only constant in life is your consistent need to grow, change, and improve.*

Boredom and a lack of fulfillment will forever remain unknown to you as long as you continue to consistently grow, change, and improve. No matter how good your life is right now, it can and should be improved upon. The Japanese refer to this process of consistent improvement with a word called *kaizen. Kaizen* reminds you to live this day to the best of your ability.

Dynamic speaker Jim Rohn talks about the necessity of consistently doing your best. He states that doing your best has nothing to do with your income level. For instance, if you are truly doing your best while earning only $10,000 a year, then you are far better off than the person who has grown complacent while earning $50,000 a year.

Whenever you choose to halt your progress and admire all of your accomplishments, your competition will pass you by. It happens in the business arena, athletic field, career world, classroom or any other aspect of your life. This is not to say that life is about rivalry and competition or that you should not enjoy your successes. You simply need to strive for excellence by consistently improving upon your personal best in every department of your life.

"The bad man is the man who, no matter how good he has been, is beginning to deteriorate, to grow less good. The good man is the man who, no matter how morally unworthy he has been, is moving to become better."
John Dewey

The common maxim "If it's not broken, don't fix it" is totally inaccurate. Today, you must improve upon everything in your life regardless of its current effectiveness.

Consider how quickly brand new computer programs become obsolete. A year is actually a long time for a computer company to market one particular program. The thriving companies in the computer industry realize that creating merely one product is not enough. Instead, they improve upon each one of their products and create new products just to stay alive in the marketplace. They realize that only through consistent progress and improvement can they continue to thrive in such a competitive industry.

YOU MUST PROGRESS AT THE INDIVIDUAL LEVEL BEFORE YOU CAN PROGRESS AT THE RELATIONSHIP LEVEL

Relationships are another part of life that must be consistently growing, changing, and improving in order to be fulfilling. It is not enough to be satisfied with the quality of any of your relationships. Instead, you must consistently add more value to each of your relationships by growing, changing, and improving at your personal level. This remains true regardless of whether the relationship in question is a marriage, family, partnership, or friendship. All relationships consist of two or more separate people with two or more separate desires and needs. Although your partners can help you to meet your personal needs and desires, they cannot meet them for you.

Before any relationship can really make noticeable progress, everyone involved must disclose their most important desires, aspirations, goals, and dreams to each other. Growing relationships cannot exist with stagnant people. In addition, each person must also be taking actions to achieve their desired result. In the case of a marriage, your spouse could not fully love you or even know the real you until you decided to do the things that you alone feel inspired to do. The only way you can share more with others is by first being true to yourself. You must accept your true "calling" from life. Failing to do so will create a void in your life that will never be filled by any type or amount of relationships.

> **"The wall to love is self-hatred; in order to let love in, the wall must come down."**
> Harville Hendrix

All growth must begin with you. You alone are responsible for the quality of relationships you develop throughout your life's journey. Don't blame your partner for a failing relationship if you are not consistently making yourself into a more valuable asset.

Strong interpersonal relationships also call for mutual support among everyone involved. Each person must be encouraged to pursue their own unique aspirations. It is hard enough for one person to motivate herself to take action. She certainly does not need anyone else pulling her down.

Jason is a great example of a someone who really needed support and did not get it. For quite some time, he was dreaming about opening a bagel shop in the local shopping complex. Even though this was quite a big step for him, he finally persuaded himself to do it. Unfortunately, his wife, Nancy, refused to support him. As a result of Nancy's disapproval, Jason decided not to open the bagel shop.

The tragedy of this story occurred several months later when Jason couldn't seem to show his love and affection to Nancy the way he once did. Although Jason never traced this mysterious lack of affection for his wife back to Nancy's discouragement, it was nonetheless the reason for Jason's lack of love. Unconsciously, Jason held back his love for Nancy. He couldn't fully love someone who didn't encourage him to pursue his dreams. In this case, Jason would have been wise to pursue his dream in spite of his wife's disapproval. By doing so, he at least would have had peace within himself.

Every day marriages are breaking up, strong friendships are crumbling, and family ties are being broken as a result of people who will not support their friends, lovers, family members, etc., when they pursue their dreams. The bottom line is that each person must take the initiative to pursue her own dreams and, equally as important, support others while they pursue their dreams. Mutual support is the key to building a strong foundation in which any relationship can flourish.

ONE WALL AT A TIME

As you begin your wall smashing journey, you must realize the importance of focusing your power upon one wall at a time. Surely, you can recall a time when you had a lot to do and you ended up getting nothing done. Why did this happen? Wasn't it because you had so much to do that you didn't even know where to start? Keep in mind how simple it is to overwhelm yourself when you become concerned with too many walls at once. Guard yourself against overwhelm by focusing your power upon the single most important wall in your life.

Remember back to the time of your childhood when you would use a magnifying glass to focus the sun's rays to burn a blade of grass. What was the key to this experiment? Wasn't it to tilt the magnifying glass at just the right angle and then to hold it steady as you focused the sun's power upon the one blade of grass? Well, the same concept is used in wall smashing. The key is to carefully focus your mental and physical powers upon one wall at a time.

When the sun's rays are shedding light upon all things, they have much less power. However, when the rays focus upon a certain object, they become many times more powerful. The sun always had this type of power and potential; all it needed was someone to come along and properly focus it. Your mind and body are no different. They have power even greater than that of the sun. All you need to do is properly focus this power upon what is most important in your life and then, apply the ideas and strategies included in this book.

First and foremost, you must remember that the enemy of overwhelm is defeated by doing one thing at a time. The most effective way to handle an important wall in your life is to focus all of your energy upon that wall until it is well under control before scattering your power upon other walls. Give the truly important walls in your life the time and attention that they require and you will eventually receive a great return on your investment.

Another mistake that you can easily make is to rush the smashing of a particular wall. Instead of thoroughly smashing a wall once and for all, you might rush the process and fool yourself into believing that you effectively handled the situation. For example, have you ever found yourself spending five minutes communicating with your son or daughter about a problem that really required an hour or two of your time? Or hastily moving through an important settlement when it would have been best to meet on several different occasions? Or hurrying the completion of a major project to finish in a few days when it really required a few weeks to finish properly? Experiences like these can be tempting to rush through and then pretend that you have thoroughly handled them. Unfortunately, when you sloppily rush through a situation, you end up wasting your time because the problem will only resurface with even more intensity in the future.

> ### *"You can't plant the seed and pick the fruit the next morning."*
> Reverend Jesse Jackson

Learn to take the proper amount of time to deal with the important walls in your life. This way, you will always be heading in the right direction. By doing first things first, your life will unfold in perfect order. Think about the way a baby must learn how to sit up before she can crawl, crawl before she can walk, and walk before she can run. Life is no different from this scenario. Certain obstacles must be overcome before you can move to something else.

---

*As for everything you do now,
there once was a time when you couldn't do it!*

Regardless of where you are on your particular journey through life, make sure that you always enjoy your current place of progress. Remember, life is a cycle. There are times when you need to rest and there are times when you need to take action. Learn to enjoy both ends of the cycle. A great friend of mine recently gave me some useful advice. He simply said, "Be where you are." How profound!

GETTING THE POWER OF MOMENTUM TO WORK FOR YOU

By focusing your power upon one wall at a time, you begin to create natural momentum in your life. Suddenly, those obstacles that once challenged you, now seem almost routine. It is a fact of life that everything picks up speed and momentum once it is set in motion. A small snowball that is rolled down a mountainside ends up becoming a gigantic snowball before it reaches the bottom. In a similar manner, you can put the power of momentum to work in your own life by consistently taking action toward the attainment of your dreams.

Wall smashing momentum is basically created by following the prevailing theme of this book, "Whatever you fear is what you need to do next." By following this strategy, you will soon harness the power of momentum. Suddenly, you will find yourself acting upon walls much larger than you ever imagined yourself acting upon. Take a moment and visualize yourself in the following example:

After several weeks of intense study and application, you finally master a very challenging computer software program. As a result of your newfound expertise, you decide to advertise at the local college as a tutor for this particular program. Little by little your clientele builds and your momentum increases. Within a short period of time, you begin teaching small groups of students at a time. Soon, it becomes apparent that you have a very natural talent for teaching computer courses. Wisely, the college offers you a teaching position. As word of mouth continues to spread about your skills, various small businesses ask you to conduct various training programs for their employees. Then, larger companies begin to inquire about your services. Within a few years, a major publisher asks you to write a book about computers.

Writing a book about computers is quite an achievement. Nonetheless, your success is traceable back to the point in time when you learned your first computer program. Achieving that initial goal was the little "snowball" that began all of your momentum in the computer field. In fact, anyone who has experienced noteworthy achievements can trace their success back to a simple starting point.

Test yourself to see if you are really making good use of momentum in your life. Look at your life four years ago and figure out exactly what kind of life you were living. Do this by briefly commenting on each of the eleven departments of your life as it was four years ago:

> Career (your income, your level of fulfillment, your goals)
> Contribution (your level of happiness, your impact upon others, the amount of time, money, or skill you used to help others)
> Education (the amount and types of books you read, the courses you've taken, the training you received, the degrees you've earned)
> Exploration (the places you've visited, the unique experiences you've had)
> Family (your level of intimacy, your parenting skills, your example, your level of fulfillment)
> Health (your eating habits, your exercise habits, your personal habits, your energy level)
> Investments (your net worth, the diversity of your investments, your knowledge level)
> Recreational (the sports and activities that you play, what you do in your "free" time, your hobbies)
> Relationships (your level of intimacy with certain people, your skills at making new friends, your personal growth, the number of

close friends you have, how you perceive the environment, your level of self-esteem)

> Spiritual (your relationship with your creator, the level of peace within yourself, your attitude toward life)

> Time Management (your level of stress, your level of control over your life, your habit of doing the most important thing first, your biggest concerns)

Once you feel that you have accurately noted the type of person you were four years ago, then proceed to refer back to the list and write down the type of person you are today. If you get stuck on either part of this exercise, get a loved one to help you. Many times, a loved one can see things about you that you cannot notice for yourself.

Once you have completed your two lists, compare them to each other. Four years is plenty of time to see either remarkable growth or terrible stagnation in your life. If the two lists are extremely similar, you can rest assured that you have not tapped into the awesome power of momentum during those four years. On the other hand, if your second list is much more dynamic than your first list, then you will know that you have been harnessing the power of momentum for the past four years.

Maybe you were unemployed four years ago, collecting $325.00 a week in unemployment, but now you are earning $850.00 a week working at a job that you love. In this case, you have shown progression in your career department. On the other hand, four years ago, you may have had intentions of attending several different religious services to find one that was right for you. But now, it is four years later and you still have not visited any of the churches on your list. In this case, you would have neglected an aspect of your spiritual department. Whatever the case, take a good hard look at each of your life departments—the facts will speak for themselves.

AS YOU MAKE PROGRESS, YOUR DESIRES AND DREAMS WILL GROW

At this moment, you are not capable of dreaming your greatest dream! The reason is simple. Some of your dreams can only be recognized once you reach a certain point in your journey. You must first make progress toward your current goals and dreams before you can uncover the other fantastic dreams and desires that are buried deep inside you.

For example, several years ago, Clarence decided to pursue his financial goal of earning over $40,000.00 a year. After a long hard struggle, Clarence finally achieved his goal. Suddenly, he gained a whole new sense of self-confidence which prompted him to pursue a new goal of earning over $60,000.00 a year. The intriguing part of this example is that several years ago Clarence was not capable of realistically pursuing a goal of earning $60,000.00 a year. It was just too much for his subconscious mind to support. But thanks to progress, Clarence can now realistically pursue a goal of this magnitude.

> *Your dreams and desires grow with*
> *every step that you take.*

It is totally natural for you as a human being to desire to do more, earn more, see more, learn more, and basically become more as you make greater progress along your journey through life. This human tendency is very healthy and is an important element of the law of growth. Aristotle taught this same principle over 2300 years ago. He believed that human beings have an inner urge that compels them to consistently seek higher levels of achievement and greater feelings of fulfillment. To Aristotle, it was only natural for people to desire to tap into more and more of their potential.

For many years as a youngster, I did not believe that I could water-ski backwards on a pair of "trick skis." Nevertheless, as I began to improve at water-skiing, the "impossible" began to seem possible. Then, one day I felt the urge to ski backwards. Although I crashed numerous times, I began to acquire a better sense of balance. My confidence also began to improve and I really began to believe that I could possibly acquire this skill. After spending several more days at the lake water-skiing, I finally did the "impossible." I actually skied backwards.

It is now about a year later and thanks once again to the magic of incremental progress, I now believe that it is possible for me to ski backwards on a single "trick ski" (something else that I never would have imagined I could do). My water-skiing experiences have helped me to realize that with consistent progress I am capable of doing many things that I once considered to be unattainable.

"We know what we are, but not what we may be."
William Shakespeare

Another example that accurately illustrates how progress can cause your desires and dreams to grow is the amazing story of Terry Fox. Terry was a talented Canadian athlete who developed cancer and was forced to have one of his legs amputated. His athletic career, as he knew it, was over. Nonetheless, he worked hard and eventually learned to walk with his artificial leg. Then, he learned to jog. After a while, Terry even progressed to the point where he could run with his new leg. As a result of his progress, Terry was inspired with a special dream. His dream was to run the whole way across Canada in order to raise one hundred thousand dollars for youth cancer research.

Despite encountering all the usual causes of retreat including feeling overwhelmed by the task at hand, feeling disappointed because of his disability, being discouraged by his family, and failing to attract the support of any national fund-raising organizations, Terry Fox began to pursue his dream. Starting at the Atlantic Ocean, he began to run across Canada. Each day he took action toward the attainment of his dream. By the time Terry had run for approximately one year, he achieved his dream of raising one hundred thousand dollars. But, instead of halting his progress, he continued his quest across the country with a new dream of raising one million dollars. Then, in a short period of time, even his new dream of raising one million dollars increased to $24.1 million dollars—one dollar for every person who lived in Canada. As his momentum and progress increased, so did his dreams.

Unfortunately, before Terry Fox could finish his amazing crusade, the cancer had spread into his chest and he was forced to stop. Shortly thereafter, Terry Fox died. Amazingly, his dream of raising $24.1 million dollars was still reached by the Canadian people. Terry Fox proved to the world what can be accomplished with consistent progress. Today, the legacy of Terry Fox lives on in the hearts of millions of Canadians and Americans alike. He is truly a national hero. Thanks to the "Terry Fox Marathon of Hope" many young children stricken with cancer have benefited from Terry's contributions.

YOU WILL NEVER REACH YOUR FULL POTENTIAL WHILE LIVING ON THIS PLANET

Even if you were to become someone as influential as Terry Fox, you still would not come anywhere close to reaching your full potential. Inside you will always be vast gold mines of untapped potential awaiting your discovery. There is literally no end to the progress that you can make in your life.

> *"A man's reach should exceed his grasp,*
> *or what's a heaven for?"*
> Robert Browning

Possessing this unlimited potential allows you to become as dynamic as you want to be. You can soar to any heights, explore any depths. Indeed, you have the ultimate freedom, the freedom to pursue your dreams, the same freedom that cost many of your ancestors their lives! What do you suppose your ancestors would say to you today if they knew how you were using their gift? Would they be proud of the ways that you use your freedom or would they be ashamed about the ways you abuse it?

Use your freedom to become someone like Ben Franklin, Leonardo da Vinci, Mother Teresa, Thomas Jefferson, Galileo, Winston Churchill, Jonas Salk, Copernicus, or Abraham Lincoln. Become someone who consistently follows your passions. The walls facing you today are really no different from those faced by the great men and women of the past. Your ancestors didn't have constant emotional support while they pursued their goals. Neither did they have an abundance of finances, nor did they have all the right resources. Yet, they still managed to make progress toward their dreams. And you can do the same! You may or may not end up becoming famous, but that is not important. All that matters is if you are making progress toward your most precious dreams. This alone will give you fulfillment.

Human beings need to progress toward their own unique aspirations of greatness. Look at what has happened to many of the communist countries. Communism is crumbling because individuals want the freedom to progress to higher levels of personal achievement. The common ownership of all things only discourages individual progress from any single person. Remember, our ancestors died to give us the freedom to be great. Let's make sure we were worth dying for!

Greatness for you might be having a four member family that lives in a small farmhouse in the country. Maybe greatness is volunteering at your local fire department, restructuring the subjects taught in our public school system, creating a way to make our environment cleaner, or improving transportation in our big cities. The possible scenarios for greatness are literally endless. Only you know what is "great" for you.

"Eye hath not seen, nor ear heard, neither have entered into the heart of man, the things which God hath prepared for them that love Him!"
First Corinthians 2:9

Pursue whatever greatness means to you. Do whatever it is that you love and do it with all of your heart, all of your mind, and all of your body. Get rid of your silly beliefs that are blocking you from achieving your dreams. Learn that it's OK to earn a tremendous amount of money, receive a high-ranking position in society, marry someone of another race, or adopt a group of orphan children from another country. Learn that it is OK to remain a virgin for as long as you desire or to be the student who would rather spend an evening at the library instead of a "keg party." This is your life. Make sure that you spend it doing the things that you love the most.

PROGRESS CREATES COMPOUNDING JOY

Joy is the natural result of doing something that once challenged you. Babies feel joy as they learn to walk. Parents feel joy as they see their children graduate from school. Athletes feel joy as they win the title. Joy exists all around you. In fact, every time you act upon a wall in your life, you access some degree of joy.

Compounding joy occurs when your current joys begin to stack on top of your past joys and in essence, build upon each other. By itself, your current level of joy is like a drop of water, but coupled with your past joys, it becomes like a raging flood of fulfillment.

The principle of compounding is most common in the financial world. Suppose you invest $2,000 per year in an IRA that earns 15% per year. This means that you would earn $300 per year in interest on your $2,000 investment. But, with the power of compounding, instead of earning merely $9,000 in interest over a thirty year period, you would earn an amazing $1,108,000 in interest. Even though you only saved $60,000 over the thirty year period, you still would earn over $1.1 million dollars in interest. Compounding is effective since it earns interest on each of your contributions and then reinvests the interest to increase the grand total of your investment. Getting "interest on your interest" is what eventually makes you rich.

Similarly, every joy that you create for yourself today will also compound with all the joys of your past. Eventually, you will find yourself feeling deep levels of joy that could not be felt from any one experience. Within a short period of time, you will have created for yourself a level of wealth that no amount of money could ever buy.

HOW TO HANDLE SUCCESS AND AVOID COMPLACENCY

Thomas Carlyle, the famous Scottish historian and social critic, once said, "Adversity is hard on a man; but for one man who can stand prosperity, there are a hundred that will stand adversity." I don't know about you, but I had to read the preceding quotation by Carlyle about twenty times before I finally understood what he meant by it. But once I thought about the quotation, I was fascinated by its accuracy. Carlyle, in essence, is alerting us about the dangers of achieving our original goals and then becoming complacent. He warns us that prosperity is much harder to handle than is adversity. Adversity forces us to improve our lives whereas prosperity and success can easily tempt us to become stagnant, which violates the law of growth.

Let's say you have just smashed a very challenging wall in your own life and you are thrilled about your success. What should you do next? Well, begin by jumping up and down and shout for joy. Bask in your glory. Throw a party. Make sure you celebrate your victories. Celebrating is an important part of success.

On the other hand, be extremely careful not to overdo your celebrating. The time frame immediately following your success is the most dangerous time in the process of wall smashing. It is tempting to bask in the limelight for an extended amount of time. Yet, this could cause you to run face first into an unexpected wall. To remind yourself about this potential danger, remember the champion cyclist who won a grueling race only to crash as she waved to the crowd. This will help you to guard against getting too caught up in your celebration.

The wisest approach to success is to celebrate as you continue to take action upon the next wall along your journey. This way, you can celebrate your victories while you are still heading in the right direction. In addition, you will not run the risk of crashing into your next wall without being properly prepared for it. The times when you let your guard down and become complacent are usually the same times when you end up getting hurt in some unexpected way.

> *There is no greater accomplishment*
> *than to live until the day that you die!*

Former Los Angeles Lakers basketball coach Pat Riley wrote about the dangers of complacency in his book, *The Winner Within*. He admitted that after his team defeated the Boston Celtics for the championship in 1985, his 1986 team became complacent. Riley claims that his 1986 team simply failed to dream a bigger dream. As a result, the Los Angeles Lakers lost their title even though they probably had the most talented team in the league. Riley's team proved that all teams, organizations, and individuals alike must continue to make progress on a daily basis if they want to maintain their elite status.

Suppose there are two equally talented teams who are preparing to play each other for the title. The first team is *defending* the title while the second team is *fighting for* the title. How can you tell who is going to win? Well, the team that is *fighting for* the title is playing "to win" and will likely win as a result. On the other hand, the team who is *defending* a title is playing "not to lose" and will likely lose as a result. What a difference there is between these two attitudes!

If you ever find yourself uninspired to fight for some type of "title," maybe your heart is telling you to move on to something else. It is very common in our society for an executive to retire from one company so that she can go to work for another company. This is usually done to avoid complacency and to gather new learning experiences in the process. After all, a new company brings with it new walls to smash which means more opportunities for a person to expand and diversify herself. Diversity is a great way to guard yourself against the trap of complacency.

Basketball great Michael Jordan is an example of one such person who had the courage and wisdom to pursue a new dream instead of drifting into complacency. Jordan retired from professional basketball after he led the Chicago Bulls to an unprecedented third straight championship season. He did so because he lacked the motivation and inspiration that once drove him to excel at basketball. Instead, his motivation was pulling him in another direction. Michael Jordan had a dream to play professional baseball for the Chicago White Sox.

As a result of his new dream, Jordan demoted himself from the glory of being the "Most Valuable Player" on a world championship basketball team to the ranks of being a mediocre player on a minor league baseball team. Nevertheless, Jordan was happy because once again he felt inspired. He was motivated to put forth tremendous amounts of effort every day to make his dream come true. He put all of his heart and soul into baseball, but in the end, it just was not meant to be. Michael Jordan came up a bit short of achieving his baseball dream.

Although he never did achieve his dream of playing professional baseball for the Chicago White Sox, he did successfully avoid the pitfalls of complacency that would have occurred had he remained in basketball. But most importantly, he regained his inspiration and motivation for basketball, which prompted him to return to the Chicago Bulls.

Since his return to professional basketball, Michael Jordan has once again become a dominant player in the league. In 1996 he even led his team to another NBA championship and once again received the Most Valuable Player award. In fact, many basketball analysts claim that the 1996 Chicago Bulls might have been the greatest team in the history of basketball. Some analysts have even speculated that Michael Jordan could possibly be the greatest basketball player ever to play the game.

Many people believe that once they achieve their "ultimate goal," they will be happy. This is not true. Many millionaires have reported that the attainment of their financial goals was a big letdown. After the process of making the money was over, they felt empty. On the other hand, people who are committed to making consistent progress in their life are rarely at a loss for joy. They understand that real security is not found in financial independence, retirement, prestige, or even power. Rather, they realize that it can only be experienced while they are making steady progress toward a worthwhile dream. In fact, best-selling authors and dynamic businessmen Earl Nightingale and Dexter Yager have both defined success as "the progressive realization of a worthwhile dream."

> *PROBLEM: Arriving at a goal is not as much fun as the process of getting there.*
> *SOLUTION: Make sure you are always in the process of pursuing a goal.*

ENJOY YOUR JOURNEY

In the midst of all that's going on in your life, it is so easy to forget to enjoy yourself. You might be one of the many people who are already tremendously successful in every department of your life, yet you still may not feel genuinely happy. You might live in a nice house located in a nice neighborhood. You might have a college degree, an above-average paying job, smart children, and many close friends. You might even contribute to your community and go on several vacations a year. But, you still might not feel as though you are really enjoying your life.

In this case, you should adopt a "fisherman's mentality." Aren't fishermen always happy when they are fishing? It doesn't matter how many fish they catch. To them, a day outdoors is always an enjoyable experience. Fishermen do not force themselves to catch a certain number of fish before they are allowed to be happy. They simply enjoy every moment of their adventure.

The funny truth is that even if you do not fish you are still, in essence, a fisherman. Every wall you ever encounter serves as a metaphor for a day of fishing. On your "fishing trip," you can either choose to enjoy the process of wall smashing regardless of the speed of your current progress or you can choose to sulk in misery because you did not catch enough "fish."

Thomas Edison is a great example of someone who so loved what he did that it did not matter how fast he progressed. As long as Edison was inventing, he was happy. He experienced his greatest joys during the process of inventing, not from the glory that followed a successful invention. When Edison finished inventing something, he would often sell it off to other people so that he could have more free time to pursue other inventions.

The truth is, Edison could have been a greater financial tycoon than even Rockefeller himself, but Edison was hungry for the joy of inventing more than he was hungry for financial gain. Edison simply acquired a comfortable amount of money to live on and spent the rest of his life doing what he loved. The application of this strategy eventually allowed him to claim over 1,000 patents and, more importantly, to live a truly dynamic life.

Unfortunately, many people tend to have a mentality that makes it extremely difficult for them to enjoy their journey. In my own life, I used to think that I would start enjoying myself as soon as I got my business out of "the red," earned a certain amount of income, found the right girlfriend, bought or sold particular pieces of real estate, and weighed 162 pounds with nine percent body fat. I was gravely mistaken! Nothing could have been farther from the truth. Even as I smashed many of my walls and achieved certain goals and dreams of mine, I discovered that I still did not feel as though I was enjoying my life. It seemed as though I would never be satisfied.

Fortunately, I came to the realization that the only way to enjoy my life was to delight in it right this very moment regardless of the walls that were facing me. After all, I knew that there would always be walls in my life. As soon as I smashed one, another one would unexpectedly surface. As a result, I learned to enjoy my journey much more than any destination. This one simple adjustment in my thinking transformed my entire life and gave me the inspiration to write this book. Now, I enjoy every step of my wall smashing journey. Instead of perceiving the walls in my life as my enemy, I now perceive them as my teacher. I have learned to soak up all of the fearful emotions of overwhelm, disappointment, discouragement, and failure as well as the joyful emotions of excitement, adventure, passion, and love.

Life is supposed to be enjoyable. Therefore, pursue a dream that brings joy into your life. It is absurd to fill your days with activities and events that have no special meaning to you.

Consider the man who gets two weeks of vacation each year from a job that he hates. Over the course of ten years, this man will endure 500 weeks of painful work while he only gets 20 weeks of pleasurable vacation. This man is not enjoying his journey. He is merely *surviving* for 50 weeks a year so that he can *live* for the two remaining weeks of each year. This man has a 25 to 1 ratio of unhappiness to joy. How could someone justify such an imbalance?

Nonetheless, many people continue to spend large amounts of their time devoted to activities, jobs, and obligations that they do not enjoy. These are the same people who believe that they will be happy when they achieve some preconceived destination. It is a tragedy in the way that these people work themselves "into the ground" for as many as fifty years only to find out that it was their journey that they were really supposed to enjoy.

> *"Work hard for many years at your job. Then, someday you can retire and begin to enjoy your life."*
> The great joke of the twentieth century.

The only way to avoid such a tragedy is by courageously pursuing your dreams. If you hate your current job, then you had better start saving your money or doing whatever it takes so that you can put yourself in a position to begin to pursue your real dreams. If you are not willing to leave your present job, then at least change your attitude about it.

There is no reason you cannot enjoy yourself at this very moment. You do not have to make some predetermined number of sales, earn a certain amount of money, get married, graduate, or anything else before you can enjoy yourself. You simply need to make a committed *decision* to enjoy yourself in this very moment regardless of what is going on in your life. Learn to live *in* the moment instead of living *for* the moment. This way, you will not force yourself to achieve some ridiculous level of success before you stop to enjoy your life.

As a human being, you are supposed to enjoy yourself regardless of the walls in your life. Doing so will prepare you to receive life's greatest reward, a....DYNAMIC CHARACTER.

CHAPTER 14

DYNAMIC CHARACTER: THE REASON FOR BECOMING A WALL SMASHER

"Sow a thought, reap a belief, sow a belief, reap an action; sow an action, reap a habit; sow a habit, reap a character; sow a character, reap a destiny."
An ancient truth

There is no escaping the inevitable. You are a finite being and therefore, you must die. It does not matter if you are wealthy, famous, or influential, you cannot escape the hand of death. The only question left to answer is, "What do you get to keep when you die?"

Well, by looking at life with an objective viewpoint, it becomes apparent that you will not be taking your physical body with you when you depart from Earth. It's also plain to see that you will not be taking any of your material possessions either. In fact, you will lose every material possession that you even think you own, including your new luxury car, your $2,500.00 wedding ring, the $60,000.00 balance in your savings account, and your gorgeous three-bedroom split-level house overlooking the lake. Everything will disappear in a moment's notice.

> *Do you really own the things you think you own?*

So, what's left that you can take with you when you die? What is your reward for living a dynamic life? It surely won't be anything tangible.

The only logical conclusion is that it must be something intangible, something invisible to the human eye, something embedded deep within your soul. Will it be your fame in the community? How about the title that precedes your name? Will it be your reputation, your power, or even your prestige? No! At best, your fame, titles, reputations, power, and prestige are relative and have no lasting value. Even if you could take these things with you, they would be of no benefit to you whatsoever. But isn't there at least one possession that you can retain when you die, one possession that can be your reward for all the obstacles you have overcome in your life?

The good news is that there does exist one genuine possession that you can take with you when you die, one belonging that is truly your own—your character. Your character is the sum total of both your good and bad qualities. It is the one and only possession that you are permitted to take with you beyond the realm of life as you know it.

Since your character is your last and only real possession, there is only one decision left for you to make, "What type of character will you create for yourself?" Only you can decide what kind of person you will become. You can choose to disobey the guidance of your fear and create a weak character or you can obey the guidance of your fear and create a strong, dynamic character. In short, you are free to create whatever type of character you desire.

"I have a dream! That my four little children will not be judged by the color of their skin, but rather by the content of their character."
Martin Luther King Jr.

Character is indeed your most valuable asset. It is the essence of your being, the person you are. Character is your unique trademark that distinguishes you from everyone else on this planet. It is much more than your reputation. Your reputation is merely what people *think* you are. Your character, on the other hand, is what you *know* you are. The whole world could think of you as a great person, but if you have harmful intentions, then you have a flawed character.

"Your reputation functions under favorable circumstances, but your character functions under all circumstances."
Unknown

Character is the truth of your being. It is what you are when nobody is looking. You might be able to manipulate your employees, your customers, your spouse, your children, your parents, your coaches, your teachers, your police officers, or even the IRS into believing you are something that you are not, but you cannot manipulate the essence of your character. Your character is the foundation of your being. It is an exact replica of the person you have become.

> *Character is what you are in the dark.*

A DYNAMIC CHARACTER IS FORMED WHEN YOU ALIGN THE POWER OF YOUR HEART, MIND, AND BODY IN THE SAME DIRECTION

When you align your heart, your mind, and your body in the same direction for your good and the highest good of all living creatures, you become the most powerful person in the world. By listening to your heart, believing with your mind, and acting with your body, all of your power is channeled in one direction. As best-selling author Dr. Stephen Covey would say, you become "principle centered," your compass always points true north, you always do what is right.

> *"Who you are speaks so loudly*
> *I can't hear what you're saying."*
> Ralph Waldo Emerson

Mother Teresa is a great example of someone with a dynamic character. Her character is so pure and focused that people have claimed to literally feel her passion and energy as she approached them. She can transform the atmosphere of a room merely with her presence. Everything about Mother Teresa says love and caring. Although she started out as nothing more than an ordinary person, she has since become extraordinary by listening to the inspiration of her heart, creating supportive beliefs, and taking action to make her dreams come true. This is what has allowed her to make such a tremendous impact upon the less fortunate in the world. Thanks to her dynamic character many impoverished countries of our world are beginning to receive health care, food, and most importantly, love.

Another great example of someone who created a dynamic character is Mohandas Gandhi. Here is a person who despite being born into a "low ranking" merchant caste in India, almost single-handedly led his country to independence from Britain in 1947—one year before his death. Most importantly, he accomplished this remarkable feat without the use of violence. You may ask, "How could one person lead his country to freedom without the use of violence?" The answer to this question lies in the power he accessed by having his heart, mind, and body all aligned toward his dream of nonviolent freedom. Everything about Gandhi said freedom and nonviolence.

Gandhi began his journey first by listening to his heart. He realized that the only way he could live a truly dynamic life was by acting upon the things that were most important to him, the things he was most passionate about. In this case, his heart was inspiring him to free the people of India without the use of any violence. This was his dream, his passion, his purpose for living.

Next, he aligned the power of his mind to his dream of nonviolent freedom by creating beliefs like:

- I am willing to pay whatever price it takes to accomplish my dream.
- By going out into the rice paddies and gathering one person at a time, I can eventually get the support of the entire country.
- I can master myself by mastering my fears.
- One *committed* person is more powerful than ten thousand people who are merely *interested*.
- It is possible to achieve freedom without the use of any violence.
- It is an honor to bring freedom to India.
- Nonviolence is many times more powerful than violence.

By creating beliefs like these, Gandhi got the power of his mind to support the inspiration of his heart. This assured him that whenever he encountered a wall he would be motivated to smash through it, instead of retreating from it.

Finally, Gandhi combined the inspiration from his heart and the beliefs from his mind and he went out into the world and took action. Despite being personally humiliated by his countrymen, ejected from first-class train compartments, beaten for refusing to give up his seat on a stagecoach, and repeatedly thrown into prison where he suffered intense physical and mental abuse, Gandhi continued to take action.

Relentlessly, he would focus his actions upon what he considered to be the truth. Along the way, he became known as Mahatma—"The Great Soul." And in the end, though he held no sort of political office, Mahatma Gandhi accomplished his dream. He freed the Indian people from England's political domination without the use of violence. Yes, one man armed with a passionate inspiration, strong effective beliefs, and a willingness to take action eventually dismantled the entire British army. But, more importantly, Gandhi also created a dynamic character for himself that would outlast his life on Earth.

Although inspiration and belief are vital in the formation of character, you must still have the courage to "do the thing you fear." You must take action. Life cannot be experienced solely in your heart or mind. You must physically venture out into your dynamic zone to experience life. Although you certainly can create a perception of reality in your mind, the physical world is still the only place to test those perceptions.

> *Action is the ingredient that makes life real.*

Life is not about getting ready to get ready. Life is for living right now. This is not preseason. This is your Super Bowl and the clock is ticking. The only way to make your life dynamic is to go out into the physical world and make it happen.

During times when you feel fearful, it's so easy to let your mind persuade you to give up on your dreams. This is especially true if you still have any beliefs like, "When I feel fear, I should avoid taking action." In this case, it is vital for you to realize that your heart is more genuine than your beliefs. Your heart is your center for inspiration. It is your connection, your bond to your creator. No one really knows how you get these inspirations, but they should be treated as something sacred, something divine nonetheless. Never let some ridiculous belief cause you to give up the pursuit of your heart's desires!

"The heart has reasons of its own, which the head can never understand."
Pascal

Emotionally, you can hurt your heart when you choose not to act upon a particular inspiration. Inspirations are unique gifts that are yearning to be expressed. No one else in the whole world has the exact same inspirations as you do. Therefore, it is your responsibility to your creator, to yourself, and to all of society to develop these inner passions. Inspirations give meaning and purpose to your life. Any time your actions are not in alignment with your inspirations, you sacrifice your individuality.

> *It's easier to SAY what you believe*
> *than to BE what you believe.*

227

It is amazing how many people live their entire life with their actions and inspirations pulling in opposite directions. Then, when they become ill and contemplate the possibility of death, they go on a wall smashing rampage and begin to do all the things they should have been doing for all the years beforehand. These types of people procrastinate for their entire life until they reach a point in time when they cannot afford to procrastinate for another moment.

Sandy is an example of someone who did this in her own life. Recently, she was diagnosed with a terminal case of melanoma cancer and was told by her doctors that she had only two months to live. Upon hearing this, Sandy began to take action upon many of the inspirations that she had ignored up to this point in her life. She began by forgiving her sister for the "garage incident." She also told her twin daughters that she loved them—something she had not done in ages. She even went so far as to tell her husband about the affair she had ten years ago that had been eating away at their marriage ever since.

Although it is great that Sandy finally chose to smash her walls, she does regret the fact that it took a death sentence for her to take action. For years, Sandy lived with a void in her life because she did not exhibit the courage to align her heart, mind, and body in one common direction.

To avoid a terrible situation like Sandy's, you can ask yourself one key question every day, "Am I living the same way I would if I only had one week to live?" Asking yourself this key question and acting upon your honest answer will guarantee that you honor the unique inspirations and dreams that have been bestowed upon you, before it is too late.

WALLS REVEAL YOUR CURRENT LEVEL OF CHARACTER

Once upon a time, there was a wealthy, wise, old woman who needed to hire a limousine driver to take her from city to city so that she could attend her various business meetings. Her objective was to hire the safest and most reliable driver that she could possibly find, someone with impeccable character. After all, she was putting her life in the hands of the driver who got the job. In order to accomplish her objective, she was willing to pay this person a very handsome salary.

As a result of the very generous wages that she was offering, hundreds of people applied for the job. After reviewing the applications and conducting dozens of interviews, the wise, old businesswoman narrowed her selection down to the four most qualified applicants. From there, she decided to test the remaining applicants to see which one of them was most qualified. So, she gathered the four finalists together and explained to them the rules of the particular test that she was going to give to them.

The test consisted of each applicant driving from the woman's suburban mansion to her downtown business office. Each of the applicants were instructed to make the best time that they possibly could, even if that meant driving faster than the speed limit, coasting through stop signs, or blatantly running red lights. To say the least, the applicants looked confused over such an unusual testing procedure.

Nonetheless, the first driver began his test. As fate would have it, he encountered quite a bit of fog which prevented him from going any faster than 75 miles per hour in the 65 mile per hour zone. Even though his speed was a bit dangerous, he decided that the job was worth the risk. Anyway, he made up some time by running a few red lights along the way. His time ended up being 40 minutes.

In the meantime, the fog lifted and the second driver began his test. He knew the first driver finished in 40 minutes and that he had to beat his time in order to get the job. Unfortunately, heavy rains occurred the moment he began to drive. Nonetheless, he was determined to get the best time. Despite the low visibility and the slippery roads, this driver still managed to travel nearly 80 miles per hour for most of his journey. He also ran a few red lights and ended up scoring a time of 38 minutes.

It was now time for the third driver to take his test. He knew that he had to complete his test in less than 38 minutes to get the job. As he began to drive, the rains increased and heavy winds soon followed. The driving conditions were treacherous. Debris was scattered all over the roads, visibility was low, and some parts of the road were flooded. Nonetheless, he was willing to do whatever it took to get the job. Despite the horrendous driving conditions, he somehow managed to beat the time of the previous driver by 30 seconds.

By this time, the winds and the rains had stopped, the sun came out, and all the debris was removed from the road. Amazingly, the fourth and final driver had the opportunity to take his test in ideal driving conditions. The first three drivers were furious. They knew that the fourth driver would easily achieve the fastest time and consequently get the job.

But, to the amazement of the first three drivers, the fourth driver never traveled above 65 miles per hour, the legal speed limit. He also stopped at every red light along the way. He didn't even coast through a stop sign. In short, he was the epitome of safe drivers. Of course, he also had the slowest time of the four drivers.

Out of curiosity, the wise, old woman asked the fourth driver, "Why did you drive so slowly and safely when you were told by me to drive as fast as possible?" The fourth driver replied, "If you want to hire me for the job, this is how I will drive for you. In fact, I would have traveled much slower yet if I had to drive in the same dangerous conditions as did the three previous drivers. You see, my actions are based upon my character, which is the foundation of my being. I know that I was instructed to go as fast as I can, but that contradicted my character and my character is much more important than any job."

Can you guess who got the job? I think it was an easy choice for the wise, old woman!

This story is a great example about the way that walls can reveal a person's character. The first three drivers showed the wise, old woman that they would break the law and compromise their own morals in order to get a certain job. On the other hand, the fourth driver proved that he would not compromise his own morals regardless of who told him to do so. As a result, the wise, old woman succeeded in finding the safest and most reliable driver, someone with a dynamic character, someone worthy of receiving a very high salary.

Your character reveals itself when you face great walls. Viktor Frankl, survivor of a Nazi concentration camp and author of the monumental bestseller, *Man's Search For Meaning*, reported how the filth and disgust of Auschwitz clearly revealed the character of those held in bondage. Frankl goes on to say, "…people became more different; people unmasked themselves, both the swine and the saints." Never did character, both good and bad, shine so brightly as it did in the disgust of those German death camps. After being stripped, beaten, verbally abused, and malnourished, Viktor Frankl and others like him were left with nothing but their character. Frankl's unique experience of facing some of life's greatest challenges proved the awesome power that walls have to reveal character.

The great quality about character is that it goes wherever you go. No matter how bad things get, you always retain your character. By creating a dynamic character for yourself, you can draw upon it in the middle of any adversity and use it to pull yourself through the hard times. It doesn't matter if you encounter financial challenges, emotional challenges, social challenges, or physical challenges; a dynamic character has the power to save you.

WALLS GIVE YOU THE OPPORTUNITY TO STRENGTHEN YOUR CHARACTER

Not only do walls reveal your existing character. They also give you the opportunity to refine and strengthen it. This process is likened to the procedure a fine piece of steel goes through when it is heated and chilled over and over as a means to create superior strength. By exposing the steel to extreme temperatures, both hot and cold, it becomes stronger. Likewise, every time you encounter adversity, you become like a fine piece of steel in that you keep getting stronger and stronger.

Without walls, your character would never be tested. Eventually, you would drift into the complacency of your comfort zone and adopt a weak character. As a result, this world would have failed you. Since character is your only real possession, you need walls in order to maintain, test, and improve upon your existing character.

> *The true test of your character is the size of wall it takes to cause you to retreat.*

Let's suppose you receive an inspiration to organize a nonprofit organization in your community. When you tell your friends about your dream, ninety-five percent of them laugh at your idea and tell you that it will not work. They tell you stories about someone else who "tried" to do something like that before and failed.

In a situation like this, you are up against a wall. Do you listen to the opinions of your friends or do you continue to follow the inspiration of your heart? Your decision will result in either a strengthened character or a weakened character. You will either become the type of person who regards the opinions of your friends as more important than your own personal dreams or you will become the type of person who regards your dreams as more important than the discouragement you receive from others. You alone must decide if you are willing to let someone else tell you what is and what is not possible in your own life.

Another example of how walls can strengthen character can be found in a junior high school classroom. Shelly is a math teacher who has a room full of students in her class. It is getting very close to the end of the grading period and she still has a substantial amount of material to cover with her students. To say the least, Shelly feels a bit rushed. Suddenly, one of the students raises her hand and asks a question that Shelly has already answered a few days ago. Even though the student's request was sincere, Shelly is tempted to berate the child for not paying attention when she first answered the question. At this moment, Shelly will either strengthen her existing character by taking the necessary time to answer the student's question or she will weaken her existing character by yelling at the student. What will she do?

The same is true for the woman who loses her husband of forty years to cancer. Her character will either be strengthened or weakened by this experience. She can either choose to express her grief, pick herself up, and move on or she can choose to deny her grief, retreat into her comfort zone, and consider her own life to be over. It is moments like these that this woman will set the tone for the rest of her life.

Even a common situation such as a tennis match can provide you with an opportunity to strengthen your character. Suppose you are losing by one game and you are forced to make a tight call on a ball that landed on the very edge of the line. It would be easy to call the ball "out" since your opponent didn't get a very good view of the shot. You are faced with a wall. Will you make the accurate call and risk losing the game? Or will you manipulate your opponent by making the wrong call and give yourself a better chance to win? Your choice will either strengthen or weaken your character. What will you do?

There are an endless number of opportunities for you to strengthen your existing character. The deciding factor is how you choose to act upon the particular situation.

WHAT TYPE OF CHARACTER DO YOU HAVE?

It may be possible to fool the entire world into believing you have a dynamic character, but you cannot fool yourself. You are the only one in this world who truly knows what kind of character you possess. Many people may recognize bits and pieces of your character throughout their interactions with you, but only you truly know your own character.

Take a moment and answer the following questions to determine whether or not you have a dynamic character:

- Do I like the person I have become?
- Can I look at myself in the mirror and say, "I love you," with sincerity?
- Would I want my children to become someone like me?
- What would the world be like if everyone were just like me?
- How would an encyclopedia entry objectively comment on my life?

The preceding questions were designed to help you to see what quality of character you currently possess. Once you realize what kind of character you possess, you can free yourself to make any necessary changes. The first step involved in any type of change is always to recognize the thing that needs to be changed. Fortunately, character is something that you have complete control over, something that you can change at will.

Consider for a moment the differences between a thermostat and a thermometer. A thermostat *can* control and change the temperature inside an entire building whereas a thermometer *is* controlled and changed by the temperature of the building. If you had to honestly classify yourself as either a thermostat or a thermometer—which one would it be? Are you like a thermostat in the way that you decide in advance that you will feel excited, energetic, and joyful amidst the walls that surround you? Or are you like a thermometer in the way that you let circumstances determine how you will feel? I sincerely hope that by this point in the book you have learned to act like a thermostat.

Decide right now about what type of character you will create for yourself. Don't become another person whose behavior and attitude depends upon what day it is or what they are doing. Surely, you have encountered such people in your life. They are the ones who act polite and cheerful at the party on Saturday night, but act rude and grouchy at work on Monday morning. They treat you like gold at church on Christmas morning, but turn around and treat you like dirt on the morning of April 15th as you stand in line to mail your taxes.

As you begin to take charge of your life, you will soon realize that character is not about putting on a show for your friends and relatives on holidays or special events. Nor is it about acting a certain way at church on Sundays or during a meeting with "important" people. Instead, you will realize that your character is the person you are, the essence of your existence. Slowly, you will begin to act with integrity in all that you do. No longer will there be "special" events where you act any differently than you normally would.

Your character is the foundation for your life. Build it much like you would construct the foundation of your house. Remember, foundations must be built strong enough to withstand the adversity of the inevitable storms. If your character is weak, then you will crumble whenever you encounter adversity.

Create the quality of character for yourself that is strong enough to deny the request of your friend to take two newspapers out of the newspaper bin even though you only paid for one. Adopt a dynamic character that is capable of telling your dating partner that you are not yet ready to have sex if that is how you feel. Mold your character in a way that you could easily resist a bribe of $50,000.00 to assist in transporting stolen goods. Develop a character that is above racial prejudice. Foster the type of character that allows you to be honest with your children about the issues in your own life. Remember, you alone are responsible for the quality of character that you create for yourself!

CHARACTER AND MATERIAL POSSESSIONS

In order to create a dynamic character for yourself, you do not necessarily have to forsake all of your material possessions. It is entirely possible for you to create a dynamic character while simultaneously enjoying an abundance of material possessions in the process. There is absolutely nothing wrong with enjoying material possessions. Material possessions, in and of themselves, are not evil. It is the abuse of material possessions for your own personal greed that causes them to become evil. With this in mind, do yourself a favor and get rid of any belief that suggests material possessions are evil. The truth is, material possessions, money included, can do a lot of good in the hands of wise people.

> *Money is the root of an abundance of good when it is used wisely for the good of society.*

Nothing is wrong with spending $150.00 to buy some really neat Easter decorations for a display in your front yard or spending $21,000.00 for a nice boat if you enjoy water-skiing and fishing. You deserve to have all the material possessions that you desire. Just be sure that you never buy material possessions as a means to inflate your ego or to infer that you are better than someone else. Material possessions exist as a means of enjoyment and goodwill. They do not exist as a means of comparison and competition against your peers. The day you lose your temper because your boat is no longer faster than your brother's boat is the day you have gone "overboard" with material possessions.

"All unhappiness is caused by comparison."
The Buddha

If you have a poor self-image, a new outfit is not the answer. If you are mean and cruel, a new house on the other side of the city won't improve your attitude. If you feel old and "washed up," a new luxury car won't change your beliefs about yourself. In fact, there are no types or amounts of cars, boats, or houses that will ever make up for a weak character! If you think you are incomplete without a certain material possession, then you have a major crack in the armor of your character.

Character cannot be bought, it can only be expressed from the inside out. You cannot create a dynamic character for yourself by eating out at fancy restaurants. Neither can you do so by purchasing a condo at the ski resort, wearing expensive jewelry, or attending elegant parties. Character is totally independent of everything that you own and any event that you attend.

> *"...what a man IS contributes more to his happiness than what he HAS."*
> Arthur Schopenhauer

One way to guard yourself from falling into the trap of materialism is to remind yourself about where you came from and how truly fortunate you are to have all the "toys" that you currently possess. In my own life, I periodically take my old beat-up cargo van out to run errands as a way to remind myself of the days when I lived in the back of that van. It's a very humbling experience. It also reminds me about how fortunate I am to enjoy my current lifestyle.

Another good example of someone who uses this strategy to remind himself and his family about where they came from is a man I will call "John." John and his family are the classic "rags to riches" story. They started out with nothing but a dream and today, they are multi-millionaires. As a way to guard against greed and a lack of appreciation for all of their material possessions, John and his family take one day out of the year and return to the farm where they once worked. For exactly eight hours in the blistering heat of summer, they voluntarily shovel cow manure.

This annual ritual of theirs is actually a great concept! It sparks vivid memories for John and his family about what their life was like before they became financially independent. It also reminds them how hard they had to work to get to their current level of financial comfort. Consequently, when they return to their beautiful suburban mansion to soak in their whirlpool, they seem to enjoy it a little bit more than usual.

> *"What shall it profit man if he gains the whole world, but loses his soul?"*
> Jesus Christ

YOU HAVE ALREADY WON

The greatest honor in the universe is the opportunity to be you! No one else on this planet could ever become the type of person that you are capable of becoming. Even if you have an identical twin, there still exists no other person with the exact same resources as you.

With such a unique design, it's a shame how many people long to become someone other than themselves. People fantasize about becoming just like their "role model" who is a musician, actor, entrepreneur, or athlete. Little do they know that even if their fantasy would come true, they would still be terribly unhappy. They do not realize that happiness is only possible when they are being their own unique self. This is not to say that it is wrong to learn from a particular role model. It is only wrong to model them too closely.

Use every moment of your life to become more of yourself. Live your life in such a way that at the end of all of your exploring you will discover yourself and know yourself for the first time. Don't be all things to all people. Focus your energy upon becoming your own unique person. Desiring to please everyone will assure but one thing, you will grow to despise yourself.

> *You can thank your creator for the gift of life by actually living it.*

Your best strategy is to surround yourself with people who support you in becoming the best possible you. Encompass yourself with people with whom you can discuss both your fears and your dreams. Regardless of how strong you are as an individual, you need the support of others. No one is strong enough to look life straight in the eye at every moment of every day. You will need someone to lean on at times.

Hang in there through all the temptations to retreat. Defy the odds and continue to chip away at your walls of fear. With every positive action that you take, your character will shine more and more brightly. With every step of progress that you make, you will become more and more beautiful. And within a short period of time, your entire life will become dynamic. Joy will pervade every cell of your body. Then, when the day finally comes that you must pass on to the next dimension, you will know beyond a shadow of a doubt that you possess life's ultimate reward a....**DYNAMIC CHARACTER!**

ABOUT THE AUTHOR

Sean Hockensmith is an author, speaker, and consultant. His specialty is helping others to overcome their fears and achieve their dreams. Every year, Sean impacts the lives of thousands through his speeches and books.

Sean resides in Windber, Pennsylvania. Sean and his wife Gina share their home with three kids, two dogs, a rabbit, and a cat.

Website: www.seanhockensmith.com
Email: sean@seanhockensmith.com

DYNAMIC LIFE PUBLISHING

Dynamic Life Publishing is a company dedicated to supplying YOU with practical, effective strategies that will allow you to improve the quality of your life today.

For inquiries into the speaking and consulting services of Sean Hockensmith, please visit Sean's website at www.seanhockensmith.com.

You can order additional copies of "Smashing the Wall of Fear" by turning to the last page of this book.

Dynamic Life Publishing
429 Clearwater St.
Johnstown, PA 15904

GLOSSARY

Ability: What you are capable of doing.

Adapt: Adjusting yourself to cope with change.

Assertiveness: Actively displaying your genuine self.

Attitude: The way you choose to interact with some aspect of life.

Avoidance: An unwillingness to face something.

Blame: Giving away your personal responsibility for something and consequently leaving yourself powerless to make any changes.

Can't: You either don't *want* to do something or you don't know *how* to do something.

Change: Doing something different.

Character: The sum total of both your good and bad personal qualities.

Codependency: Living your life through someone else. Failing to make your own unique contributions to the relationship.

Cognitive Dissonance: A conflict between your beliefs and actions in which your mind prompts you to accept the most familiar.

Comfort Zone: A metaphor for a place where you can rest, relax, and recuperate. A place where you can easily handle everything in your life.

Communication: Mutual understanding.

Complacency: Choosing not to make any additional progress because you are satisfied with your current level of achievement.

Compounding joy: When your past joys combine and multiply with your current joy to create a deeper sense of joy in the present.

Conditioning: A preprogrammed response in your nervous system that causes you to feel certain emotions when you encounter specific stimuli in your environment.

Conscious Mind: Your "thinking mind" that is used to direct the awesome power of your subconscious mind.

Contribution: Wisely giving of your time, your skills, and/or your money to improve the quality of life for another person.

Conviction: The most intense type of belief.

Courage (Bravery): Taking action in the presence of fear.

Decision: Making an absolute commitment to produce a certain result.

Defense: A belief or behavior used to protect yourself from a real or imagined danger.

Denial: Refusing to acknowledge the existence of something.

Determination: Taking consistent action until you accomplish a specific objective.

Discipline: Controlling your behavior by focusing your actions upon your objective.

Dream: The unique aspirations and desires that exist within you.

Dynamic action: Smart, small, consistent action.

Dynamic: Anything that is growing, changing and improving.

Dynamic life: A life filled with joy.

Dynamic zone: A metaphor for the vast unfamiliar, unexplored, unknown area located directly outside the edge of your comfort zone. It's the place where you take action upon your walls of fear and pursue your dreams.

Ego: Your "false self." Perceiving yourself inaccurately.

Emotion: A biochemical response in your brain linked to certain stimuli. Emotions involve changes at the physiological level and produce feelings of pleasure and pain.

Emotional: Having to do with your feelings. Commonly linked to your heart.

Emotional reasons: Personal reasons that motivate you to make a change in your life.

Entrepreneur: Someone who creates wealth by adding value to society.

Escapism: Removing yourself from a painful situation and substituting it with what you perceive to be a more pleasurable situation.

Excellence: Consistently improving upon your personal best.

Excuse: A reason for failure.

Faith: Believing something will happen without having complete proof that it will.

Fantasy : A dream that you choose not to pursue.

Fear: A friendly emotion that protects and guides you. It is activated by the expectation of a real or imagined threat of losing your current state of comfort.

Feeling: A physical sensation resulting from a reaction to a thought.

Financial: Having to do with money.

Flexibility: Adapting yourself to certain changes while maintaining physical, mental, and emotional control.

Freedom: The opportunity to step into your dynamic zone to pursue your own unique dreams.

Goals: Benchmarks along the way to achieving your dreams.

Grace: The unconditional love of your creator.

Greatness: Achieving the things that you consider to be great.

Habit: Consistently engaging in a certain behavior or thought process.

Happiness: Feeling good in the present moment regardless of what is going on around you.

Hard work: Focusing a significant amount of energy upon doing something that you already know how to do. Hard work is most effective when it is preceded by "smart work."

Health: A feeling of inner peace between your body and mind.

Hedonism: Seeking out cheap, instant pleasures solely for your own personal benefit without considering the well-being of others involved.

High Self-esteem: Seeing yourself as an extremely valuable part of life.

Insanity: Consistently taking the same actions and hoping for a different result.

Insight: Gaining a deeper understanding about something.

Integrity: Acting in accordance to what you value the most.

Intellect: The capacity to understand information and to gain knowledge.

Intelligence: The ability to recognize and resolve problems.

Intention: Making definite plans to produce a certain result.

Intuition: Immediate knowledgeable guidance that comes to you without the use of rational thought. Commonly referred to as your sixth sense.

Irrational: Illogical reasoning.

Joy: A natural high that you feel when you tap into more of your potential.

Kaizen: A Japanese word for small, consistent improvement.

Knowledge: Obtaining specific information.

Lazy: An unwillingness to take the necessary actions to achieve your dreams.

Life: The greatest gift you could ever receive.

Love: Sharing joy with yourself and with others.

Low Self-steem: Seeing yourself as having very little value in life.

Meditation: The act of deliberately calming your mind.

Memory: Storing and retrieving information in your mind.

Mental: Having to do with your mind.

Metaphor: A term used out of context for sake of a comparison.

Mind: The part of the brain responsible for all aspects of thinking.

Negative emotions: See page 90.

No self-esteem: Seeing yourself as having no value in life.

Obsession: Compulsively occupying your mind with a certain thought.

Pain: An unpleasant sensation.

Panacea: A magical remedy for all of your diseases and problems.

Panic attack: An overwhelming sense of fear characterized by the belief, "I've got to get out of here!"

Paradigm: The way that you perceive a particular aspect of your life.

Perception: The way that you interpret or understand any given situation.

Personality: The unique way that you consistently interact with other people.

Philanthropist: Someone who works to improve life for everyone.

Philosophy: An organization of knowledge.

Phobia: A habitual, involuntary, and irrational fearful reaction to a specific stimulus.

Physical: Having to do with your body.

Planning: The process of designating a specific time in the future that you will take a particular action.

Pleasure: A pleasant sensation.

Positive emotions: See page 106.

Positive thinking: Choosing to think about the things you want rather than the things you do not want.

Power: Your ability to take action.

Procrastination: A method used to avoid taking certain actions.

Progress: The result of growth, change, and improvement in your life.

Psychology: The study of mental, emotional, and physical processes in order to learn more about feelings and behaviors.

Purpose: The unique mission that your creator has instilled upon you.

Rational: Supported by concrete reasons.

Reality: Your own unique personal perception about life.

Rejection: Being excluded from someone or something.

Relationship: The specific ways that you deal with yourself, other people, animals, and/or your environment.

Reputation: The unique way that a particular person or group of persons regards your actions.

Retreat: When you quit taking action upon your wall of fear.

Ritual: A behavior that is conducted the same way at the same time and/or at the same place.

Self-esteem: The amount of general value that you place upon your life.

Self-image: The unique way that you perceive yourself in any specific situation.

Selfishness: Caring solely for yourself while disregarding the needs of others.

Sensation: A physical feeling that stems from the stimulation of a sense organ.

Skilled: Acquiring the necessary expertise to perform a certain task well.

Smart work: Gaining new knowledge that allows you to work more efficiently.

Social: Having to do with yourself and the other people in your environment.

Spiritual: Having to do with your relationship with your creator.

State of mind: The present emotional or mental condition of your mind.

Stretching: Participating in an unfamiliar activity.

Subconscious mind: An unconscious mechanism that acts like a computer by storing all of your past experiences and beliefs. It is programmed by your conscious mind and carries out its orders perfectly.

Success: Achieving a preconceived level of accomplishment.

Talent: Unique natural ability.

Teach: To instruct someone about the application of certain knowledge.

Try: Going through the motions without giving it all of your effort.

Visualization: Focusing the power of your thoughts on the outcome that you desire to experience.

Wall: A metaphor for any obstacle in your life that is currently preventing you from achieving your dreams.

Wall building: Ignoring important issues in your life.

Will: Your intention to produce a specific result.

Wisdom: (common sense) The accumulation of both knowledge and experience.

INDEX

INDEX

INDEX

BIBLIOGRAPHY/RECOMMENDED READING

Allenbaugh, Eric. *Wake-Up Calls: You Don't Have to Sleepwalk Through Your Life, Love, or Career.* New York: Fireside, 1994.

Anthony, Robert. *Advanced Formula for Total Success: For Success-Minded People Who Want to Go Beyond Positive Thinking.* New York: Berkley Books, 1988. ---- *50 Ideas That Can Change Your Life!: An Indispensible Guide to Happiness and Prosperity.* New York: Berkley Books, 1987. ---- *The Ultimate Secrets of Total Self-Confidence: A Proven Formula that Has Worked for Thousands. Now It Can Work for You.* New York: Berkley Books, 1984.

Bell, Jesse Grover. *Here's How By Who's Who.* Lakewood, OH: Bonne Bell Inc., 1968.

Borysenko, Joan. *Minding the Body, Mending the Mind.* New York: Bantam Books, 1988.

Bradshaw, John. *Homecoming: Reclaiming and Championing Your Inner Child.* New York: Bantam Books, 1992.

Branden, Nathaniel. *How to Raise Your Self-Esteem: The Proven Action-Oriented Approach to Greater Self-Respect and Self-Confidence.* New York: Bantam Books, 1988.

Brodie, Richard. *Getting Past OK: A Straightforward Guide to Having a Fantastic Life.* Seattle, WA: Integral Press,1993.

Brown, Les. *Live Your Dreams.* New York: Avon Books, 1994.

Buscaglia, Leo. *Born for Love: Reflections on Loving.* New York: Ballantine Books, 1994.

Carnegie, Dale. *How to Win Friends and Influence People.* New York: Pocket Books, 1982.

Chopra, Deepack. *Unconditional Life: Discovering the Power to Fulfill Your Dreams.* New York, Bantam Books, 1992. ---- *Ageless Body, Timeless Mind: The Quantum Alternative to Growing Old.* New York: Harmony Books, 1994.

Cohen, Alan. *Dare to Be Yourself: How to Quit Being an Extra in Other People's Movies and Become the Star of Your Own.* New York: Ballantine Books, 1994.

Cousins, Norman. *Anatomy of an Illness as Perceived by the Patient: Reflections on Healing and Regeneration.* New York: Bantam Books, 1991.

Covey, Stephen R. *The 7 Habits of Highly Effective People: Powerful Lessons in Personal Change.* New York: Fireside, 1990. ---- *Principle-Centered Leadership.* New York: Fireside, 1992.

DeAngelis, Barbara. *How to Make Love All the Time.* New York: Dell Publishing, 1991.

Durant, Will. *The Story of Philosophy: The Lives and Opinions of the World's Greatest Philosophers from Plato to John Dewey.* New York: Pocket Books, 1953.

Dyer, Wayne W. *Your Erroneous Zones: Step-by-Step Advice for Escaping the Trap of Negative Thinking and Taking Control of Your Life.* New York: HarperPerennial, 1991. ----- *Pulling Your Own Strings: Dynamic Techniques for Dealing with Other People and Living Your Life as You Choose.* New York: HarperPerennial, 1991. ---- *The Sky's the Limit.* New York: Pocket Books, 1981. ----*You'll See It When You Believe It: The Way to Your Personal Transformation.* New York: Avon Books, 1990.

Frankl, Viktor E. *Man's Search for Meaning.* New York: Pocket Books, 1985.

Foundation For Inner Peace. *A Course in Miracles.* Mill Valley: Foundation For Inner Peace, 1993.

Fulghum, Robert. *It Was on Fire When I Lay Down on It.* New York: Ballantine Books, 1991.

Gawain, Shakti and Laurel King. *Living in the Light: A Guide to Personal and Planetary Transformation.* Novato, CA: Nataraj Publishing, 1992.

Getty, J. Paul. *How to be Rich: His Formulas.* New York: Jove Books, 1983.

Givens, Charles J. *Super Self: Doubling Your Personal Effectiveness.* New York: Simon & Schuster, 1993.

Griessman, Eugene B. *Time Tactics of Very Successful People.* New York: McGraw-Hill, Inc.,1994.

Hansen, Mark Victor and Jack Canfield. *Dare To Win.* New York: Berkley Books, 1994.
---- *Chicken Soup for the Soul: 101 Stories to Open the Heart and Rekindle the Spirit.* Deerfield Beach, FL: Health Communications, Inc., 1993.

Harris, Thomas A. *I'm OK - You're OK: The Transactional Analysis Breakthrough That's Changing the Consciousness and Behavior of People Who Never Before Felt OK About Themselves.* New York: Avon Books, 1973.

Hay, Louise L. *You Can Heal Your Life.* Carson, CA: Hay House Inc., 1994.

Hedges, Burke. *Who Stole the American Dream?: The Book Your Boss Doesn't Want You to Read.* Charlotte, NC: InterNET Services Corporation, 1993.

Helmstetter, Shad. *You Can Excel in Times of Change: Anticipate the Best and Get It—With the Six Key Steps for Taking Charge of Change.* New York: Pocket Books, 1992. ---- *What to Say When You Talk to Yourself.* New York: Pocket Books, 1987.

Hendrix, Harville. *Keeping the Love You Find: A Guide for Singles.* New York: Pocket Books, 1993.

Hill, Napoleon. *Think and Grow Rich.* Hollywood, CA: Wilshire Book Company, 1966.

Hubbard, L. Ron. *Dianetics.* Los Angeles, CA: Bridge Publications, Inc., 1992.

Huber, Cheri. *The Fear Book: Facing Fear Once and for All.* Mountain View, CA: Keep It Simple Books, 1995.

Jeffers, Susan. *Feel the Fear and Do It Anyway: Dynamic Techniques for Turning Fear, Indecision, and Anger into Power, Action, and Love.* New York: Ballantine Books, 1988.

King, Barbara. *Transform Your Life.* Marina del Rey, CA: Devorss & Company, 1989.

Kouzes James M. and Poshner Barry Z. *The Leadership Challenge.* San Francisco: Jossey-Bass, 1987.

Kubler-Ross, Elisabeth. *On Death and Dying: What the Dying Have to Teach Doctors, Nurses, Clergy, and Their Own Families.* New York: Collier Books, 1993.

Kushner, Harold. *When All You've Ever Wanted Isn't Enough: The Search for a Life that Matters.* New York: Pocket Books, 1987.

Mackay, Harvey. *Swim with the Sharks without Being Eaten Alive: Outmanage, Outmotivate, and Outnegotiate Your Competition.* New York: Ivy Books, 1991.

Maltz, Maxwell. *Psycho-Cybernetics.* New York: Pocket Books, 1969.

Mandino, Og. *The Greatest Salesman in the World: You Can Change Your Life with the Priceless Wisdom of Ten Ancient Scrolls Handed Down for Thousands of Years.* New York: Bantam Books, 1985.

Mason, John L. *An Enemy Called Average: Don't Settle for an Average Life - God wants to Launch You Past the Middle to the Top.* Tulsa, OK: Insight International,1990.

Maxwell, John C. *The Winning Attitude: Your Key to Personal Success.* Nashville, TN: Thomas Nelson., Inc., Publishers, 1993.

May, Rollo. *Man's Search for Himself.* New York: Delta Books, 1973.

McGinnis, Alan Loy. *Confidence: How to Succeed at Being Yourself.* Minneapolis, MN: Augsburg Publishing House, 1987.

McWilliams, Peter and John-Roger. *Life 101: Everything We Wished We had Learned about Life in School - But Didn't.* Los Angeles, CA: Prelude Press, 1991. ---- *Do It!: Let's Get Off Our Butts.* Los Angeles, CA: Prelude Press, 1991.

Murphy, Joseph. *The Power of Your Subconscious Mind*. New York: Bantam Books, 1982.

Nightingale, Earl. *Lead the Field*. Chicago: Nightingale-Conant (Audiotape), 1986.

Padus, Emrika. *The Complete Guide to Emotions and Your Health: Hundreds of Proven Techniques to Harmonize Mind & Body for Happy, Healthy Living*. Emmaus, PA: Rodale Press, 1992.

Peale, Norman Vincent. *The Power of Positive Thinking*. New York: Ballantine Books, 1992.

Pearsall, Paul. *The Pleasure Principle: Discovering a New Way to Health*. Chicago: Nightingale-Conant (Audiotape), 1994.

Peck, M. Scott. *The Road Less Traveled: A New Psychology of Love, Traditional Values and Spiritual Growth*. New York: Touchstone/Simon & Schuster, 1980.

Piering, Tim. *Breaking Free to Mental and Financial Independence*. Sierra Madre, CA: Sunwest Publishing Company, 1990.

Ringer, Robert J. *Million Dollar Habits*. New York: Ballantine Books, 1991.

Robbins, Anthony. *Unlimited Power*. New York: Ballantine Books, 1987. ---- *Awaken the Giant Within: How to Take Immediate Control of Your Mental, Emotional, Physical, and Financial Destiny*. New York: Fireside, 1992. ---- *Powertalk*. With Deepak Chopra. Robbins Research International, Inc. Volume 22, 1993.

Rohm, Robert A. *Positive Personality Profiles: "D-I-S-C-O-V-E-R" Personality Insights to Understand Yourself... and Others*. Atlanta, GA: Personality Insights, Inc., 1994.

Schuller, Robert H. *Move Ahead with Possibility Thinking*. New York: Jove Books, 1978. ---- *Be an Extraordinary Person in an Ordinary World*. New York: Jove Books, 1986.

Schwartz, David J. *The Magic of Thinking Big*. New York: Fireside, 1987.

Seigel, Bernie S. *Peace, Love, and Healing: Bodymind Communication & The Path to Self-Healing: An Exploration*. New York: Harper and Row, 1989. ---- *Love, Medicine, & Miracles: Lessons Learned about Self-Healing from a Surgeon's Experience with Exceptional Patients*. New York: Harper and Row, 1990.

Shinn, Florence Scovel. *The Game of Life and How to Play It*. Marina del Rey, CA: Devorss & Company, 1925.

Swindoll, Charles R. *Hand Me Another Brick: Principles of Effective Leadership: How to Motivate Yourself and Others*. Nashville, TN: Thomas Nelson, Inc., 1990.

Sylver, Marshall. *Passion Profit & Power*. Del Mar: Sylver Enterprises (Audiotape), 1993.

Viscott, David. *Winning*. New York: Pocket Books, 1987. ---- *Risking*. New York: Pocket Books, 1979. ---- *Feel Free*. New York: Pocket Books, 1987. *Taking Risks*. Chicago: Nightingale-Conant (Audiotape), 1991.

Waitley, Denis. *The Winner's Edge*. New York: Berkley Books, 1983. ---- *The Psychology of Winning: Ten Qualities of a Total Winner*. New York: Berkley Books, 1984. ---- *The Psychology of Human Motivation*. Chicago: Nightingale-Conant (Audiotape), 1991.

Williamson, Marianne. *A Return to Love: Reflections on the Principles of <u>A Course in Miracles</u>*. New York: HarperPerennial, 1993.

Wright, H. Norman. *Afraid No More!: Gaining the Faith You Need to Live Fully and Confidently*. Wheaton, IL: Tyndale Books, 1992.

Yager, Dexter R Sr. and and Doyle Yager. *The Business Handbook: A Guide to Building your Own Amway Business*. Charlotte, NC: InterNet Services Corporation, 1993.

Ziglar, Zig. *Top Performance: How to Develop Excellence in Yourself and Others*. New York: Berkley Books, 1987.

<u>ORDER FORM</u>

Please send me the following books:

QUANTITY   **AMOUNT**

___ **Smashing the Wall of Fear** ($13)   _____

___ **A Teen's Guide to Smashing the Wall of Fear** ($10)   _____

Total for book(s) _____

Shipping: $3 first book _____

$1 each additional book (Maximum of $9) _____

Pennsylvania residents add 6% sales tax _____

TOTAL AMOUNT ENCLOSED (U.S. FUNDS) _____
*Make checks payable to **Dynamic Life Publishing**

PLEASE PRINT CLEARLY

Your Name: _____

Address: _____

City: _____State: _____Zip: _____

*** Fill in the following information if you are paying by credit card:

Which credit card are you using? ____Visa ____MasterCard

Card number: _____

Name on card: _____ Exp. Date: ____ / ____

Cardholder Signature: _____

***Mail this order form to:

**Dynamic Life Publishing
429 Clearwater St.
Johnstown, PA 15904-1340, USA.**

***FAX orders to 814-467-0753

***Phone orders to 1-888-925-5762

THANK YOU FOR YOUR ORDER!

ORDER FORM

Please send me the following books:

QUANTITY   **AMOUNT**

___ **Smashing the Wall of Fear** ($13)   _____

___ **A Teen's Guide to Smashing the Wall of Fear** ($10)   _____

Total for book(s) _____

Shipping: $3 first book _____

$1 each additional book (Maximum of $9) _____

Pennsylvania residents add 6% sales tax _____

TOTAL AMOUNT ENCLOSED (U.S. FUNDS) _____
*Make checks payable to **Dynamic Life Publishing**

PLEASE PRINT CLEARLY

Your Name: _____

Address: _____

City: _____State: _____Zip: _____

*** Fill in the following information if you are paying by credit card:

Which credit card are you using? ____Visa ____MasterCard

Card number: _____

Name on card: _____ Exp. Date: ____/ ____

Cardholder Signature: _____

***Mail this order form to:

Dynamic Life Publishing
429 Clearwater St.
Johnstown, PA 15904-1340, USA.

***FAX orders to 814-467-0753

***Phone orders to 1-888-925-5762

THANK YOU FOR YOUR ORDER!